EMOTION AND THE RESEARCHER: SITES, SUBJECTIVITIES, AND RELATIONSHIPS

STUDIES IN QUALITATIVE METHODOLOGY

Series Editor: Sam Hillyard

STUDIES IN QUALITATIVE
METHODOLOGY   VOLUME 16

EMOTION AND THE RESEARCHER: SITES, SUBJECTIVITIES, AND RELATIONSHIPS

EDITED BY

TRACEY LOUGHRAN
University of Essex

DAWN MANNAY
Cardiff University

United Kingdom – North America – Japan
India – Malaysia – China

Emerald Publishing Limited
Howard House, Wagon Lane, Bingley BD16 1WA, UK

First edition 2018

Copyright © 2018 Emerald Publishing Limited

Reprints and permissions service
Contact: permissions@emeraldinsight.com

British Library Cataloguing in Publication Data
A catalogue record for this book is available from the British Library

ISBN: 978-1-78714-612-9 (Print)
ISBN: 978-1-78714-611-2 (Online)
ISBN: 978-1-78743-262-8 (Epub)

ISSN: 1042-3192 (Series)

ISOQAR certified
Management System,
awarded to Emerald
for adherence to
Environmental
standard
ISO 14001:2004.

Certificate Number 1985
ISO 14001

INVESTOR IN PEOPLE

CONTENTS

PART III
SUBJECTIVITIES AND SUBJECT POSITIONS

LIST OF CONTRIBUTORS

Sophie Bowlby is a feminist social geographer whose research focuses on care, especially in relation to access, friendship and bereavement. Whilst retired, she has continued to research at the University of Reading, UK, and as Visiting Professor at Loughborough University, UK. She is co-author of *Interdependency and Care Over the Lifecourse* (Routledge, 2010).

Katherine Carroll is Research Fellow at the School of Sociology, Australian National University, Australia. She conducts sociological research on the banking and donation of female-specific reproductive tissues in relationship to motherhood. She has recently received an Australian Research Council grant to extend her research with both bereaved mothers and their health professionals on the topic of lactation and milk donation after infant loss.

Andrea Davies works as a Clinical Psychologist and Systemic Psychotherapist in Adult Mental Health Services for Abertawe Bro Morgannwg University Health Board, UK. She currently works with people admitted to a mental health ward and a Psychiatric Intensive Care Unit. Andrea has a specialist interest in working with people experiencing psychosis and those deemed 'hard to engage'.

Caroline Day is a children and youth geographer whose research focuses on transitions to adulthood, aspirations and care in sub-Saharan Africa, particularly Zambia. She is currently a Senior Lecturer in Human Geography at the University of Portsmouth, UK, and has also worked as a researcher for non-governmental organisations Barnardo's and Centrepoint.

Janet Fink is Professor of Childhood and Personal Relationships in the School of Education and Professional Development, University of Huddersfield, UK. Her research spans the disciplinary boundaries of sociology and social history and draws on mixed methods to explore the everyday relationships and experiences of children, young people and couples.

Lauren Fowler is a Clinical Assistant Professor of Neuroscience at the University of South Carolina School of Medicine in Greenville, SC, USA. She researches the effects of fatigue on empathy and performance in medical, military and law-enforcement personnel. She has served as a consultant for the US Air Force and has published in the journals *Behavioral Neuroscience* and *Primate*.

Aimee Grant is a Wellcome Trust ISSF Fellow at the Centre for Trials Research, Cardiff University, UK. Her interests are qualitative methods, stigma, pregnancy and motherhood. Her sole-authored methodology text *Doing EXCELLENT Social Research with Documents: Practical Examples and Guidance for Qualitative Researchers* will be published by Routledge in 2018.

Amie Scarlett Hodges is a Senior Lecturer in the School of Healthcare Sciences, Cardiff University, UK. Her research interest focuses around the sociology of health and illness, including children, young people, families, sibling performance, social interaction, places, spaces and respiratory health. She uses participatory, creative and visual methods within her work.

Łukasz Krzyżowski is Assistant Professor at AGH University of Science and Technology in Kraków, Poland. His research interests are transnational migration, old age and elderly care provisions, intergenerational solidarity, social networks and mixed-methods research.

Geraldine Latchem-Hastings is Senior Lecturer in the School of Healthcare Sciences, Cardiff University, UK. Her primary research is focused on health-care law, ethics and professional socialisation related to physiotherapy as a healthcare profession. Her secondary research focuses on creating digital learning spaces to facilitate allied health professionals, midwives and nurses learning to meet the challenges of modern healthcare practice.

Agata Lisiak teaches migration and urban studies at Bard College Berlin, Germany. She is interested in everyday urban cultures, visual cultures, spatialities and visualities of migration, and developing methodologies for research-ing said issues.

Tracey Loughran is Reader in History, University of Essex, UK. She is the author of *Shell-Shock and Medical Culture in First World War Britain* (Cambridge University Press, 2017) and co-editor (with Gayle Davis) of

The Palgrave Handbook of Infertility in History: Approaches, Contexts and Perspectives (Palgrave, 2017).

Kate Mahoney is a Post-Doctoral Research Assistant in the Department of History, University of Essex, UK. Her research examines feminist health activism in twentieth-century Britain. Her publications include *The Politics of Authenticity: Countercultures and Radical Movements across the Iron Curtain, 1968–1989* (Berghahn Books, 2018), co-edited with Joachim Häberlen and Mark Keck-Szajbel.

Dawn Mannay is a Senior Lecturer at Cardiff University, UK. Dawn recently edited a collection, *Our Changing Land: Revisiting Gender, Class and Identity in Contemporary Wales* (University of Wales Press, 2016) and wrote the sole-authored text, *Visual, Narrative and Creative Research Methods: Application, Reflection and Ethics* (Routledge, 2016).

Mary Morris works as a Senior Lecturer and Consultant Systemic Psychotherapist at the Family Institute in the University of South Wales, UK. She trains systemic psychotherapists and counsellors to qualifying level and beyond, as well as practicing as a psychotherapist herself. She has a particular interest in collaborative, social constructionist approaches to both education and psychotherapy, and is a Fellow of the Higher Education Academy.

Erin Roberts works within an interdisciplinary space in the School of Social Sciences at Cardiff University, UK. With a background in Human Geography, specialising in cultural, rural and energy geographies, she explores how relationships – with people, places and things –shape household energy demand across Wales.

Lisa Sheppard is a Lecturer in Welsh in Cardiff University, UK. Her research examines the portrayal of Wales's racial, ethnic and linguistic minority communities in contemporary Welsh- and English-language literature. Her monograph on the fictional portrayal of Welsh multiculturalism since 1990 will be published by University of Wales Press in 2018.

Sally Bishop Shigley is Professor of English at Weber State University, USA. She is currently pursuing research on the role of reading literature and empathy. She has published on topics from short fiction to poetry and health humanities.

Deborah Tout-Smith is Deputy Head and Senior Curator, Home & Community, in the Humanities Department of Museums Victoria, Australia. She has curated major exhibitions including *World War I: Love & Sorrow* (2014) and co-curated *The Melbourne Story* (2008). Deborah is Vice-President of ICOM Australia.

Lisa-Jo K. van den Scott is an Assistant Professor at Memorial University of Newfoundland, Canada. She has published in journals such as *The Journal of Contemporary Ethnography*, *The American Behavioral Scientist* and *Symbolic Interaction*. She is currently an Associate Editor for *The Journal of Empirical Research on Human Research Ethics*.

ACKNOWLEDGEMENTS

In editing this collection, *Emotion and the Researcher: Sites, Subjectivities and Relationships*, there are many people who should be thanked and acknowledged. As much of our initial engagement with questions of emotion, relationality and the ways in which methods travel across disciplinary boundaries began in our involvement with the Families, Identities and Gender Research Network, we will begin with this acknowledgement.

We both co-convened the interdisciplinary Families, Identities and Gender Research Network (FIG) at Cardiff University, with our colleagues Dr Siwan Rosser, Dr Melanie Bigold, Dr Katherine Shelton and Dr Stephanie Ward. We held a number of events that invited cross-disciplinary perspectives on the immensely complex topics of families, identities and gender, which foregrounded many of the issues that led to the creation of this volume. Papers presented at the series of 'Emotion and the Researcher' workshops, co-convened with the Women's History Network (West of England and South Wales), generated many of the following chapters. In the later workshop series, 'Constructing and Deconstructing Selfhood', we were joined by Dr Agata Lisiak. We are grateful for funding for this later event from the Economic and Social Research Council's Wales Doctoral Training Centre. We would also like to thank all of the presenters and delegates at these workshops. Even those who did not write chapters were in many ways the guiding muse for this collection.

It is also important to thank all of the individual authors for engaging with the project and offering a set of diverse and thoughtful accounts and reflections, drawing on their extensive knowledge and expertise. The authors have recounted their own experiences of research, generously sharing their approach to their craft and the uncertainties, concerns, enjoyments and questions it entails. Many of the contributors are friends and colleagues that we met through the workshops in Cardiff and at other international conferences. However, we feel that we have come to know the authors more closely through the editing process. We have a deep respect for the research and scholarship of all the authors in this collection, and we were privileged that they accepted the invitation to be part of *Emotion and the Researcher*. Overall, the authors' enthusiasm for the collection and their carefully crafted responses have engendered an inspiring set of chapters, and, in reading them, we have gained a wealth of knowledge, developed more nuanced understandings of emotion and gained a deeper appreciation of its place within and beyond interdisciplinary applications.

Dr Mike Ward was particularly helpful in selecting a publisher and providing advice drawn from his own experience publishing in Emerald's *Studies in Qualitative Methodology* series. We are grateful to Dr Sam Hillyard and Dr Philippa Grand for their invaluable help and guidance in developing the initial proposal for this book, and for their ongoing support and encouragement. The wider editorial team at Emerald should be acknowledged for their involvement, particularly Rachel Ward, who worked with us patiently to attend to all the essential administrative tasks that were necessary to move forward. We are also indebted to a wide range of authors and inspiring speakers and although we cannot name them all individually, much of their work is cited in the book.

Lastly, we would like to thank all our great friends and family. We are unable to acknowledge everyone, but those who are constantly involved in the emotional tapestry of our lives we would like to mention, in alphabetical order, with much love; David, Jamie, Jordon, Matthew, Sherelle, Tahlia, Taya, Tilleah, Tim, Toyah, Travis and Travis Jay.

LIST OF FIGURES

LIST OF ABBREVIATIONS

BAME	Black and Minority Ethnic
CDA	Critical Discourse Analysis
CF	Cystic Fibrosis
EMG	Electromyography
ERC	European Research Council
GSR	Galvanic Skin Response
HP	Health Professional
NGO	Non-Governmental Organisation
PHP	Pre-Healthcare Professional
RG	Remedial Gymnast
RMIT	Royal Melbourne Institute of Technology
UN	United Nations
WLM	Women's Liberation Movement
WTC	Women's Therapy Centre

FOREWORD

By Janet Fink

In an article about the role of emotions in feminist research, Kristin Blakely (2007, p. 60) asks the question:

> Suppose we turn the focus inward, reflecting not on the research but actually how we respond to our research, and suppose that we feel the research instead of just thinking it?

This provocation to suppose is part of a wider argument that emotionally engaged research 'opens up space for new questions, ideas and interpretations' (Blakely, 2007, p. 65), and it is just such a determination to suppose that is at the core of this important new interdisciplinary collection and its careful interrogation of the place of emotions in empirical research and the production of knowledge.

Given that, if we are sufficiently attentive to their presence, the complex dynamics of emotions can be traced, inter alia, through the development of research funding bids, responses to peer reviews, applications for ethical approval, fieldwork relationships, interpretations of data and the dissemination of findings – in short, 'the everyday' of our research practices – it is surprising that so few collections such as this exist. It is especially so since some of the most constant features of qualitative research are the emotional labour (Hochshild, 1983) demanded by its research practices (particularly when feminist in principle) and the emotionally fraught ethical dilemmas (Guillemin & Gillam, 2004) that emerge, often unpredictably, at every stage of the research process. Yet, at the same time, it is arguably not so surprising that such collections do not have a more visible presence on our bookshelves and in our libraries. As researchers we regularly have to negotiate feelings of respect, guilt, anger or anxiety in making decisions about what is 'the unsayable and the unspeakable'; 'who to represent and how' and 'what to omit and what to include' (Ryan-Flood & Gill, 2010, p. 3). It is not always easy to be open and transparent about such decisions or the emotions that inflect them, and so secrecy, silences and omissions can be recurrent aspects of our research,

research practices and research outputs (Ryan-Flood & Gill, 2010). However, as Sara Ahmed (2010, p. xvii) reminds us:

> 'secrets' aren't simply information or details that are passed or not passed. A secret might be something we keep from ourselves, something that is too hard or too painful to come to light.

It is noteworthy, then, that the authors in this collection *have* brought into the light aspects of their research and of themselves as researchers that they have found difficult to bear or to question, and they have been carefully reflexive about the reasons for this. They thus offer richly detailed examples to readers of how not only to 'trouble' taken-for-granted research practices, in which the researcher is assumed to maintain a neutral and objective standpoint, but also to reflect on the social, political and ethical relations of research generally. Crucially, at the core of these examples are wider theoretical and methodological debates about the meanings and study of emotions (Bailey & Barclay, 2017; Brownlie, 2014; Burkitt, 2014; Lupton, 1998; Smart, 2007) and the importance of presenting thick, vibrant accounts of research encounters and the embodied, sentient lives of research participants (Back, 2013; Gabb & Fink, 2017).

This collection thus echoes the content and concerns of papers presented at two workshops, titled 'Emotion and the Researcher', which were co-hosted in 2014 at Cardiff University by its Families, Identities, and Gender Research Network (FIG) and the Women's History Network (West of England and South Wales). As a member of the audience at one of the workshops and presenter at another, these events were deeply memorable for a number of reasons. First, they provided a 'safe place' for presentations in which emotions generated in and by different research topics, methods and collaborations could be shared with colleagues. Second, the audience was able to respond in kind by relating their own emotional responses to the presentations and the ways their research had evoked similar or different feelings. Third, for some presenters and audience members, these interactions enabled an often long overdue opportunity to acknowledge and process feelings generated either in the field, in the archive, during analysis or when writing up findings. And fourth, the workshops illustrated that 'emotionally sensed knowledge' is never readily or simply attained, not least because 'the epistemological status of such knowledge is always complex, uncertain and provisional' (Bowlby & Day, [this volume], p. 129). The trope of 'journeys' was thus regularly drawn upon in discussions as a way of examining the many different and sometimes arduous paths taken to develop the skills of emotional, ethical and caring reflexivity (Rallis & Rossman, 2010) and of elucidating how emotion is woven into the spatial and temporal dimensions of qualitative research as well as academic research careers.

Like the two workshops, this edited collection will productively animate and engage those just embarking on their research careers as well as those who have undertaken multiple projects. The authors encourage us to witness how re-focusing our analytic lens onto the secret, liminal or elided emotional landscapes of our research results in richer and more complicated understandings of epistemology, methodology, reflexivity and ontology. They have thus successfully and powerfully answered Blakely's (2007, p. 60) question about what happens when *we feel the research instead of just thinking it*.

REFERENCES

Ahmed, S. (2010). Foreword. In R. Ryan-Flood & R. Gill (Eds.), *Secrecy and silence in the research process* (pp. 1–12). London: Routledge.

Back, L. (2013). *The art of listening*. London: Bloomsbury Academic.

Bailey, M., & Barclay, K. (Eds.). (2017). *Emotion, ritual and power in Europe, 1200–1920: Family, state and church*. Basingstoke: Palgrave Macmillan.

Blakely, K. (2007). Reflections on the role of emotion in feminist research. *International Journal of Qualitative Methods*, 6(2), 59–68.

Bowlby, S., & Day, C. (2018). Emotions, disclosures and reflexivity: Reflections on interviewing young people in Zambia and women in midlife in the UK. In T. Loughran & D. Mannay (Eds.), *Emotion and the researcher: Sites, subjectivities and relationships* (Vol. 16). Studies in Qualitative Methodology (pp. 127–142). Bingley: Emerald.

Brownlie, J. (2014). *Ordinary relationships. A sociological study of emotions, reflexivity and culture*. Basingstoke: Palgrave MacMillan.

Burkitt, I. (2014). *Emotions and social relations*. London: Sage.

Gabb, J., & Fink, J. (2017). *Couple relationships in the 21st century: Research, policy, practice*. Basingstoke: Palgrave Macmillan.

Guillemin, M., & and Gillam, L. (2004). Ethics, reflexivity, and 'ethically important moments' in research. *Qualitative Inquiry*, 10(2), 261–280.

Hochshild, A. R. (1983). *The managed heart*. Berkeley, CA: University of California Press.

Lupton, D. (1998). *The emotional self*. London: SAGE.

Rallis, S. F., & Rossman, G. B. (2010). Caring reflexivity. *International Journal of Qualitative Studies in Education*, 23(4), 495–499.

Ryan-Flood, R., & Gill, R. (Eds.). (2010). *Secrecy and silence in the research process*. Abingdon, Oxon: Routledge.

Smart, C. (2007). *Personal life: New directions in sociological thinking*. Cambridge: Polity.

INTRODUCTION: WHY EMOTION MATTERS

Tracey Loughran and Dawn Mannay

THE RESEARCHER'S STORY

All researchers have stories to tell about why they chose to research particular topics. In some cases, there is a direct and uncomplicated link between personal experience and research agenda. We are not surprised to find that the sociologist who interrogates the relationship between class, inequality and education was once a child, 'working-class, troubled, difficult, out of place in schooling, a fighter but also a survivor' (Reay, 2017, p. 2), or that the historian of self-harm is scarred by self-inflicted wounds (Chaney, 2017, pp. 7–17 and 236–243). In other cases, the connections between researcher and subject are more oblique. Who would have guessed that a career in neuroscience hinged on a moment of boredom during a family holiday, when a young girl resorted to reading her grandfather's books, and became captivated by a volume on the brain (Fowler & Shigley, 2018 [this volume]). How could anyone else know that, as an unhappy adolescent, the historian of the First World War found a distorted mirror of her own pain in the symptoms of traumatised soldiers (Loughran, forthcoming)?

Whether such tales confirm expectations or provoke astonishment in the audience, they usually hold profound emotional resonance for the teller. As researchers, many of us feel intensely vulnerable about the prospect of telling our own stories, even if we firmly believe that our research is embedded in our

Emotion and the Researcher: Sites, Subjectivities, and Relationships
Studies in Qualitative Methodology, Volume 16, 1–15
Copyright © 2018 by Emerald Publishing Limited
All rights of reproduction in any form reserved
ISSN: 1042-3192/doi:10.1108/S1042-319220180000016001

selves. These stories are not peripheral to our research. They are about where it starts and what keeps us going in the face of obstacles that sometimes feel insurmountable. Yet, for the most part, when we present our research to audiences we deliberately exclude the stories that suffuse that work with meaning.

The same pattern is evident when we think about emotion in the research process. From our own experiences, and from our conversations with colleagues and students, we know that undertaking research is often an intensely emotional experience (Ehn & Löfgren, 2007). There is the frustration at data that will not yield easy answers, the anger at an aggressive question at a conference, the despair when reviewers do not like your work, and, of course, the joy when suddenly all the pieces fall into place and that tricky problem somehow resolves itself. Emotion is not an intrusion into the research process, but a constitutive element of it. So why do we so often pretend it is not there?

'OBJECTIVITY', SUBJECTIVITY AND EMOTION

All academic disciplines have their own conventions for organising research: particular boundaries, methodologies and technical vocabularies. These conventions amount to different ways of organising our mental worlds. They shape the way we see our subjects, the way we speak about them, and the extent to which outsiders can understand us. Most disciplines employ, at least to some extent, techniques that work to conceal the presence of the researcher, or to contain it within certain boundaries. Even when methodologies are used that directly influence the generation of evidence, such as ethnographic or oral history interviews, researchers sometimes apologise for their own presence in the text, try to write it out, or acknowledge their emotional responses entirely through the frame of risk to the data (Fitzpatrick & Olson, 2015, p. 49). Our common working practices create the impression that the researcher is an unfortunate necessity for the production of research, rather than its beating heart.

This embarrassment is, in many ways, a hangover from the nineteenth century, when the human sciences emerged in their distinctively modern forms. As the ideal of scientific objectivity took shape from the mid-nineteenth-century (Daston & Galison, 2007), it became the idol of emergent disciplines with ambitions to scientific status (Smith, 1997, pp. 3–35). This epistemological framework held that the particular researcher was incidental to the generation of universally valid data. Any researcher employing a properly scientific method should be able to replicate the same results, and researchers not employing a properly scientific method would not produce data worth replicating. The worldview that relegated subjectivity to the status of dirty secret also outlawed demonstrable emotion. In the dominant Darwinian paradigm of the late nineteenth-century, emotion was associated with children, women and non-white races (Darwin, 1872; Lutz, 1986, pp. 289–290), and seen as opposed to the rational intelligence of European manhood. Emotion tainted research.

For good or ill, in the nineteenth century, the ideals of objectivity and the scientific method revolutionised approaches to the study of human life. Despite serious challenges in recent decades to their hegemony, these ideals still influence academic research in all kinds of ways, both acknowledged and implicit. One of the most far-reaching effects is that researchers still struggle to acknowledge and explore their own emotions and subjectivity in ways that enrich their research. As Clifford Geertz (1995, p. 120) lamented in relation to difficulties in theorising field research as a mode of enquiry, 'We lack the language to articulate what takes place when we are in fact at work. There seems to be a genre missing'. In other words, most of us find it difficult to 'show our workings', to account for how the inner states we experience shape and alter our research, even when we fully accept that the 'unseen lens' of emotion 'colors all our thoughts, actions, perceptions and judgments' (Goodwin, Jasper, & Polletta, 2001, p. 10). This volume is an attempt to find this missing genre; to work out exactly what it is we lack, and how we might fill this gap.

EMOTIONAL TURNS

This volume is, therefore, another contribution to the 'emotional turn' within the social sciences and humanities over the past three decades. The roots of this 'emotional turn' spread far and wide, but for current purposes, two particular drivers are especially important. The first is the intellectual purchase of post-structuralism across all fields since the 1980s (Howarth, 2013); the 'cultural turn' was a necessary precondition for its emotional successor (Roseneil & Frosh, 2012). The notion that all knowledge is culturally constructed encouraged research into aspects of experience previously perceived as fixed and ahistorical, including the body and emotions (Rubin, 2002, p. 83), and simultaneously undermined academic claims to objectivity and neutrality. In the wake of this intellectual revolution, and with the realisation that subjectivity had been hiding in plain sight all along, it suddenly seemed necessary to probe the historical and contemporary construction of emotion.

Despite the resurgence of neuroscientific perspectives on emotion within some fields (Damasio, 1999; Rose & Abi-Rached, 2013), and to a certain extent even within popular culture, research in the social sciences and humanities has succeeded in challenging universalist and transhistorical conceptions of emotion (Connolly, 2011; Leys, 2011). There now exists an enormous wealth of research on how emotion operates in specific social, cultural and historical contexts, and it is difficult for even the most hard-bitten neuroscientist or cognitive psychologist to deny that the cultural mediation of emotion has differed greatly according to time and place (Reddy, 2001; Ticiento Clough & Halley, 2007).

The second important driver in the turn to emotion, and one inextricably linked to the development of the 'cultural turn', is the wider social change that has influenced both the make-up of the academy and the perceived legitimacy of different approaches to academic scholarship. Since the 1960s, as 'minorities' (women, gay and Black and minority ethnic scholars) have claimed their rights to a place within the academy, they (we) have vociferously challenged an 'objectivity' that is perceived as the sole preserve of white middle-class men – those who 'never even notice what it means to inhabit that category' because their inhabiting of it 'is never called into question' (Antwi, Brophy, Strauss, & Troeung, 2013, p. 124). These marginalised groups did not only dissect the ideal of objectivity, but in prising open its carapace generated new approaches that emphasised the unavoidability of emotion and subjectivity within research (Harding, 1987). Individuals and groups perceived as fatally aligned with emotion, and therefore as incapable of attaining rationality and objectivity, could only stake their claims to rights, power and voice by attacking the entire worldview that assumed 'objectivity' was possible for some but not others (Rowbotham, 1973, pp. 34–35). Feminist scholars ripped away the veil of science to unmask vested patriarchal interests; post-colonial theorists revealed the rational Enlightenment subject as standing not on the shoulders of giants, but the corpses of dispossessed imperial subjects (Narayan, 2012, p. 147; Taylor, 2012, p. 197). In doing so, they laid bare 'the ideological functions of emotions' as a concept within 'a system of power relations' that its use helps to maintain (Lutz, 1986, p. 288).

Our volume picks up the story from this point and pursues one corollary of these revelations of the impossibility of objectivity. Acceptance of the social construction of all knowledge led many scholars to re-engage with questions of emotion and subjectivity, from several different perspectives. Some chose to assert the irreducibility of biological expressions of emotions and to separate out this terrain from the cultural expressions that *could* be studied (Hofman, 2016, p. 15). Others, following to its logical conclusion the argument that we all necessarily speak from a specific subject position, argued that explorations of subjectivity could even enrich and deepen understanding

(Eley, 2005, pp. 169–172; Miller, 1991, p. 20). These scholars sought new tools, such as the application of psychoanalytic theory outside therapeutic contexts, to shed light on inner states (Hunt, 1990, pp. 109–110). For at least some of these scholars, the turn to subjectivity and emotion provided a means of escaping post-structuralism's relentless emphasis on textuality, and recovering something of the 'real'. It also provided, at least potentially, a way to recognise that research 'involves complicated issues of identification and recognition, and is not itself outside the circuit of psychic exchanges, of projection and introjection' (Dawson, 1994, p. 240).

This approach to subjectivity is only one part, but perhaps the most controversial, of the 'emotional turn'. There are many potential objections, beyond a rearguard defence of scientific 'neutrality', to approaches that make subjectivity central to scholarship. The use of psychoanalytic theory beyond the therapist's couch is perceived as particularly problematic, and from several different perspectives: because the theory is valid in the clinical context, but untried and untestable elsewhere; because the unconscious is, by its very nature, inaccessible to consciousness; or because the fundamental premises of psychoanalysis, including the existence of the unconscious, are unproven. Where scholars do not trespass on the territory of the unconscious, their critics might argue that while explorations of individual subjectivity can tell us much about one person, they are not replicable to other people or contexts, and so can tell us little about wider experiences. (This is, in many ways, simply a new twist on the old criticism that the case study always remains exceptional, and its findings cannot be applied to wider contexts.) Finally, even those scholars seduced by promises of deeper understanding fear that analysis of the subject position will slide into pure subjectivity, and read as self-indulgence rather than the attempt to reach another kind of truth (Roper, 2014, pp. 186–187). As Renato Rosaldo (1993, p. 7) suggested in his seminal essay on grief and a headhunter's rage, trying to avoid the 'slippage from the ideal of detachment to actual indifference', carries the risk for 'the self-absorbed Self to lose sight altogether of the culturally different Other'.

These multiple objections help to explain why, while we now know much about the operation of emotion at different sites in contemporary and past societies (Matt, 2011; Stearns, 1994; Stearns & Stearns, 1988), for the most part researchers have proved reluctant to cross-examine their own emotional motivations, or how their emotional relations to their research topics affect their methodologies and findings. Where researchers do reflect on the role of emotion in the research process, these insights are often either scattered, concentrated within or perceived as only relevant to specific research fields, such as autoethnography, participatory approaches or oral history. It is still difficult to find a place for the researcher within the results of research. Despite the widespread acceptance that the subjectivity of the researcher is, at least to some degree, inescapable, scholars troubled by this problem still most often choose to book-end their results with a discussion of the 'I' who created it, rather than to integrate the 'I' within it. We return to Geertz's identification, more than 20 years ago, of a missing 'genre', and add that there is still no established, immediately recognisable and easily replicable way of placing the researcher within research. What can we do about this?

EMOTIONAL JOURNEYS

This volume is an attempt to resolve some of these problems, and it is the result of a long journey. For several years, we (the volume editors) co-convened the interdisciplinary Families, Identities and Gender Research Network (FIG) at Cardiff University, with our colleagues Melanie Bigold, Siwan Rosser, Katherine Shelton, and Stephanie Ward. As a group, we spanned many different disciplines: English literature, history, social science, psychology, and Welsh studies. We created FIG because of our dawning realisation that although we shared common interests, even within the context of one institution it was difficult to reach across disciplinary confines. As we held more events that invited cross-disciplinary perspectives on the immensely complex topics of families, identities and gender, the similarities and differences between disciplines began to trouble some of us. We became intrigued by what different traditions take for granted or dispute, the ways in which ideas and methods remain confined or travel across disciplinary boundaries, and the very different uses of apparently similar terms across diverse fields.

This curiosity led us to hold two linked workshops in 2014 on 'Emotion and the Researcher'. One of our main aims in these workshops was to interrogate the operation of 'objectivity' as an ideal and a guiding principle of research, perceived as essential to maintaining scholarly standards, across diverse disciplines. Our frank and often passionate discussions within FIG had convinced us that emotions are always present during the research process and affect the final outcomes, but that disciplinary conventions often work to disguise the emotional impetus behind research. The workshops proved immensely stimulating, as speakers from diverse academic institutions and disciplinary fields discussed, shared and debated the emotional lifeworlds of their research. The excitement of the event generated interest to create a book, and the proposal attracted international scholars who were also looking for a platform to share the lived experience of being a researcher.

In each chapter in this volume, authors reflect on their own experiences of research and generously share their approach to their craft, and the uncertainties, concerns, enjoyments and questions it entails. The contributors are based in departments and schools of Geography, Healthcare Sciences, History, Literature, Medicine, Sociology, and Welsh; in the museum sector; in an institute for psychotherapy, training and consultation; and on a University Health Board. The volume, therefore, brings together disciplines (from the social sciences, humanities and healthcare) that do not usually form part of the same field of enquiry. This provides a unique opportunity for reflection on differences between and similarities across disciplinary boundaries, and sheds new light on common problems and opportunities stimulated by emotion in research. We further consider the revelations this approach offers in our Afterword, but emphasise here that in exposing readers to different disciplinary practices, we hope to encourage them to reflect on the often unacknowledged assumptions within their own fields.

We therefore have three main aims in this volume. The first is to explore how emotion operates throughout the research process. To this end, we have divided the book into three sections, each hosting five chapters, which respectively deal with research relationships, sites and subjectivities. These themes are inevitably interrelated, but shifting the focus to a different aspect of the research process in each section underlines our central finding that emotion is always and inescapably present in research, as well as demonstrating how 'emotional entanglements evolve and transform over time and in different spaces of the field' (Laliberté & Schurr, 106, p. 75). Our second goal is not only perhaps the simplest, but also the most enjoyable: to share methodologies, case studies and experiences from different fields, and in this way to demonstrate the invigorating effects of cross-disciplinary ways of thinking and working. Finally, we want to develop techniques and languages for acknowledging, understanding and consciously integrating emotion into every step of the research process. Each chapter in this volume, therefore, amply confirms Coffey's (1999, p. 158) assertion that 'emotional connectedness to the process and practices of fieldwork, to analysis and writing is normal and appropriate' and 'should be acknowledged, reflected upon, and seen as a fundamental feature of well-executed research'.

REFLEXIVITY AND RESEARCH RELATIONSHIPS

Our first section, 'Reflexivity and Research Relationships', examines how researchers' personal and political identifications influence their relations with research participants. Each chapter focuses on the affective elements of negotiation within professional and personal research relationships. Importantly, these chapters explore research both within and beyond the field, examining the role of reflexivity in active research relationships, in the process of analysis and in the everyday encounters, interactions and recollections which act on and through the researcher.

Lisa-Jo K. van den Scott's opening chapter on reflexivity and role transitions in the field illustrates the transient and shifting nature of research relationships where researchers are neither total 'insiders' nor 'outsiders' in relation to the individuals they interview (Song & Parker, 1995, p. 243). The chapter documents how van den Scott's transition from the role of friend to that of researcher in the Inuit community in Arviat, Nunavat, and how this transition was further complicated by her social location as a Western outsider. Here, van den Scott reflects on how she encountered, embraced, and even celebrated the exotic, and the importance of adopting an attitude of learning (Spradley, 1979). Appreciating and communicating the honour, enjoyment and terror of researching and representing community lives, the chapter concludes that, 'Research is a messy roller coaster. But what a ride!'

Agata Lisiak and Łukasz Krzyżowski follow with their chapter on emotional support within a research team. The chapter disrupts the idea of researcher 'nearness' based on a shared country of origin, demonstrating that epistemic privilege can be dangerous because it produces a false binary, Polish/non-Polish, 'which silences the multifaceted nature of identities, lifestyles and perspectives' (Mannay, 2010, p. 92). Lisiak and Krzyżowski reflect on their experiences as Polish migrants conducting interviews with other Polish migrants, describing how their participants positioned them as 'like them', and assumed that their own racist, Islamophobic, homophobic, xenophobic, classist, or misogynist perspectives were shared. Their commitment to the wider aims of the research project meant that the authors felt unable to counter these claims. This was emotionally challenging, yet they were able to negotiate these difficulties by drawing support from each other. They share this story to highlight the importance of collegiality when carrying out emotional labour, despite the often anti-collegial and hypercompetitive landscape of academia.

In her chapter on the positional self and researcher emotion, Amie Hodges examines how the researcher's presence can impact on emotional hierarchies, norms and everyday interactions within families. Focusing specifically on how the researcher's presence influences sibling relationships, Hodges communicates how children with cystic fibrosis often take centre stage in family life. In bringing the voices of non-cystic fibrosis siblings to the fore, her research destabilised the existing family equilibrium. Initially, this generated anger, hostility and defensiveness, but later resulted in partial resolution of unequal sibling relationships. The chapter argues that reflective metaphorical expression can be applied as a method of processing and coping with the emotional impacts of unforeseen and unexpected interactions, and at the same time engender more nuanced understandings of family life.

Kate Mahoney's chapter also acknowledges the salience of hierarchy but her chapter on the emotional entanglements generated by researching the British women's movement returns to an emphasis on the research/researched dyad. The social category of researcher often acts as an important basis for the distribution of status, and access to power, where the researcher is positioned as holding more power than the research participant. However, for Mahoney, her positive emotions, including feelings of excitement, reverence, commonality and being a 'fan of feminism', reversed this position and curtailed critical questioning in the interview setting. Examining the interactional features of positive emotional exchanges, Mahoney argues that historians' personal identifications can inspire research, but unless acknowledged and questioned, the same identifications can work against the desired end of producing critical histories.

The final chapter in this section is Dawn Mannay's exploration of the telling and silencing of trauma in interviews with marginalised mothers. This account moves away from positive emotions to consider the emotional impacts of topics that are hard to speak of and hard to bear. Considering the nature of the interaction between researchers and participants, Mannay argues that psychoanalytically informed frames of analysis can engender a more nuanced understanding of the relationality and emotionality of qualitative research. Rejecting the 'image of dispassionate science' (Rogers-Dillon, 2005, p. 445) conducted by disconnected researchers devoid of any feelings that could contaminate the integrity of the data, the chapter examines feelings of helplessness, anger, guilt and resolution, drawing attention to their emotional weight but also their reflexive value.

EMOTIONAL TOPOGRAHIES AND RESEARCH SITES

The second section, 'Emotional Topographies and Research Sites', considers the operation and communication of emotion across diverse research sites. The chapters explore the emotional resonances of research across different disciplines and domains, including online media, museums, home communities and non-Western cultures. The authors explore the boundaries of insider and outsider positioning, and the emotions of sadness, anger, helplessness and hope, across private and public spaces in their roles of researcher, writer and curator.

Katherine Carroll begins this shift of focus with her opening chapter on public emotion in applied sociology, which is based on her experience of researching breastmilk donation after infant death. Although early infant death is always a devastating experience, Carroll argues that 'heartfelt positivity methodology' (adopting a positive approach) shows that breastmilk donation after early infant death can provide some bereaved mothers with feelings of pride, productivity and a sense of purpose. Moving beyond the initial fieldwork, Carroll explores the emotional afterlife of this work and its relational affects in three spaces: the audience at an international milk banking conference, a national stakeholder meeting and academic peer review.

Erin Roberts also considers how emotions come into play both in fieldwork and after researchers have left the field. Roberts draws on her experience of conducting a bilingual study of rural household energy consumption in the community where she was born and raised to consider issues of nearness and distance. Documenting the emotional intricacies of doing research 'at home', Roberts introduces the concept of the transient insider to reflect on forms of comfortable uncomfortableness, and the weight of responsibility in telling other people's tales. The notion of transience employed across the chapter emphasises a fluid understanding of positionality, which displaces fixed binaries to illustrate the complexities and multiplicities of space, place and belonging.

Caroline Day and Sophie Bowlby reflect on their experiences both home and away in interviewing young people in Zambia and women in midlife in the UK. The chapter examines the 'translation' of interpretations of emotional responses from one cultural context into another within and beyond the face-to-face encounter of the interview. Day and Bowlby examine cultural sensitivity within the fieldwork and the process of making emotional sense of people's stories, exploring their own positioning, how to react 'appropriately' to distressing accounts, the issues raised in using an interpreter in foreign language encounters and the guilt of actual and perceived privilege. The chapter illustrates the entwinement of emotional and professional complexities and demonstrates the importance of researchers sharing their own uncertainties around fieldwork and interpretation.

The following chapter contends that participant absent research can generate equally complicated emotions. Aimee Grant demonstrates how data collection techniques framed as 'passive' affect researchers' emotional lifeworlds. The realm of online communication can no longer be seen as a hermeneutically separate space; rather, in this digital age, portals to the virtual world mediate and shape 'real' life experiences. Reflecting on her analysis of user-generated data from an online news site and Twitter, Grant examines the emotion work required in participant absent research. Documenting the physiological impacts of anger, experienced through an elevated heart rate, and the shift from revulsion to desensitisation, Grant's chapter illustrates how physical distance cannot negate the psychological nearness, and associated affective disruption, of emotive online accounts.

Deborah Tout-Smith's chapter moves from the online world to the public space of the museum to consider how emotion can be harnessed to communicate the impacts of historical events on everyday lives to contemporary audiences. The emotional aspects of museum work have received relatively little attention, but Tout-Smith argues that to develop deeper understandings of the past, exhibitions must not simply curate and display inert objects. In the exhibition 'World War I: Love & Sorrow' that she curated for Museums Victoria, Tout-Smith strategically deployed emotion to present an honest, graphic and challenging account of the experience of the First World War. In this chapter, she draws on surveys and qualitative interviews with exhibition visitors to show how the personal stories and objects displayed in the exhibition built empathy and an appreciation of the impacts of war on individuals and families, both in the past and in the present.

SUBJECTIVITIES AND SUBJECT POSITIONS

The final section, 'Subjectivity and Subject Positions', examines tensions between researchers' emotional and political identifications and the 'translation' of subjectivity into established scholarly conventions. Researchers routinely turn their attention to the lives of others who then feature in their written accounts, but within the constraints of academic publishing they are less prone to represent 'themselves as social and cultural products, producing social and cultural products' (Richardson, 1997, p. 1). As in the previous sections, the authors reject the ideology of the rational, detached and objective researcher, but here they also draw on personal experiences to emphasise the positive value of emotions and subjectivities in the research process.

Sally Bishop Shigley's and Lauren Fowler's opening chapter reflects on their collaborative investigation into whether reading literature increases empathy in health professionals. The authors reflect on their journeys into academia and their differential positionings as neuroscientist and literature scholar. As well as considering the potential dissonance between literary approaches and quantitative measures, and how this can be resolved in research design, the chapter puts forward a passionate plea for collaborative ways of working: 'interdisciplinary work, interpersonal trust and a willingness to be vulnerable opens us up to see and imagine things that we would not have access to if we restricted ourselves to our disciplinary world view'.

The next chapter returns to some of the issues explored in the previous sections around both insider/outsider status, and the difficulties generated by positive emotional orientations to research participants. Lisa Sheppard explores how her identity as a second-language Welsh speaker affected her doctoral study and her actions as an early career researcher. Sheppard links her academic interest in hybrid identities, multilingualism and multicultural- ism to her personal history in which different languages symbolise different emotional relationships and different kinds of national identity. As an emerg- ing academic in the close-knit Welsh literary world, Sheppard experienced an affective disjuncture between her belief that criticism is essential to the development of a robust and inclusive literary and critical culture, and her understandable reluctance to speak critically about the work of writers she knew and liked.

Similar issues resurface in Geraldine Latchem-Hastings' account of ethi- cal practice in healthcare research on paediatric physiotherapy. The work of the physiotherapist entails close and prolonged physical contact with patients and their families, which is necessarily imbued with emotion. The emotional resonances of these encounters inevitably infiltrated Latchem-Hastings' interviews with physiotherapists, but as a former paediatric physiotherapist herself, Latchem-Hastings also had to negotiate thorny problems of nearness and distance, acceptance and judgement, and trust and suspicion through- out these interview encounters. The chapter argues for the importance of structured attention to emotional responses in the field, close examination of how and why researchers make particular theoretical interpretations from participants' narratives, and reflection on the relations between researchers and participants. Working through feelings of guilt, anger and frustration, Latchem-Hastings invites the reader to consider the importance of 'reflect- ing on ethically important, and at times uncomfortable, moments in the research process'.

Mary Morris' and Andrea Davies' chapter continues with the theme of reflexivity in relation to their use of a collaborative 'second-person' methodol- ogy within an action research framework. The chapter explores the historical legacies of positions that align masculinity (and science) with rationality and objectivity, and femininity with irrationality and subjectivity. In this world-view, 'the feminine' is a contaminant of empirical purity. Morris and Davies make gender central to their self-reflexive practices, acknowledging and connecting with emotions in the fields of clinical and systemic psychotherapy. They conclude that although 'entrenched vocabularies' around gender and research still exert too much influence within their discipline, these vocabularies can be challenged by collaborative, reflexive and feminist practices of the kind undertaken in this chapter.

Closing the section, Tracey Loughran considers the interaction of subjectivity, class and education in British 'autobiographical histories'. Loughran details how her own experiences of class and higher education affected her reading of Carolyn Steedman's *Landscape for a Good Woman* (1986), and how the text provided a way to understand and reflect on her own 'inbetween-ness' as an educated working-class woman. The chapter explores who has the authority to speak, the ways in which some voices become silenced and how methods of writing that acknowledge emotion and vulnerability can challenge the accepted order and insist marginalised voices are heard.

Overall, this volume argues that the presentation of research as 'objective' conceals the subject positions of researchers, and the emotional imperatives that often drive research. In this sense, the erasure of the researcher from published accounts of research can be more misleading, or perhaps even dishonest, than acknowledging her/his presence. In this collection, we engage with the emotional experiences of researchers working in different traditions, contexts and sites, and demonstrate their centrality in data production, analysis, dissemination and ethical practice. We never lose sight of 'the rich lived *practice* of emotion culture' (Ikegami, 2012, p. 352). This sustained focus on the emotional position of the researcher and the role of emotion in the research process, rather than on the constitution or operation of emotion in research participants or in contexts 'out there' has a further effect. It breaks down the artificial division between researchers and their participants that much research on emotion still assumes, and therefore unintentionally reifies. We are therefore able to shift 'between the position of participant and observer/listener, constantly reflecting upon how we know about things, and how to view the knowledge we produce' (Edwards & Robbens, 1992, p. 2). In this way, reflection on emotion within research has the potential to lead to new methodologies and practices (Laliberté & Schurr, 2016, p. 73). The volume is therefore a sustained plea for the need to find a new place for emotion in research; to research and write in ways that are more honest, more revealing, and have greater potential to disrupt the established workings of knowledge and power.

REFERENCES

Antwi, P., Brophy, S., Strauss, H., & Troeung, Y-D. (2013). 'Not without ambivalence': An interview with Sara Ahmed on postcolonial intimacies. *Interventions*, *15*(1), 110–126.

Chaney, S. (2017). *Psyche on the skin. A history of self-harm*. London: Reaktion Books.

Coffey, A. (1999). *The ethnographic self, fieldwork and the representation of identity*. London: SAGE.

Connolly, W. (2011). I: The complexity of intention. *Critical Inquiry*, *37*(4), 791–798.

Damasio, A. (1999). *The feeling of what happens: Body and emotion in the making of consciousness*. New York, NY: Harcourt Brace.

Daston, L., & Galison, P. (2007). *Objectivity*. Brooklyn, NY: Zone Books.

Darwin, C. (1872). *The expression of the emotions in man and animals*. London: John Murray.

Dawson, G. (1994). *Soldier heroes: British adventure, empire and the imagining of masculinities*. London: Routledge.

Edwards, R., & Ribbens, J. (1998). Living on the edges: Public knowledge, private lives, personal experience. In J. Ribbens & R. Edwards (Eds.), *Feminist dilemmas in qualitative research: Public knowledge and private lives* (pp. 1–23). London: SAGE.

Ehn, B., & Löfgren, O. (2007). Emotions in academia. In H. Wulff (Ed.), *The emotions: A cultural reader* (pp. 101–117). Oxford: Berg.

Eley, G. (2005). *A crooked line: From cultural history to the history of society*. Ann Arbor, MI: University of Michigan Press.

Fitzpatrick, P., & Olsen, R. E. (2015). A rough road map to reflexivity in qualitative research into emotions. *Emotion Review*, *7*(1), 49–54.

Fowler, L., & Shigley, S. B. (2018). The expectation of empathy: Unpacking our epistemological bags while researching empathy, literature, and neuroscience. In T. Loughran & D. Mannay (Eds.), *Emotion and the researcher: Sites, subjectivities and relationships* (Vol. 16). Studies in Qualitative Methodology (pp. 179–196). Bingley: Emerald.

Geertz, C. (1995). *After the fact: Two countries, four decades, one anthropologist*. Cambridge, MA: Harvard University Press.

Goodwin, J., Jasper, J. M., & Polletta, F. (2001). Introduction: Why emotions matter. In J. Goodwin, J. M. Jasper, & F. Polletta (Eds.), *Passionate politics: Emotions and social movements* (pp. 1–24). Chicago, IL: University of Chicago Press.

Harding, S. (1987). Introduction: Is there a feminist method?. In S. Harding (Ed.), *Feminism and methodology: Social science issues* (pp. 1–14). Bloomington, IN: Indiana University Press.

Hofman, E. (2016). How to do the history of the self. *History of the Human Sciences*, *29*(3), 8–24.

Howarth, D. R. (2013). *Poststructuralism and after: Structure, subjectivity and power*. Basingstoke: Palgrave Macmillan.

Hunt, L. (1990). History beyond social theory. In D. Carroll (Ed.), *The states of 'theory': History, art and critical discourse* (pp. 95–111). Stanford, CA: Stanford University Press.

Ikegami, E. (2012). Emotions. In U. Rublack (Ed.), *A concise companion to history* (pp. 333–353). Oxford: Oxford University Press.

Laliberté, N., & Schurr, C. (2016). Introduction: The stickiness of emotions in the field: Complicating feminist methodologies. *Gender, Place and Culture*, *23*(1), 72–78.

Leys, R. (2011). The turn to affect: A critique. *Critical Inquiry*, *37*(3), 434–472.

Loughran, T. (forthcoming). Absent families and the present self: Personal reflections on emotion and writing a history of trauma in the First World War. In J. Damousi, D. Tout-Smith, & B. Ziino (Eds.), *World War I: Love & sorrow*. Melbourne: Museums Victoria.

Lutz, C. (1986). Emotion, thought, and estrangement: Emotion as a cultural category. *Cultural Anthropology*, *1*(3), 287–309.

Mannay, D. (2010). Making the familiar strange: Can visual research methods render the familiar setting more perceptible?. *Qualitative Research*, *10*(1), 91–111.

Matt, S. (2011). Current emotion research in history: Or, doing history from the inside out. *Emotion Review*, *3*(1), 117–124.

Miller, N. K. (1991). *Getting personal: Feminist occasions and other autobiographical acts*. New York, NY: Routledge.

Narayan, Y. (2012). The cultural turn, racialisation and postcoloniality. In S. Roseneil & S. Frosh (Eds.), *Social research after the cultural turn* (pp. 144–159). Basingstoke: Palgrave Macmillan.

Reay, D. (2017). *Miseducation: Inequality, education and the working classes*. Bristol: Policy Press.

Reddy, W. (2001). *The navigation of feeling: A framework for the history of emotions*. Cambridge: Cambridge University Press.

Richardson, L. (1997). *Fields of play: Constructing an academic life*. New Brunswick, NJ: Rutgers University Press.

Rogers-Dillon, R. H. (2005). Hierarchal qualitative research teams: Refining the methodology. *Qualitative Research*, *5*, 437–454.

Roper, M. (2014). The unconscious work of history. *Cultural and Social History*, *11*(2), 169–193.

Rosaldo, R. (1993). *Culture and truth: The remaking of social analysis*. With a new introduction. Boston, MA: Beacon Press.

Rose, N., & Abi-Rached, J. M. (2013). *Neuro: The new brain sciences and the management of the mind*. Princeton, NJ: Princeton University Press.

Roseneil, S., & Frosh, S. (2012). Social research after the cultural turn: A (self-) critical introduction. In S. Roseneil & S. Frosh (Eds.), *Social research after the cultural turn* (pp. 1–15). Basingstoke: Palgrave Macmillan.

Rowbotham, S. (1973). *Woman's consciousness, man's world*. Harmondsworth: Penguin.

Rubin, M. (2002). What is cultural history now?. In D. Cannadine (Ed.), *What is history now?* (pp. 80–94). Basingstoke: Palgrave Macmillan.

Smith, R. (1997). *The Norton history of the human sciences*. New York, NY: W.W. Norton & Company.

Song, M., & Parker, D. (1995). Commonality, difference and the dynamics of discourse in in-depth interviewing. *Sociology*, *29*(2), 241–256.

Spradley, J. P. (1979). *The ethnographic interview*. New York, NY: Holt, Rinehart and Winston.

Stearns, P. (1994). *American cool: Constructing a twentieth-century emotional style*. New York, NY: New York University Press.

Stearns, C., & Stearns, P. (1988). *Emotion and social change: Toward a new psychohistory*. New York, NY: Holmes & Meier.

Steedman, C. (1986). *Landscape for a good woman*. London: Virago.

Taylor, B. (2012). Historical subjectivity. In S. Alexander & B. Taylor (Eds.), *History and psyche: Culture, psychoanalysis, and the past* (pp. 195–210). Basingstoke: Palgrave Macmillan.

Ticiento Clough, P., & Halley, J. (Eds.). (2007). *The affective turn: Theorizing the social*. Durham, NC: Duke University Press.

PART I
REFLEXIVITY AND RESEARCH RELATIONSHIPS

CHAPTER 1

ROLE TRANSITIONS IN THE FIELD AND REFLEXIVITY: FROM FRIEND TO RESEARCHER

Lisa-Jo K van den Scott

ABSTRACT

Purpose – *Occasionally, we find our social roles transitioning from friend to researcher. This chapter is a reflexive account of one such transition. The author examines the emotions, the concerns and the rewards and stresses of this shift in her relationship with individuals and community.*

Methodology/Approach – *The author moved to Arviat, Nunavut, in 2004 and gradually found her inner sociologist could not be contained. Through a process of consultation with the Inuit community in which she was residing, she transitioned from the role of friend to that of researcher. This was complicated by her social location as a Western outsider who had been accepted as a community member.*

Findings – *Reflexivity is a key component of mitigating the challenges which arose and pursuing ethical research, as well as managing the dynamic range of experiences and feelings which emerged during this process.*

Keywords: Emotions in the field; Inuit; reflexivity; researcher role; insider/outsider status

Emotion and the Researcher: Sites, Subjectivities, and Relationships
Studies in Qualitative Methodology, Volume 16, 19–32
Copyright © 2018 by Emerald Publishing Limited
All rights of reproduction in any form reserved
ISSN: 1042-3192/doi:10.1108/S1042-319220180000016002

INTRODUCTION

I eyed the black, gelatinous meat warily, trying not to let my uncertainty show on my face. It was a bright May day, and we were visiting friends out on the sea ice during the annual fishing derby. I had just been offered *igunak*: raw, aged walrus meat. I could feel their questions: 'How would the *qablunaaq* [a person from South of Churchill, Manitoba, usually white] cope?' 'Would she try the delicacy, or judge the eating of raw meat?' I smiled my gratitude, sank to my knees in front of the meat sitting in a grocery bag on the snow, and cut myself a slightly too generous piece with a nearby *ulu* (a curved, Inuit knife). Fear rose up. Would I get sick from raw, aged meat? If I did not try it, how would that impact on my friendships there? Could I actually get it down with a pleasant expression on my face and would a slip make it worse than not trying it? I put the meat into my mouth and chewed once, twice, and swallowed the rest of it whole. To my surprise, I found that if I had been accustomed to the texture, I would have found the taste pleasurable. But, as it rested against my tongue, invoking the palette of a distant place and culture, it was quite challenging.

When I got home, I called one of my good friends (an Inuk friend) and told her what I had eaten. She was impressed and told me she would not go near the stuff! Rather like blue cheese, you love it or you hate it. Nevertheless, I had made an impression for being willing to try *igunak*. That was 12 years ago, and I am still relieved that I was able to partake in the offered food. Since then, however, I have been quite aware that this 'commitment act' (Emerson, Fretz, & Shaw, 1995), which was in the context of friendship, helped pave my way to being a researcher in this community. This chapter is a reflexive account of my transition from friend to researcher in a remote Inuit hamlet in Nunavut, Canada.

I moved to Arviat, Nunavut, in 2004 and gradually found my inner sociologist could not be contained. Through a process of consultation with the Inuit community in which I was residing, I transitioned from the role of friend to the role of researcher. This was further complicated by my social location as a Western outsider who had been accepted as a community member prior to the transition to researcher. I examine the emotions, the concerns and the rewards and stresses of this shift in my relationship with individuals and the community. Reflexivity is a key component of mitigating the challenges which arose and pursuing ethical research, as well as managing the dynamic range of experiences and feelings which emerged during this process.

Arviat, Nunavut, is home to roughly 2,500 people. It is only accessible by airplane and maintains one of the more traditional Inuit ways of living in Nunavut. Inuktitut is still the dominant language and traditional foods common. The government of Canada forcibly settled the citizens of Arviat, *Arviammiut*, into this community during the late 1950s through the mid-1960s. All names here are pseudonyms.

NEW FRIENDS

I moved to Arviat in the capacity of the music teacher's wife. My status there as a married woman allowed me into settings which otherwise would have been restricted. For example, I could interact with men in a business capacity without worrying that people would talk. There were single Western women living in town as teachers or government workers, but they were either considered to be of low moral fibre, or were restricted to only interacting with other women. Soon I found work as a substitute teacher and then as an instructor at Nunavut Arctic College.

When I initially arrived, I had just completed my MA in Ancient Greek and had no sociological research intentions. I did not intend to make the Inuit my object of study, nor to become a scholar of the social processes at play within the community. I built trust-based relationships, friendships and worked to embed myself in the community as an active participant, learning the language as well as involving myself with sewing seal-skin boots and spending time with Elders.

I had been in Arviat for two weeks when a woman who had heard of my father (a well-known academic and fellow Bahá'í) was visiting the community. She called one evening and told me she had been hired to facilitate meetings between Elders and youth within the community. She invited me to join these meetings, and I was therefore extremely fortunate to be presented to the Elders en masse. This helped me formally enter the community in the role of 'learner' (van den Hoonaard, 2012), with the proper respect due to the Elders.

In my first lunch with them, I was put to the test and engaged in my first commitment act (Emerson et al., 1995). The meal was entirely traditional, consisting of *muqtaaq* [whale blubber], both cooked and raw, caribou meat (raw), dried raw fish and bannock. The food was offered to me. In that moment, they were testing not only whether I would be willing to try foods they knew to be 'offensive' relative to my cultural sensitivities, but also whether I would judge them for eating such foods, as so many have before. I gamely tried all of the foods offered, with a smile on my face. From that moment on, the interactions of the Elders with me changed. Where they were polite before, now they were warm and accepting. I was officially welcomed into the community.

That evening I was invited to the drum dance, along with my husband, who showed he was game to try drumming while I was game to try throat singing and Ayaya songs, the traditional songs the women sing while the man drums. At the end of the week-long meetings, we returned from my first land trip and traditional feast. With several of us piled on the back of an ATV, as we bounced along the dirt track, dust gritting in my teeth, eyes, ears, and nose, one of the women who works regularly with the Elders told me, to my surprise, that they were thinking of electing me to Sivullinut, the Elders' council.

I was the first non-Inuk, first non-Elder on the council. We served each other well. They facilitated my immediate access to and acceptance by the community, while I helped them navigate the world of bureaucracy in filling out funding applications. I was surprised and grateful to be treated with the full respect of the others. I did not yet know Inuktitut when I started on the council. They would consult for about 20 minutes, and then wait while the entire conversation was translated for me. I would respond and that would be interpreted. Then it would be a smoke-break. They could have gone to smoke while the translation was done for me, but they waited patiently through the English they did not understand and were later always patient with me as I bungled through learning the language in my first year there. With no textbooks, one can only learn the Arviat dialect of Inuktitut through conversation and perseverance.

It was thus that I became quickly involved in the affairs of the community. Soon after, I volunteered at the drop-in centre and taught cross-stitch. The next day, I had a young girl at my door wanting to learn more. The following day there were three of them. Over my five years of living there, I had over 150 girls and a few boys come through my living room to participate in what developed into an after-school program for at-risk youth, including a few sleepovers where 15 sleeping bags lined my living room floor with girls ranging in age from 7 to 13. Children, whom the teachers defined as unable to concentrate, would stitch with deep concentration for hours on end. Eventually, we also did math, photography and cooking. By involving myself with the children, I inadvertently made many ties within the community. Above all, I was able to show that I could have a full, crazy, messy house 'just like an Inuk', as one of the Elders said when she dropped by with some paperwork and saw 10 girls hanging out at my house.

During my first few years in Arviat, I had found a place for myself in the community, and a circle of good friends. I built these relationships with the same intentions as I would build relationships anywhere I have moved: to have a healthy, participatory social life in which I felt a sense of belonging; to have an emotionally satisfying life. Gradually, however, sociological questions began to crop up, and I wanted to explore these questions as a researcher. In hindsight, the formation of these good-faith, reciprocal (Fine, 1996), trust-based relationships benefited not only my participants, myself and my research, but adheres to recommended practices in working with aboriginal communities (Brook & McLachlan, 2005; Caine, Davison, & Stewart, 2009; Castleden, Sloan Morgan, & Lamb, 2012; Wong, Wu, Boswell, Housden, & Lavoie, 2013). Over several years, I watched my friends navigating their everyday spaces and eventually, I began to think about how to transition into the role of researcher.

FINDING MY INNER SOCIOLOGIST

I had noticed from the start, as I was welcomed into different homes, the ways in which Inuit people treated their walls varied tremendously. The most dramatic decoration that pushed my sociological imagination to the fore was Lily's wall. She had viscerally taken control of her wall and, with rocks from the tundra, carved traditional scenes into it and created an impressive mosaic. She engaged with her built environment and used it to express her Inuit identity. Her home, in particular, stood out. Some other homes had completely bare walls, often grimy with dirt or holes, while still others had collages of family photographs, attached with tape or push pins, and other paraphernalia creating a chaotic scrapbook of their lives. I knew there was a sociological story here, and I determined to learn what it was. What did this built environment mean to them? And, ultimately, how do the Inuit negotiate and perform their Inuit identities while living inside *qablunaaq* structures and spaces?

While many of my participants were confused as to my interest in walls and space and place, they were eager to help me with my schooling, as well as to share their lived experiences within and without their homes. I am humbled by their candidness and their acceptance of me as a researcher within the community. Not all researchers are accepted with open arms in Nunavut (Caine et al., 2009; Collings, 2009). During an interview with Lily, another Elder arrived and saw that Lily was in the middle of being interviewed. The newcomer installed herself on the couch (Lily and I were seated at the table) and crossed her arms and glared at me. I suggested to Lily that I return the next day to complete the interview. At first she encouraged me to go on, but the Elder glared and huffed and made quite a show of disapproval, such that I soon told Lily I thought it would be better if I came back the next day.

She agreed and I stood to leave. Before leaving, I thought it wise to go say hello to the Elder since I knew her. Her children and grandchildren had learned stitching from me and had also been my husband's students.

I approached the couch rather cautiously as her glare was intense and her body posture defensive and almost aggressive. While I said hello to her in Inuktitut, I undid the bun in my waist-length hair since it was slipping. My intention was to re-bun it quickly as I paid my respects to the Elder. As soon as my hair came tumbling down around me, the Elder recognised me. Her entire demeanour and body posture changed instantly. She jumped up from the couch and hugged me and started laughing, saying that she thought I was just a usual researcher. There was much laughter and joking, and she sat back down and insisted that we continue the interview, apologising for trying to cut it short. In the end, I stayed for tea and visited with Lily and the other Elder, rather than intrude on their visiting time with the interview. I returned the following day to complete the interview.

Instances like this reassured me that my Inuk neighbours were not treating me as they treated other researchers who were not seen as part of the community. Having the community accept trust-based relationships with me, although I was never able to actually be Inuk, gave me a special insider/outsider position as a researcher which is rare. I was fortunate to already be considered a member of the community when I began to transition into the role of researcher. As such, I was able to consult with both the Elders and my Inuit friends as I made the decision to become a researcher. I was, therefore, committed to engaging with them with all the respect due to research participants as experts in their own lives (Becker, 1967; van den Hoonaard, 2012).

FROM FRIEND TO RESEARCHER

I lived and worked among the Inuit for a full five years. The Elders were used to researchers doing work that they did not entirely agree with, but I wanted to avoid this. When I decided to transition into the role of researcher, I was able to have conversations with the friends I had made. While they were encouraging, it was the Elders who emphatically supported the idea. They asked my husband and me to travel south and to talk about the Inuit of Arviat. We were living among them and could bring context with our stories, rather than simply glorifying a quick trip full of exotic experiences. As the years went by, they began introducing us to visiting outsiders as their 'researchers'. In my third year in Arviat, I brought a group of dancers to do dances in the schools about social issues. When we had a performance just for the Elders, they lined up and gave hugs to all the dancers. One of the Elders hugged me without really looking (I had been standing next to one of the dancers). Another Elder gave her a friendly nudge and told her that I was one of them, so why was she hugging me? Peals of laughter ensued.

I obtained a research licence from the Nunavut Research Institute, which allowed me to conduct formal interviews and ethnography. After I moved away, I later returned for two trips, totalling three months, where I embarked on intensive ethnography, taking notes each night into the early hours of the morning. My participant observation included attending public gatherings, such as dances and feasts; participating in the daily life of the community, for example, grocery shopping, a highly social event in Arviat; attending gatherings specifically involving traditional activities, such as drum dances, as well as weddings and funerals; taking walks to participate in the street activities; and, finally, spending time visiting my friends and acquaintances. I approached my participants with an attitude of learning, rather than an attitude of studying (Spradley, 1979; van den Scott, 2013).

Because I was interested in the use of space, the interactions of the family and the performance of Inuitness, I spent several hours each day visiting. I chose the three families to whom I had grown close and, as they represented a cross-section of socio-economic status and of familiarity with Western practices, I focused my visiting attention on them for the most part, although I also took the time to visit several other families relatively frequently during my time there. From the initial interest in 2004 that children had shown in me, as I was often the only white person who had been to their home, I became commonplace. I took field notes on all of these visits, often noting deep informal conversations as part of my observations.

My participants, my friends, knew I was also there as a researcher. Because of my application to the Nunavut Research Institute, when I came for a research trip, everyone in town knew why I was there (van den Scott, 2012). To help mitigate this sense of descending on the community, I frequently talked about how genuinely lucky I felt that my school allowed me to come back to do research. Overall, my reappearance, however, was seen as the fulfilment of a promise to return to visit, which many people make when they move away and almost no one follows up on. I presented the research as a means to an end of visiting and the community was supportive of my return to school, and happy that I kept my word and returned as I said I would. On one of these trips, when my husband, also a researcher, drum danced, the Elders changed the song that they sing from the standard one for *qablunaaqs* to 'The One about the Man Who Does What He Says He Will Do'. This also happens to be the song of one of the families with whom we are closest.

In all cases, both in visits and in formal interviews, I encouraged story-telling. To have approached them in a strictly formal manner would have destroyed the ease with which the participants, who knew me from my time living in the community, answered my questions and told me relevant stories. I felt this was important as when I had lived there in the past, some who had participated in other research projects told me afterward that they had merely told the researcher what he or she thought the researcher wanted to hear. To overcome this in my own work, in addition to supplementing interviews with ethnographic data as well as informal conversations, I took pains to make the interviews as relaxed as possible. When I was interviewing Hyacinth, for example, she seemed quite nervous. She had once helped me get on some hockey gear for a tournament in which I was participating as an instructor at the Arctic College. The scene had been hilarious pandemonium. I had pulled some borrowed equipment out of a bag and could not figure out what piece was supposed to go where. The women in the locker room descended on me, laughing and gleefully taping my equipment to me since most of it was too big to stay on otherwise. Rather than continue the interview, I reminded Hyacinth of this story. We laughed long and hard and, after that, she relaxed into the interview and engaged in story-telling herself. I relied on the friend-ships I had made to make my role as a researcher easier and more comfort-able for all concerned. Laughter was an integral part of my interactions and experiences in Arviat. With the possible exception of Stebbins' (1990) study of stand-up comedians, I dare say my participants and I laughed a good deal more than most.

RESEARCHING MY FRIENDS AND THEIR FRIENDS

Close But Not Too Close

My friends all knew that I was now researching Arviat. I wondered what would change. I worried that my friends could get mad at me (they still could). I knew that my presence now meant something different and that even if they forgot sometimes that I was a researcher, I could not. I could not assume that they had that at the forefront of their minds all the time. I needed to be reflex-ive about my new role. That meant deciding what information made it into my field notes. Would being a friend affect my findings? Of course – but in which way? How much? What should I do? I lost many nights of sleep worrying about how to honour my trust-based relationships since being a researcher can sometimes be equated with being a 'fink' (Fine, 1993; Goffman, 1989) – after the generous gift of willingness on the part of my participants (Jacobs, 1980), I worried about the 'agony of betrayal' (Lofland, 1971).

In the end, I resolved to be ever-vigilant about being reflexive in each stage of my research. Not only was I a researcher, but I was a white researcher immersed in a colonial setting, turning my scientific gaze to look at the Inuit. I dedicated myself to an attitude of learning (Spradley, 1979; van den Scott, 2013) and tried to remind myself as frequently as possible that while these were still my friends, a part of me was now an external intrusion in their personal lives and that I would have to manage that going forward. Turning away from traditional approaches of study and embracing a methodology of learning and treating participants as experts in their own lives allowed me to manage this balance to the best of my ability and to honour my promises to the Elders.

My friendships did shift and change as I, and they, tentatively embraced my new role. I found that my closest friends were reluctant to be formally interviewed, having already revealed things to me which would make them more uncomfortable imagining me in the role of researcher. For example, a close friend who had confided in me was nervous about being interviewed. She consented to the interview itself, but said no when I asked to photograph her home. I considered this to be fantastic as many Inuit have a great deal of trouble saying no to *qablunaaqs*. My experiences told me that I was enough a part of the community and had developed my trust-based relationships to the point where I could be relatively confident that if a participant who was also a friend really wanted to say no, he or she would. In general, however, I learned that interviewing my closest friends was neither fruitful nor comfortable for either of us.

Some of my interviews were set up by friends trying to help me get as many interviews as possible. My participants in this case would still know much about me, as Arviat is a small community and I had lived there for five years, but we had not built up trust-based relationships in the past. Nevertheless, I found that they were as consistent as my other participants in welcoming me and encouraging me with my work. Only one participant was reluctant. I felt part-way through the interview that she had wanted to say no, but did not know me well enough to know how. She was giving curt answers and her body language was defensive and nervous. After realising how uncomfortable she was early on, I severely truncated the interview so as to leave as soon as possible without offending her or intruding more in her life. I could not rush out, however, because I did not want her to think I was not interested in her as a participant or that she had somehow been a failure as an interviewee. To this day, I sometimes think of her and hope that I found the right balance for her. I have seen her since and she has been warm, so I take heart in that. One of the key elements of reflexivity, however, is acknowledging when I have been in the wrong and doing my best to own the how and the why of that situation.

The most eager group of participants consisted of friends who were close, but not too close. Many close-but-not-too-close friends wanted to help me because the idea of going back to school is a trope within the community rhetoric. It is an idea they are familiar with and generally approve of. This group was strikingly generous with their time and their openness. I remember the painful modesty with which Samuel told me about the effects of over-crowding and how they had to share bathwater to wash all their kids, and that some of the children had to bathe elsewhere. His dignity under such cir-cumstances, and his willingness to lay bare for me embarrassing and painful details for the sake of my research was humbling. This pattern repeated over and over with these close-but-not-too-close friends. I did not have private information about trouble in their personal lives which they would not want a researcher to be aware of, and yet I understood their often difficult social context. Because they liked me, knew me and we shared mutual respect, they often disclosed information in interviews that was deeply private and personal – but they could set the pace and decide when to give me that information.

Money and Respect

While it is commonplace for researchers to pay participants in Arviat, as a friend and community member I felt uncomfortable doing this. I did not want our relationships to turn into financial transactions. Additionally, it is docu-mented that research involving money in the North is not necessarily reli-able (Collings, 2009). I felt that it was more consistent with Inuit traditional practices to bring gifts. Arviat is known for its sewing. I therefore brought various fabrics with me on my trips. These were fabrics that people could not find in Arviat or were several yards of a fabric that would have cost them triple and sometimes quadruple the amount that I had paid. I also bought a few harmonicas and some guitar strings. When interviewing women, I would bring several choices of fabric with me based on what I already knew of the participant. At the start of the interview, I would tell them (since it was true) that my research was only partially funded and I could not afford to pay for interviews (the common rate being $50–75/h) and asked if that was okay. At the end of the interview, I pulled out the fabric and said that I had a gift thanking them for participating. This is consistent with traditional practices around obtaining knowledge from others. When interviewing men, I would bring fabric in case they wanted it for their wives or sisters, as well as a harmonica and guitar strings. Which gift they chose varied. The women were, in general, enthusiastic about the fabric, immediately telling me what they might do with it.

When interviewing Elders, I was the most nervous about not bringing money. They understand that *qablunaaqs* show respect for the worth of something, even knowledge, with money. Some of them make a fair amount of money each year giving interviews. All the Elders whom I approached agreed to be interviewed for free. One Elder pushed my hands away, when offered the gift, telling me that I was a friend and did not need to pay or give her gifts for her stories. This heartened my hopes that I was not offending them and was getting accurate data (Collings, 2009), and also deeply touched me. It is unheard of for an Elder to give knowledge away. In the end, I showed her the intended gift, some fringe that was highly valued in the community and hard to come by, and she relented and accepted the gift. As I left, she gave me a *kunik* (nose kiss), as she had done on a few other occasions.

In one home, after I interviewed an Elder, he started talking about researchers coming to town and being disrespectful and bad researchers. I asked him if there was anything I should be doing differently. He looked surprised and told me that no, I was doing everything right and that he was comfortable with me as a researcher (Field Notes, Oliver's Interview). My emotions certainly got a workout; I felt sick when I thought he was talking about me and then ready to weep with relief when he affirmed my role as researcher. These moments of relief, however, were also opportunities to understand how easily things could go wrong and how important it was to reflect on my actions and interactions and to make constant adjustments in response.

The biggest methodological challenge was overcoming the assumptions of judgement which tinge all interactions between Inuit and *qablunaaq*. The historical contingencies which bear on my interactions with *Arviammiut* include countless instances of personal judgement on the part of *qablunaaqs* against the Inuit I am in dialogue with, as well as institutional structures which are inherently judgemental of the Inuit. The Inuit in Canada now call themselves Inuit because the word Eskimo actually is a twist on the Cree word for 'rawmeat-eater'. The word 'Inuit' means 'people'. They are saying, 'we are people, not savages'.

Every time I would interact with someone in Arviat, I had to be aware of their trepidation that I would be judging them. This is why it was so important for me to eat raw meat – to show that I did not judge them for it.

Partaking in traditional activities such as sewing seal-skin boots, which included my chewing on the seal skin to soften it, also helped to show that I did not pass judgement on these forms of traditional behaviour that have so often been criticised. It is impossible to overstate the extent to which this expectation of judgement shaped my interactions with community members, particularly in the first few years of my time there. As the years went by and my trust-based relationships blossomed, this threat of judgement became less salient in our interactions. Nevertheless, it was something I had to constantly keep in mind (Collings, 2009).

CONCLUDING THOUGHTS

Since the 1970s reflexivity has been increasingly encouraged in the social sciences (Puddephatt, Shaffir, & Kleinknecht, 2009). Although many have bandied about definitions, at its root this means we need to be 'self-aware and honest' (Puddephatt et al., 2009, p. 6) as we reflect on our social locations, our actions and our impact, and then we need to react accordingly.[1] The emotions we experience in the course of our research are an integral part of our lives as researchers. In approaching this chapter, I made a list of the emotions that had swamped me at various times during my work in Arviat. These include wonder, fear (of offending and of new experiences), intellectual excitement, respect, confusion, being humbled, love and loneliness. In the context of my work, these were part of confronting and overcoming a sense of the exotic. I did not want to highlight only difference between my participants and mainstream Western society. I take time to reflect before sharing stories such as the one with which I started this chapter. In my work on passive and active engagements (van den Scott, 2016), for example, I seek to analyse generic social processes, not to dwell on a sense of 'Arcticism' (Ryall, Schimanski, & Waerp, 2010). Finding myself in situations, however, which were indeed exotic to me, was a part of coming to know the community and central to my commitment acts. In reflecting on my time in Arviat and my ensuing analysis, I continue to face the challenge of moving past the sense of the exotic without discounting the reality of experiencing difference, of my own social location in that context – and, most importantly, of my participants' awareness of my social location and the meaning *for them* of how I encountered, embraced, and even celebrated the exotic.

As in all things, I recommend striving for balance. To navigate the complex emotional experiences of living and researching in Arviat, I adopted an attitude of learning (Spradley, 1979; van den Scott, 2013). An attitude of learning is conducive to constant reflexive evaluation of the emotions, concerns, rewards and stresses involved in one's research. The stories I chose to share here help to illustrate the variety of emotions I experienced and how I connected them to an attitude of learning. I was also acutely aware, and worked at remaining so, of the generosity of my participants in inviting me to learn from them and in opening themselves to my research. Balancing this humbling feeling with a respect for the integrity of my research data, which can sometimes inductively present findings that my participants may not all appreciate can be terrifying. Research is a messy roller coaster. But what a ride!

NOTE

1. For an extended discussion of the literature on reflexivity see Puddephatt et al. (2009, pp. 8ff).

ACKNOWLEDGEMENTS

This research was supported by the Social Sciences and Humanities Research Council of Canada.

REFERENCES

Becker, H. S. (1967). Whose side are we on? *Social Problems, 14*(3), 239–247.

Brook, R. K., & McLachlan, S. M. (2005). On using expert-based science to 'test' local ecological knowledge. *Ecology and Society, 10*(2), r3.

Caine, K. J., Davison, C. M., & Stewart, E. J. (2009). Preliminary field-work: Methodological reflections from northern Canadian research. *Qualitative Research, 9*(4), 489–513.

Castleden, H., Sloan Morgan, V., & Lamb, C. (2012). 'I spent the first year drinking tea': Exploring Canadian university researchers' perspectives on community-based participatory research involving Indigenous peoples. *The Canadian Geographer, 56*(2), 160–179.

Collings, P. (2009). Participant observation and phased assertion as research strategies in the Canadian Arctic. *Field Methods, 21*(2), 133–153.

Emerson, R. M., Fretz, R. I., & Shaw, L. L. (1995). *Writing ethnographic fieldnotes*. Chicago, IL: University of Chicago Press.

Fine, G. A. (1993). Ten lies of ethnography: Moral dilemmas of field research. *Journal of Contemporary Ethnography, 22*(3), 267–294.

Fine, G. A. (1996). *Kitchens: The culture of restaurant work*. Berkeley, CA: University of California Press.

Goffman, E. (1989). On field work. *Journal of Contemporary Ethnography, 18*, 123–132.

Goulet, J. (1998). *Ways of knowing: Experience, knowledge, and power among the Dene Tha*. Lincoln, NE: University of Nebraska Press.

Jacobs, S. (1980). Where have we come? *Social Problems, 27*, 371–378.

Lofland, J. F. (1971). *Analyzing social settings*. New York, NY: Wadsworth.

Puddephatt, A. J., Shaffir, W., & Kleinknecht, S. W. (2009). *Ethnographies revisited: Constructing theory in the field*. London: Routledge.

Ryall, A., Schimanski, J., & Waerp, H. H. (2010). *Arctic discourses*. Newcastle upon Tyne: Cambridge Scholars Press.

Spradley, J. P. (1979). *The ethnographic interview*. New York, NY: Holt, Rinehart and Winston.

Stebbins, R. A. (1990). *Laugh-makers stand-up comedy as art, business, and life-style*. Montreal: MQUP.

van den Hoonaard, D. K. (2012). *Qualitative research in action*. Don Mills, ON: Oxford University Press Canada.

van den Scott, L. K. (2012). Science, politics, and identity in northern research ethics licensing. *Journal of Empirical Research on Human Research Ethics, 7*(1), 28–36.

van den Scott, L. K. (2013). Working with aboriginal populations: An attitude of learning. In J. Sieber, & M. Tolich (Eds.), *Planning ethically responsible research* (2nd ed.) (pp. 128–129). Thousand Oaks, CA: SAGE.

van den Scott, L. K. (2016). Mundane technology in non-western contexts: wall-as-tool. In L. Suski, J. Moore, & G. Anderson (Eds.), *Sociology of home: Belonging, community and place in the Canadian context* (pp. 33–53). Toronto: Canadian Scholars Press International.

Wong, S., Wu, L., Boswell, B., Housden, L., & Lavoie, J. (2013). Strategies for moving towards equity in recruitment of rural and Aboriginal research participants. *Rural and Remote Health, 13*(2), 2453.

CHAPTER 2

WITH A LITTLE HELP FROM MY COLLEAGUES: NOTES ON EMOTIONAL SUPPORT IN A QUALITATIVE LONGITUDINAL RESEARCH PROJECT

Agata Lisiak and Łukasz Krzyżowski

ABSTRACT

Purpose – *This chapter explores the strategies and tactics employed by researchers when dealing with emotionally challenging situations, both in the field and in academia in general.*

Methodology/Approach – *It draws on a qualitative longitudinal project investigating how recent Polish migrants from cities that are rather homogenous in terms of ethnicity and religion make sense of, and come to terms with, the much greater diversity they encounter in German and British cities. The project adopts a mixed-methods approach that includes social network analysis, focus groups, creative methods and in-depth interviews.*

Findings – *Moving beyond the inside–outsider binary in qualitative research, the authors reflect on their management of conflicting feelings about what happens in research situations. The authors discuss interview*

Emotion and the Researcher: Sites, Subjectivities, and Relationships
Studies in Qualitative Methodology, Volume 16, 33–47
Copyright © 2018 by Emerald Publishing Limited
All rights of reproduction in any form reserved
ISSN: 1042-3192/doi:10.1108/S1042-319220180000016003

situations they found particularly emotionally challenging and the different ways they supported each other during and after fieldwork, for instance, when faced with situations in which research participants say things that are racist, Islamophobic, homophobic, xenophobic, classist or misogynist. They reflect on their use of electronic media, especially email and messenger applications, as tools which not only allow them to unpack the emotions that emerge in fieldwork, but also enable them to collaboratively reflect on their own positionalities in the field.

Originality/Value – *The chapter argues that face-to-face and virtual interactions with colleagues can create spaces of care, self-care and solidarity. These relational spaces can form integral support systems for researchers and help them to deal with both the emotionality of social-science research and the wider emotional labour of academic work.*

Keywords: Communication; emotions; fieldwork; friendship; neoliberal academia; qualitative longitudinal study

INTRODUCTION

Whereas ethical reviews and careful design of fieldwork tools are conducted under the rule 'first do no harm' to research participants (Jones et al., 2017), there is much less emphasis, if any, on researchers' self-care and care for each other (Bloor, Fincham, & Sampson, 2008; Hubbard, Backett-Millburn, & Kemmer, 2001). Despite the vast interest in reflexivity (Coffey, 1999; Shinozaki, 2012), there is still not enough critical engagement with the emotional toll academic work takes on researchers (Gill, 2010). As researchers' emotions continue to be largely overlooked or silenced, we conceived this chapter as an intervention: an attempt to bring attention to the importance of emotional support between colleagues, and an honest discussion on how it can be facilitated with the help of electronic media. Based on a qualitative longitudinal study we conducted over the past few years, we will reflect on the fieldwork situations we found particularly emotionally challenging and examine how we coped with those challenges. We find it impossible to separate the stress related to fieldwork from the stress involved in working in contemporary academia more generally. We will therefore discuss how the coping and support mechanisms developed by researchers during fieldwork can translate into tactics of emotional support in neoliberal academia and create a safe space for academics within a hostile environment.

HOW WE GOT WHERE WE ARE NOW

The authors of this chapter met four years ago as members of the ERC-funded TRANSFORmIG[1] team at Humboldt University in Berlin. The project investigates how migration changes people, their everyday lives and mindsets, especially when their new place of living differs considerably from their place of origin (Nowicka, 2015). We conducted field research with Polish migrants living in Berlin, Munich, London and Birmingham, as well as their family members and friends living in Poland. As a qualitative longitudinal study (Neale & Flowerdew, 2003), TRANSFORmIG examines changes in people's attitudes and practices that occur over time, thus bringing attention to migration as a process rather than a one-time event (Findlay & Stockdale, 2003). Aside from three waves of in-depth interviews, the project's mixed-method approach included social network analysis, focus groups and creative methods (Krzyżowski, 2016; Lisiak, 2013; Nowicka, 2015).

A longitudinal research design creates an opportunity for researchers to establish a long-term relationship with research participants, build mutual trust and respect, and, consequently, sustain a high rate of retention (Hannah, Scott, & Schmidt, 2014). The retention strategies we implemented in TRANSFORmIG relied on interpersonal skills rather than financial incentives offered to participants. Yet, building relationships with research participants can also result in negative outcomes, as it blurs the divide between the work and private lives of researchers. Compared to other qualitative approaches, it can be argued that a longitudinal design affects researchers' engagement with the lives of research participants more strongly, as we continue to meet over years and remain in contact between the interviews (Shirani & Weller, 2010).

Agata and Łukasz were involved in the design of TRANSFORmIG's research tools from the onset of the project and continued to collaborate closely throughout its three waves. Although this chapter discusses how electronic media can facilitate emotional support, we want to emphasise that direct, in-person contact is crucial for building trust and establishing a strong basis for further communication. In the first stage of the research project, Agata was living in Vienna and Łukasz was commuting between Berlin and Kraków, so we had few occasions to meet. Frequently organised video conferences worked well to keep all project members up to date with the latest developments but did not yield collaborative exchanges beyond the established framework. It was not until Łukasz came to Vienna to discuss the final version of the first-wave interview script with Agata that we could start learning from – and about – each other and, in the process, we were able to lay foundations for an academic exchange based on interdisciplinarity, openness to methodological approaches and mutual trust. From our interdisciplinary exchanges, a new version of the interview guide emerged, one that was later accepted by the entire project team and used during our field research. Regardless of the methods we had favoured prior to our meeting, we reached an agreement as to what field research meant for us, how we wanted to engage with research participants, what kind of obstacles and opportunities we should look out for and why we were doing it at all.

Certainly, our good working relationship relied also on the fact that, as post-docs, we held the same positions within the project's hierarchy, while we were not in direct competition with each other as our research foci are rooted in different fields. The mutual support, respect and trust we were able to establish – and which provided a base for friendship – are worth mentioning particularly in the time of neoliberal academia, when early career researchers need to compete in a hostile environment for very few available positions (Gill, 2010; Ivancheva, 2015; Thwaites & Pressland, 2017). Ronell (2015, p. xi) observes that 'among scholars, hanging onto a friend is laughably difficult, nearly impossible' because of the 'solitary axis' in which we spin despite the mobility contemporary academia necessitates. And yet, we purposefully seek out friends in academia as we need allies and crave kinship networks (Ronell, 2015). It is often through academic friendships that exciting and meaningful academic collaborations emerge, and it is not uncommon for close scholarly collaborations to lead to friendships. We are convinced that the practices of care and solidarity, in which we engaged throughout the project, have been crucial for an honest and meaningful scholarly collaboration (Jenkins, 2014).

EMOTION AND THE RESEARCHER: FIELDWORK

Undoubtedly, research situations can produce many different emotions in researchers and research participants alike (Bille & Steenfeldt, 2013). In this chapter, we will focus on several aspects of fieldwork which researchers may experience as emotionally challenging. Already the fact of meeting a stranger can be experienced as stressful (Kaler & Beres, 2016), and each interview necessitates considerable emotional labour (Hochschild, 1983) on the part of the interviewer. Importantly, stress may accompany not only 'negative' feelings such as fear or anger, but also the 'positive' ones such as joy and camaraderie, as the researcher may be concerned with collapsing the elements that define the interview situation (Kaler & Beres, 2016).

In classical sociological (qualitative) methodologies, an interview has certain rules such as maintaining objectivity, sticking to the interview scenario, reduced flexibility in relation to research instruments and control of the interview situation (Nilan, 2002). Kvale (2007) uses the metaphor of a 'classical' interviewer as a miner who is responsible for knowledge collection and juxtaposes it with the figure of an interviewer as a traveller involved in the process of knowledge construction. Highlighting lived experiences and the importance of feelings and empathy, postmodern methodologies seek to reduce the asymmetry between researcher and research participants and deconstruct hierarchies (Rosenau, 1992).

Research situations can be stressful for researchers because they sometimes pose real physical danger (e.g., being in a car with a participant who happens to be a reckless driver, as once happened to Łukasz) or anticipation thereof (feeling uncomfortable or anxious about conducting an interview in a private apartment). We try to limit those dangers in the preparatory phase, but we are aware that not all fieldwork situations are predictable and we need to keep our guard up. In a longitudinal study, this stress is reduced in follow-up interviews as familiarity with research participants increases, but some level of unpredictability remains: even two or three years into the project, we were surprised by what research participants said or did. We were familiar with them, but it does not mean we knew them.

Whereas we do not ascribe to the insider–outsider dichotomy (Lisiak, 2015; Nowicka & Ryan, 2015), we did occasionally find our 'Polish socialisation' and our own migration experiences helpful during data collection and analysis because it allowed us to read certain cultural codes (see Mannay & Creaghan, 2016; Roberts, 2018 [this volume]). Yet, we also experienced our 'Polishness' as challenging when our research participants assumed a range of commonalities with us based on our nationality, gender or class. These assumptions of shared 'Polish' or 'female' or 'middle-class' values were particularly difficult to cope with when research participants expressed opinions or worldviews we strongly disagreed with. In the course of the project, we repeatedly encountered racist and sexist jokes during small talk, Islamophobic statements during interviews and classist jibes over lunch or dinner (see Nowicka, 2018). Confrontation with racial, class, religious and gender prejudice and hate speech, of which the researcher can be both an object and a witness, is an emotionally and methodologically complex situation and we will explore it in more detail in the following sections.

Drawing from nearly 300 interview transcripts, field notes, emails and a messenger history, we will now present several situations that, to our mind, best demonstrate the importance of emotional support among researchers, how it emerges, how it is facilitated and what happens with it once research is over. In what follows, we will shed light on the coping mechanisms we developed during the study and discuss how to address the emotions that occur *after* a first-time interview, as well as those shaped by the researcher's expectations *before* follow-up interviews. We will focus on researchers' emotional responses to the many expressions of prejudice and hate speech we encountered during fieldwork including racism, Islamophobia, classism, sexism and homophobia (focusing on the first two), discuss some of the limitations and silencing inscribed in fieldwork and, more generally, academic work (Ryan-Flood & Gill, 2010) and demonstrate how those can be coped with – even if not entirely overcome – through regular exchanges between researchers.

COPING: AFTER AN INTERVIEW SITUATION

In May 2014, Łukasz sent an email to his TRANSFORmIG colleagues with a short update on his fieldwork in Birmingham, including the profiles of the people he interviewed – a heterogeneous group of Polish migrants when it comes to age, family, education and occupation. Łukasz observed that regardless of the many differences between them, they all have one thing in common: racism. Łukasz wrote not just about the things people said in interviews, but primarily about the small interactions with research participants which he engaged in immediately before and after an interview, and during which he encountered casual racist jokes, Islamophobic slurs and homophobic comments. One of these situations was particularly difficult:

> Today I visited one research participant to interview him. It turned out that his wife and their two small children were at home as well. I ended up not interviewing anyone because the woman insisted her husband drives her to a special store as she was expecting clients (she's a hairdresser) and she doesn't drive herself. ... So we all went together, the five of us ... I spent three hours with them altogether, then I had to rush to another interview. As we drove, every few meters the driver (our potential research participant) threatened to drive over a *czarnuch* [nigger], a *ciapak* [Paki], a *ninja* [a derogative term for a woman wearing a burka], and so on. ... At one point, stopping at a pedestrian crossing to let a black woman with pink hair cross the street, he declared: 'F*ck, it's too bad her hair is pink. Otherwise, if I ran her over, I'd fill out all the holes in the tarmac.' And now I have a problem with this couple because not only do they want to talk to me, but they also... invited me to their barbecue party with their friends. I was thinking, maybe it'd be worth engaging the people at the party in an informal discussion. What do you think? It would be more of ethnographic research, rather spontaneous, and I am not sure how it would end. I find this situation potentially ethically very difficult, hence my question to you: what to do?[2]

Whereas other research team members focused in their replies on the ethical aspects of conducting the mini-ethnographic study, Agata's email centred on the incident in the car and its emotional dimensions:

> Łukasz, what you wrote is terrible. ... I would be happy to hear you out if you need to talk about it, also in a regular manner. We could Skype if/when you want.

Though Łukasz appreciated Agata's offer, he had little time to spare during fieldwork:

> Unfortunately, time is a problem. I still have many interviews to conduct and I am leaving in a moment. I usually return back to the hotel at about 11 pm. I've been in such situations before, but not on such a great scale. Sharing these stories with the team – which is what I did in my previous email – is one way of dealing with it. Thank you for responding to it.

Lack of time – a common problem during fieldwork – may not have been the only reason Łukasz rejected Agata's offer to talk. At this time, we hardly knew each other, as Agata was still on an international fellowship and communicated with team members via Skype and email. Being honest and open about emotional reactions in the field necessitates trust and empathy. Agata could empathise with Łukasz because, as she was about to start her fieldwork, she could imagine herself in this situation and was mortified by the prospect of having to keep a blank face when confronted with verbally violent expressions. This email exchange was a first step to opening up about challenges encountered during fieldwork, doubts and hopes, little joys and stressful situations. It may have helped that Agata was a newcomer to the social sciences, with many questions that a more experienced sociologist would maybe shy away from asking. Agata's academic inhibitions were few, which encouraged Łukasz to reconsider methods and approaches he had long taken for granted.

Following this exchange, Łukasz and Agata started regularly discussing their encounters with research participants, sharing their observations and frustrations and gradually disclosing their emotional responses to what happens in the field. As we continued to spend extended periods of time on the move in various geographic locations, conducting interviews in Berlin, Munich, London and Birmingham, as well as several cities in Poland, we remained in touch on a regular basis, first by email, then mainly via a smartphone messenger application. As it turned out, the more traditional communication channels such as email, which we used with other colleagues in the project, lacked the instantaneity and quick response features which kept Agata and

Łukasz's conversations lively. We would often text right before an interview or immediately after. In a way, the texts became appendixes to our field notes, but were also different from ethnographic observations because of the instant reciprocity inherent to this mode of communication. As we regularly use the app in conversations with friends and family, using the messenger for research updates further blurred the boundaries between our work and private lives.

COPING: BEFORE (AND AFTER) AN INTERVIEW SITUATION

Preparation for fieldwork is a dynamic process that requires researchers' critical reflection, also with regard to seemingly mundane details such as the clothes we wear (Lisiak, 2015). Before we enter a research situation, we imagine it, we make assumptions and we try to be prepared for the unexpected. When Agata went to interview Laura[3] in her apartment in Berlin, she had few expectations as she knew only some very basic facts about her such as her address, family situation and the number of years spent in Berlin. Laura was chatty and demonstrated strong opinions on many issues, including what she eagerly admitted to be her favourite topic: the 'Islamisation of the West'.

> Laura: What is happening right now is a damn Islamisation of entire Europe, there's no use in fooling yourself about it. What is happening for real, in my opinion, is a beginning of the third world war, it's just it's camouflaged because, for now, no armies are entering. See, the situation right now, if you've read about it, is that every single country has a problem with Islamists. The problem is quite big and it's not just about terrorist attacks, but about the fact that now they are loudly demanding their rights. Have you ever been at the Brandenburg Gate on the weekend and not seen *islamy* [pejorative for Muslims] protesting holding those large banners of theirs?
>
> Agata: I don't think I've ever been to the Brandenburg Gate on a weekend.
>
> Laura: They're always there, *always*, and there is always police because, obviously. On any big holiday, I don't know, maybe they also protest there on weekdays. Anyway… Ever since I moved here, I have never seen the Brandenburg Gate in its full glory. In every photo I took there I have those damned *muslimy* [pejorative for Muslims], in *every* photo, it's *sick*! More than that, wherever you look, they are loudly demanding their rights. They have five kids on average and in exactly five years every third child will be born in an Islamic family. This is a humongous cultural barrier. … In every country they shout loudly about their rights, about their beliefs. If they don't like it [here], then why don't they return to their countries? After all, they have everything they want there, *but* over there it's filth, hunger, dirt, poverty and war. … But these are not intelligent people – you can count the really intelligent ones among them on your fingers. Mostly, these people, 80% of all Muslims live off unemployment benefits, 80%!

This mixture of stereotypes, fake news and outrageous exaggerations with relentless hatred – racial slurs said through clenched teeth, the grimace of disgust twisting her face and the cigarette smoke exhaled in the imaginary direction of the objects of her hatred – created a particular atmosphere Agata experienced as literally suffocating. As in the case of sensory experiences of racism in a football stadium described by Back, Crabbe, and Solomos (2001, p. x), 'the force of [the research participant's] words stained the air'. Throughout the interview Laura made several allusions to assumed shared commonality of worldviews with a fellow Pole. In turn, Agata had 'a sense of being trapped and unable to counter the voice of hate' (Back et al., 2001, p. xi). Unlike in their case, however, Agata's 'punitive silence' was not due to a fear of being physically attacked, but rather of breaking the rules of 'proper' social research.

Agata's frustration emerging from not being able to speak up to what she read as Islamophobic pronouncements was overwhelming. Ever since she can remember, Agata has been a killjoy (Ahmed, 2017) around her family, friends and strangers, calling people out on racism, anti-Semitism, sexism, homophobia and, in recent years, Islamophobia. In her new role as an interviewer (Kvale, 2007), Agata found herself stripped of not only her right, but also her duty: speaking up against prejudice and discrimination. Throughout the interview, Agata struggled to keep balance between non-intervention into the research participant's narrative, establishing rapport and staying 'true to herself' in that she refused to nod empathically at Islamophobic statements and laugh at racist jokes.

Immediately upon leaving Laura's apartment, Agata texted Łukasz to inform him how the interview went, but, primarily, to vent. She needed to share the many emotions she was feeling with someone she knew would understand because he had been in similar situations. In retrospect, looking through our messenger exchanges, we notice that much of Agata's stress and silenced anger took on a form of an intense sensory experience (Okely 2007; Pink, 2009). In her text messages, Agata remarked that the research participant made Islamophobic comments, but she focused on the olfactory sensations of the interview situation:

> 3h of listening about *Turasy* [Turks, pejorative] and islamisation of the world./On top of everything, she smokes in the apartment and has that chemical air freshener on, which smells like pseudo-flowers. I'm going home now to take a shower, I can feel those smells everywhere.

The support Łukasz offered relied mostly on listening, or, given the medium, reading about Agata's frustrations. We later talked about it in person as well, reflecting in more detail on the individual elements of the interview situation, but the immediacy the messenger application offered was crucial for Agata to cope with an emotional reaction to the self-imposed silencing.

One year later, before the second interview with Laura, Agata admitted to Łukasz she was feeling stressed about what she predicted she would hear from Laura this time – and, primarily, about not being able to react to what she expected to be Islamophobic and xenophobic statements. In the course of the second-wave interview, Laura insisted she had 'nothing against Turks because they usually have their kebab stands and they do something, but, more generally, Muslims are fucking no-goods' and 'the Roma, the Gypsies – they steal'. As Agata had been prepared to hear such statements from Laura, she felt she was able to deal with her frustration better this time, but what she recognised as a hostile atmosphere stuck to her nonetheless. As she expressed it in a text message to Łukasz upon leaving Laura's apartment: 'I smell of cigarettes, air refresher, instant coffee and nail polish./Although compared to last year's interview, this one was rather light.'

The smells listed above were not unfamiliar to Agata. In fact, she grew up around them: her aunties – and later Agata herself – would paint their nails at a kitchen table while drinking instant coffee and smoking cigarettes. Agata does not feel particularly nostalgic about these smells, but recognises them as part of her olfactory memory – those (among others) are the smells of home. Yet, these smells did not transport Agata from Laura's apartment to her childhood in Poland. Instead, she experienced them as invading, irritating and almost suffocating. Agata's bodily response to the reluctantly executed self-silencing in the face of Islamophobia resembled an allergic reaction.

Another year passed, and Agata braced herself for her final interview with Laura. In a text message sent to Łukasz on her way to Laura's apartment, Agata wrote:

A: I really don't feel like going to that interview.

Ł: It's raining :/ / So no wonder.

A: I shiver just thinking about the bile she will be pouring out.

Ł: That too.

A: I'd rather spend these 2h in the rain :(

Laura immediately started speaking about refugees. Several months before the interview, in the midst of the so-called refugee crisis (see Holmes & Castañeda, 2016), a building in Laura's neighbourhood had been turned into a reception centre for refugees – a development she detested wholeheartedly because, as she insisted, a refugee stole her phone. When Agata asked how Laura was certain that the man she saw jumping onto a subway train seconds after she realised her phone was gone was a refugee, Laura laughed with amused disbelief:

Laura: Come on! [laughter] Come on! Come *on*! It's immediately clear! For a while, there was so much *cattle* [emphasis, with disgust] around here, on the street, on the subway, it was un-be-lie-va-ble. They turned this really peaceful neighbourhood into – what happened in Berlin is a catastrophe, I'm definitely not going to stay here because, you know, ever since they brought them all over here, it's been a disaster, everywhere. Every day I listen to different stories – you know, when girls come to me to get their nails done, it's like a confession – and all of my clients have been in some unpleasant situations.

Agata: Mhm. What were some of the things that have happened to them?

Laura: Either someone harasses them, or they got mugged, or they were assaulted, or they were beaten, or, you know, every day I hear new stories.

Agata: Mhm.

Laura: The only good thing, from what I have noticed, what my clients tell me, is that if you speak German to [refugees], they totally don't give a fuck. But when you start yelling at them in Polish, then, it's, they confuse Poles with *Russkies* and are scared.

Talking about how much dirtier and more disorderly Berlin appears to her now compared to a couple of years ago (see Lisiak, 2018), Laura raised her voice and started speaking faster: 'I will always blame the refugees. I can't *stand* them, I *hate* them. I think they should be helped *over there*, not here!'

On the subway ride back home, Agata, no longer restricted by saying 'mhm', let go of her frustration in a series of texts to Łukasz, who calmly noticed: 'at least you were prepared for that'. Although she was, indeed, prepared for another outburst of Islamophobia, accusations and conspiracy theories, she still found the 'punitive silence' emotionally difficult and hard on her body. The smells she experienced as invasive stuck to her again and she was itching to remove them. Łukasz, who had been more frequently exposed to blunt expressions of racism, Islamophobia and xenophobia in fieldwork situations was able to understand Agata's frustration and to react to it in an accommodating and sensitive manner. We continued texting about the emotional toll our work takes on us, our bodies' responses, our anxieties and ideas on how to address them. Agata found the interviews with Laura emotionally difficult and felt grateful for being able to share those experiences openly with a colleague whom she trusted and whose responses she valued.

CONCLUDING REFLECTIONS ON EMOTIONS AND THE RESEARCHER IN CONTEMPORARY ACADEMIA

We conceived of this chapter as a reflection on the coping mechanisms we employ in fieldwork with regard to emotional labour. It is also a story of a friendship that emerged from intense, collegial exchanges about other people's lives and our own lives in relation to theirs; a friendship that far exceeded the mutual support framework we found necessary to deal with the emotional challenges in the field; a friendship that spilled beyond work. Over the years, we have learned each other's daily routines: which gyms we go to, what we read on the news, who we sleep with, what we like to cook or which doctors we need to see. Knowing each other's private schedules has helped us plan our work schedules: we know when it is ok to discuss work-related things with each other, even if it is in the evening or on the weekend, and when it is better to wait. It is precisely because we know and respect each other's private and work schedules that we have been able to avoid a lot of frustration.

Much has been written about how work, including academic work, tends to collapse the boundaries between work and pleasure (McRobbie, 2015). Although we fully sympathise with critiques of the colossal workload in contemporary academia that claims our late nights and weekends (Gill, 2010), we are also honest with each other that this is, in fact, how we sometimes *like* to work. Understanding the importance of finding time for rest and social life, we also recognise – and admit to each other – that we are passionate about what we do and that we are sometimes willing to work 'crazy hours'. We also admit to each other that sometimes we do *not* love what we do (Cannizzo, 2017), or that we would prefer not to do anything work-related late at night, but feel we have little choice because of the many anxieties we experience in contemporary academia (Gill & Pratt, 2008). Being honest with each other about how long and hard we work has helped us better understand the many contradictions inherent to academic work and to start to develop a certain defence mechanism against working *too* long and *too* hard – a mechanism reliant on mutual trust, solidarity and small gestures of care. Sometimes a text message sent to a colleague late in the evening – a reminder to go to sleep already – is the push we need to practice self-care (Ahmed, 2017; Lorde, 1988). Granted, these small gestures do not directly challenge the structural problems of contemporary academia (Gill, 2010; Ivancheva, 2015), and their scope is limited, but they do create spaces of care and solidarity that render academic work a less solitary endeavour (see Mountz et al., 2015).

Like any friendship, it takes work to nurture an academic friendship. It could then be argued that it requires too much work – on top of all the work that is required of us already. Whereas we do not mean to deny the extent of emotional labour that goes into maintaining a friendship, what we have tried to show in this chapter is that it is worth it. Today, with increased (and often forced) mobility of scholars, adjunctification and precarisation of academic lives, friendships in the workplace are not only anchors of sorts, but also contribute to the development of research designs, application of methodological tools and analysis. Being emotionally close to a colleague may also – as happened in our case – open up new fields of work worth exploring. And, importantly, friendship is something that – we hope – will endure once the project is over. As we write this, the project for which we work is coming towards its end. We are grateful for the many wonderful people we have met in its course, for the professional opportunities it has created for us, for everything we have learned (and we have learned a lot), but, as we once admitted to each other in a messenger exchange, to us, our friendship is the most valuable thing that has emerged from this project.

NOTES

1. European Research Council [grant number 313369] awarded to Magdalena Nowicka.
2. All the excerpts from emails and messenger exchanges were written originally in Polish and they appear here in our own translations.
3. The research participant's name has been changed.

REFERENCES

Ahmed, S. (2017). *Living a feminist life*. Durham, NC: Duke University Press.

Back, L., Crabbe, T., & Solomos, J. (2001). *The changing face of football: Racism, identity and multiculture in the English game*. Oxford: Berg.

Bille, T., & Steenfeldt, V. O. (2013). Challenging fieldwork situations: A study of researcher's subjectivity. *Journal of Research Practice*, 9(1), Article M2. Retrieved from http://jrp.icaap. org/index.php/jrp/article/view/299/301. Accessed on April 15, 2017.

Bloor, M., Fincham, B., & Sampson, H. (2008). *Qualiti (NCRM) commissioned inquiry into the risk to well-being of researchers in qualitative research, project report*. Cardiff: Cardiff University.

Cannizzo, F. (2017). 'You've got to love what you do': Academic labour in a culture of authenticity. *The Sociological Review* 66.1, 91–106, 10.1177/0038026116681439.

Coffey, A. (1999). *The ethnographic self: Fieldwork and the representation of identity*. London: SAGE.

Delamont, S. (2009). The only honest thing: Autoethnography, reflexivity and small crises in fieldwork. *Ethnography and Education*, 4(1), 51–63.

Findlay, A. M., & Stockdale, A. (2003). The temporal and social embeddedness of migration: A methodological exploration using biographical analysis. *Geography Research Forum*, 23, 4–29.

Clifford, G. (1973). *The interpretation of cultures: Selected essays*. New York, NY: Basic Books.

Gill, R. (2010). Breaking the silence: The hidden injuries of neo-liberal academia. In R. Ryan-Flood, & R. Gill (Eds.), *Secrecy and silence in the research process: Feminist reflections* (pp. 228–244). London: Routledge.

Gill, R., & Pratt, A. (2008). In the social factory? Immaterial labour, precariousness and cultural work. *Theory, Culture & Society, 25*, 1–30.

Hanna, K. M., Scott, L. L., & Schmidt, K. K. (2014). Retention strategies in longitudinal studies with emerging adults. *Clinical Nurse Specialist CNS, 28*(1), 41–45.

Hochschild, A. R. (1983). *The managed heart: Commercialization of human feeling*. Berkeley, CA: University of California Press.

Holmes, S. M., & Castañeda, H. (2016). Representing the 'European refugee crisis' in Germany and beyond: Deservingness and difference, life and death. *American Ethnologist, 43*, 12–24.

Hubbard, G., Backett-Millburn, K., & Kemmer, D. (2001). Working with emotion: Issues for the researcher in fieldwork and teamwork. *International Journal of Social Research Methodology, 4*(2), 119–137.

Ivancheva, M. P. (2015). The age of precarity and the new challenges to the academic profession. *Studia Europaea, LX*(1), 39–47.

Jenkins, K. (2014). That's not philosophy: Feminism, academia and the double bind. *Journal of Gender Studies, 23*(3), 262–274.

Jones, H., Gunaratnam, Y., Bhattacharyya, G., Davies, W., Dhaliwal, S., Forkert, K., … Saltus, R. (2017). *Go home?: The politics of immigration controversies*. Manchester: Manchester University Press.

Kaler, A., & Beres, M. (2016). *Essentials of field relationships*. New York, NY: Routledge.

Krzyżowski, Ł. (2016). Structuring social remittances: Transnational networks of Polish migrants. In M. Nowicka & V. Šerbedžija (Eds.), *Migration and social remittances in a global Europe* (pp. 71–93). Basingstoke: Palgrave Macmillan.

Kvale, S. (2007). *Doing interviews*. London: SAGE.

Lisiak, A. (2013). *Immigrant mothers as agents of change – An interdisciplinary research project*. Retrieved from http://immigrantmothers.net. Accessed on April 4, 2017.

Lisiak, A. (2015). Fieldwork and fashion: Gendered and classed performances in research sites. *Forum Qualitative Sozialforschung/Forum: Qualitative Social Research, 16*(2), Article. 14.

Lisiak, A. (2018). A sense of disorder: Orientation and migration in the 'new' west. In K. Bystrom, A. Harris, & A. Webber (Eds.), *South and North: Contemporary urban orientations* (pp. 199–215). London: Routledge.

Lorde, A. (1988). *A burst of light, essays*. London: Sheba Feminist Publishers.

Mannay, D., & Creaghan, J. (2016). Similarity and familiarity: Reflections on indigenous ethnography with mothers, daughters and school teachers on the margins of contemporary Wales. In: M. Ward (Ed.), *Gender identity and research relationships* (Vol. 14). Studies in Qualitative Methodology (pp. 85–103). Bingley: Emerald.

McRobbie, A. (2015). *Be creative: Making a living in the new culture industries*. Oxford: Polity Press.

Mountz, A., Bonds, A., Mansfield, B., Loyd, J., Hyndman, J., Walton-Roberts, M., … Winifred, C. (2015). For slow scholarship: A feminist politics of resistance through collective action in the neoliberal university. *ACME: An International Journal for Critical Geographies, 14*(4), 1235–1259.

Neale, B., & Flowerdew, J. (2003). Time, texture and childhood: the contours of longitudinal qualitative research. *International Journal of Social Research Methodology, 6*(3), 189–199.

Nilan, P. (2002). 'Dangerous fieldwork' re-examined: The question of researcher subject position. *Qualitative Research, 2*(3), 363–386.

Nowicka, M. (2015). Habitus – Its transformation and transfer through cultural encounters in migration. In C. Costa, & M. Murphy (Eds.), *The art of application: Bourdieu, habitus and social research,* (pp. 93–10). Basingstoke: Palgrave Macmillan.

Nowicka, M. (2018). 'I don't mean to sound racist but …' Transforming racism in transnational Europe. *Ethnic and Racial Studies* 41.5, 824–841, 10.1080/01419870.2017.1302093.

Nowicka, M., & Ryan, L. (2015). Beyond insiders and outsiders in migration research: Rejecting a priori commonalities. Introduction to the FQS Thematic Section on 'Researcher, Migrant, Woman: Methodological Implications of Multiple Positionalities in Migration Studies', *Forum Qualitative Sozialforschung/Forum: Qualitative Social Research*, *16*(2), Article 18. Retrieved from http://www.qualitativeresearch.net/index.php/fqs/article/view/2342/3795. Accessed on April 2, 2017.

Okely, J. (2007). Fieldwork embodied. *The Sociological Review*, *55*(S1), 65–79.

Pink, S. (2009). *Doing sensory ethnography*. London: SAGE.

Roberts, E. (2018). The 'transient insider': Identity and intimacy in home community research. In T. Loughran & D. Mannay (Eds.), *Emotion and the researcher: Sites, subjectivities and relationships* (Vol. 16). Studies in Qualitative Methodology (pp. 113–126). Bingley: Emerald.

Ronell, A. (2015). *Foreword: Friendship, authorized*. In M. Ben-Naftali (Ed.), *Chronicle of separation: On deconstruction's disillusioned love* (pp. vii–xvii). New York, NY: Fordham University Press.

Rosenau, P. M. (1992). *Post-modernism and the social sciences: Insights, inroads, and intrusions*. Princeton, NJ: Princeton University Press.

Ryan-Flood, R., & Gill, R. (Eds.). (2010). *Secrecy and silence in the research process: Feminist reflections*. London: Routledge.

Shinozaki, K. (2012). Transnational dynamics in researching migrants: Self-reflexivity and boundary-drawing in fieldwork. *Ethnic and Racial Studies*, *35*(10), 1810–1827.

Shirani, F., & Weller, S. (Eds.) (2010). *Conducting qualitative longitudinal research: Fieldwork experiences*. Timescapes Working Paper Series No. 2. Cardiff University, Cardiff. Retrieved from http://www.timescapes.leeds.ac.uk/assets/files/WP2-final-Jan-2010.pdf. Accessed on April 25, 2017.

Thwaites, R., & Pressland, A. (2017). *Being an early career feminist academic: Global perspectives, experiences and challenges*. London: Palgrave Macmillan.

CHAPTER 3

THE POSITIONAL SELF AND RESEARCHER EMOTION: DESTABILISING SIBLING EQUILIBRIUM IN THE CONTEXT OF CYSTIC FIBROSIS

Amie Scarlett Hodges

ABSTRACT

Purpose – *This chapter will discuss how the positional self and prior experiences can influence the emotional self within the research journey, for example, being a sibling and losing a sibling. It explores the researcher's emotional experience when working with children and their families, with a specific focus on the influence of the researcher presence and the sibling equilibrium.*

Methodology/Approach – *The chapter draws on the dramaturgical social interactions encountered in qualitative research which explored the experiences of siblings living in the context of cystic fibrosis. The study uses narrative inquiry and creative participatory methods to elicit sibling stories and provides insight into their worlds.*

Emotion and the Researcher: Sites, Subjectivities, and Relationships
Studies in Qualitative Methodology, Volume 16, 49–63
Copyright © 2018 by Emerald Publishing Limited
ISSN: 1042-3192/doi:10.1108/S1042-319220180000016004

Findings – *The chapter reflects on specific situations encountered on entering, engaging in and leaving the field, which had a significant emotional
impact. Two sibling vignettes will be presented along with a discussion
of how reflective metaphorical expression can be applied as a method of
processing and coping with the research context.*

Originality/Value – *The chapter argues that the positional self and prior
experiences can influence the emotional self within the research journey,
and that reflective metaphorical expression can be used as a strategy to
process thoughts and gain greater understanding of a situation as well as
to provide an emotional release for the researcher. It also suggests that
conducting research over a longer time period, as opposed to one visit, can
be beneficial in terms of participant and researcher emotional transition.*

Keywords: Sibling; dramaturgy; emotion; fieldwork; metaphorical
expression; social interaction

INTRODUCTION

A sibling can be important and influential in a person's life from the moment
they first meet, and right throughout their lifespan (Bank & Kahn, 1982;
Rowe, 2007). Being a sibling brings a lifetime journey of sharing memories
and experiences, which can be good or bad, pleasurable or painful, conflicting
or comforting. Within this relational trajectory, siblings are co-constructed
as 'co-voyagers' through their family interactions, influences and encourage-
ments as well as conflicts (Bank & Kahn, 1982, p. xvii; Edwards, Hadfield,
Lucey, & Mauthner, 2006; McGuire, Manke, Eftekhari, & Dunn, 2000).

Bank and Kahn (1982) suggest that the childhood sibling relationship
is not optional but can become so when siblings reach adulthood and then
have a choice of whether to spend time together. Regardless of whether the
sibling relationship is good, bad, indifferent or ambivalent, the sibling bond
remains because siblings formulate and influence each other's past, present and
future. Within the sibling co-voyage it is important for siblings to feel a sense of
belonging as part of a family and through connection with their sibling (Bank
& Kahn, 1982). Through these early connections, siblings formulate their
real inner most private selves (James, 1980). However, opposing this want for
togetherness, siblings can engage in an inner struggle to acquire an independent
self where their individuality is recognised (Edwards et al., 2006).

The harmonious synchronisation of the sibling relationship can be influenced by positive and negative feelings for one another that are exhibited in their

daily interactions (Brody, 1998; Edwards et al., 2006). Child siblings can spend much of their time in each other's company, and as a consequence, they become aware of each other's idiosyncrasies and learn what will please their sibling and what will not (Klett-Davies, 2008). This privileged knowledge is used when siblings choose to be a source of comfort or conflict to their brother or sister. Accordingly, siblings' experiences of each other can influence their emotional development as well as the quality of their relationship (Edwards et al., 2006).

In exploring the literature surrounding sibling relationships prior to entering the field, I became conscious of my own existential being as a sibling and of the relationship that I had had with my own sister. My childhood memories resurfaced as I reflected back on the years that had passed, and I was mindful of how I felt as both a child and adult sibling. Consequently, I realised that my researcher positioning needed to be transparent within my work, and that this reflexivity is essential in research (Cresswell, 2014; Mason, 2002).

I did not want my own sibling experience to influence my study and I wanted to make sure that I could separate being a sibling from studying siblings. I applied researcher reflexivity to separate my own voice, thoughts and feelings from those of participants through writing reflective notes and engaging in reflective discourse with my supervisors. This enabled a critical awareness of self when out in the field and in writing up my notes and transcriptions. Some of my reflections were written and performed with a metaphorical stance so I could process my own sense of being in terms of my development and progress in the research trajectory (see Hodges, 2016). Importantly, this helped me to consider my own situated position when visiting children and families within their homes, ensuring self-awareness and transparency within the research process (Hollway & Jefferson, 2007; Watts, 2009).

In the following section, my reflexive autobiographical narrative provides insight into my motivation and prior experiences and sets my positioning within my study (Durant-Law, 2005). By providing opportunities for self-knowledge through understanding prior experience and its influence on values, beliefs and decisions, autobiographical accounts enable the researcher to self-govern (Watts, 2009). They can also illustrate the interconnectedness of the researcher and the researched (Hollway & Jefferson, 2007).

MY SIBLING AND I: AN EMOTIONAL JOURNEY

As I sat in the back seat of the black car, I could see my sister looking at me from the car in front. She had short brown hair that softly framed her square-shaped face, her skin looked clear, glowing and fresh with the lightly applied makeup adding to the glow and lighting up her smile. Yes, she was smiling, but I was not. I was dazed but continued to look at her as our eyes met, we were connected with a mutual knowing.

Either side of me on the back seat were my two nieces, one with shoulder-length blonde hair and one with shoulder-length dark hair. They were looking ahead like me. The three of us looking forward, but at that moment none of us spoke a word. I eventually looked away from my sister and focused on my nieces. As I gazed at each one individually, I observed their faces and I could see two beautiful young girls, my sister's children who I was so proud of. I was proud of her for having them, as they were not only my nieces but also my godchildren. I could feel their warmth as they sat either side of me but also their chill and I felt sad for them in that moment.

I was holding their hands tightly, our fingers were entwined, cool and clammy, neither of the children were letting go, and I was not letting go either, as I knew that my sister would not want me to. The three of us sat there, we all remained connected physically and emotionally. As I looked down at their hands, I could see the silver charm bracelets on their wrists. On each bracelet was a silver star that I had bought them. The star was a symbolic representation of my sister who looked on from the car in front, now forever smiling. It was symbolic of the star I named after her and gave to her as a gift, a gift she was delighted with.

I looked at the star on each of my niece's wrists and then at each of the girls again and then back to my sister. It was a surreal moment and a life-changing one. Nothing or nobody could ever have prepared me for that day, because that was the day I lost my sister, the day I said goodbye. Sitting in that car I continued to look at the photograph that faced towards me from the car in front. It was a large photograph that she had chosen to be in the back of her car on the day of her funeral. My sister was five years older than me, and she died of lung cancer just four years before I commenced my research.

I remember a long time ago when we had the conversation where she spoke of 'if anything happens to me' and my response was 'don't talk like that, I will go before you'. I think my sister was being practical in wanting to have that conversation, especially with having the children, whereas I wanted to avoid such talk as I did not want to think about her absence from my life. If anything, I had always expected to go before her because I had always been the sickly one, enduring many hospital admissions for most of my childhood until I was 13. My sister and I were separated in those times of my hospitalisation. The longest time I was away was three months, and the shortest time was two weeks.

When I was home from hospital, life just went on and it seemed insignificant to mention. I was not one to dwell on the past, and I always strived to enjoy my health and the freedom it gave me. I focused on moving forward and moving away. Our childhood experiences had faded into the past, as we both embarked upon different life journeys. For me it was a career journey, while my sister remained in our hometown and became a wife and mother. My journey continues, but my sister's journey was cut short. She is not here, yet she is ever present because we have a 'sibling bond' (Bank & Kahn, 1982). My sister was older than me but, profoundly, now I am older than her.

THE STUDY

The study explored the experiences of non-cystic fibrosis (CF) siblings within their families, who are living with a child with the life-limiting illness of CF. Siblings had been identified as a marginalised group because their voices achieve limited recognition within the literature or family-centred care practices (Knecht, Hellmars, & Metzing, 2015; O'Brien, Duffy, & Nicholl, 2009). Family-centred care is an important aspect of children's nursing that maintains the inclusivity, dignity and respect of the whole family, and it needs to include the sibling (Kuo, Mac Bird, & Tilford, 2011). I hoped that gaining insight into sibling worlds would help inform care practices.

Narrative inquiry was used to engage siblings within the context of their family, alongside a bricolage of creative participatory methods. The sample included 10 non-CF children in middle childhood living with a brother/sister with CF. Pseudonyms were assigned to all of the participants and their families. Narrative interviews, observations, and the use of visual media provided the platform for the siblings' expression of their voices. These voices were encapsulated in the production of over 200,000 words of data, along with pictures, poems, songs and artifacts (see Hodges, 2016).

The study applied Goffman's (1959) theoretical framework of dramaturgy. This provides a metaphorical approach, where life is treated as a theatrical play in which actors take the stage to give group or solo performances (Buss & Briggs, 1984). These interactive performances can enable the actors to project a united impression of their desired self-images and words to the audience (Goffman, 1969). Thematic analysis of the observations, interviews and visual media highlighted the positions, spaces and roles encompassing siblings' overall self-presentation in their familial/cultural milieu. The following sections will reflect on the 'emotional labour' (Hochschild, 1983) of research with siblings performing on the stage set of family life within their home.

ENTERING THE FIELD

I was conscious of my positional self during my research, in terms of being a sibling, losing a sibling and my own experience of long-term childhood chronic illness that had affected my relationship with my sister. Whilst Fineman (1993) suggests that we cannot escape the personal history that defines us, it was important for me to make a clear differentiation between my voice and emotions, and those of the siblings I was working with. As well as using dramaturgy as the lens to explore sibling worlds, I used it within my own reflexive experience. I was able to present and express my emotional self through what I called dramaturge fantasia, where my metaphorical expression provided greater context, transparency and reflexivity within the work. In a similar way to Watts' (2009) use of autobiography within her research, this process enabled my greater self-understanding.

Each of my one-hour visits with the non-CF siblings took place after the children had finished their school day, between 4 p.m. and 7 p.m. In some cases, I drove very long distances to see each sibling with their family. During that time, I had an image in mind of what I will refer to, in dramaturgic terms, as the pre-performance (constructed and co-constructed social interactions and engagements) and stage set preparations (the stage set being their home) of each sibling, before I reached them.

Once I had already visited some of the children, I began to imagine a moment of dramaturge fantasia while I was driving on journeys into the field. This account was built up knowing that the children were of school age, and that I had begun from the first visits to have an understanding of their worlds, routines, family lives and how they presented themselves. I was aware that I would never be able to bring these siblings together in 'the real world' because the high risk of cross-infection in the CF context meant doing focus groups was impracticable. I was also conscious of their parallel worlds of living with brothers or sisters with CF, and of the isolation often experienced by siblings and their families within this disease trajectory.

DRAMATURGE FANTASIA

The school bell rings.

The children pack away their lessons for the day, some children are given homework and some are not.

Chairs are placed neatly under desks as teachers say 'it's home time'. The non-CF children collect their coats and bags making lots of noise and chatter. Frivolity and laughter can be heard in echoes in the corridor. As they say goodbye to their friends they are collected outside of the school by their mum and in one family by their dad. Non-CF siblings collect their brothers and sisters from different classes or different schools and they head for home either walking or by car. The school children know that they have a visitor today, all but one of the 10 non-CF siblings know.

Today is a different day, still a routine with their families, deciding whether to get changed when they get home from school, deciding whether to get something to eat, waiting while their sibling has a treatment for their CF, thinking when they should do their homework, still in their same familiar home space. Some siblings may have wanted to go out to play but choose not to because today something is different, as the protagonists are waiting.... Today THEY have a visitor! Today it is the non-CF siblings that are waiting!

My expression here is relevant because it captures the duality of my emotion.

First, there is my recognition that I am the visitor the siblings are waiting for. I knew that I was in a privileged position in being invited to spend quality time with the children and their families. It was also a position of responsibility because as a researcher I would spend time with the siblings and facilitate their journey through the research process, where they would be the creators and narrators of stories capturing their experience. Before each visit, I was filled with excitement and positive anticipation, as well as apprehension and uncertainty of what lay ahead. I had prepared my research proposal and gained ethical approval, and now here I was entering the field. This meant that my research ideas were coming into a life of their own.

Second, in capturing my emotion in the reflexive dramaturge fantasia, after having conducted first visits with some participants, I was aware that non-CF siblings were not used to having visitors. This was a different experience for them because they were used to visitors coming to see their CF sibling instead. In giving the non-CF siblings attention and the opportunity to have their moment and their say, I was bringing them to the forefront.

ARRIVING AT THE SIBLING HOMES

As I drew near to each family home, I ritualistically prepared myself for the visit ahead. I slowed down in the car, trying to get my bearings and navigate the end stage of my journey, and turned down the music to help my concentration and bring the journey's end even closer. I found the house, parked the car, turned the engine off and grabbed my large yellow research bag, as well as my handbag, a distinction that the children noticed as some tried to peer into the yellow bag during my visits.

On arrival at the family homes, as I visited at different times of the year, some days it was light, a nice sunny day and some days it was dark and freezing cold. Regardless of the day or the weather, when I walked towards each house,

I could see the siblings and, in one case, the whole family waiting for me. Some children had peering eyes looking through the front window but no full presence, a bit like the performers peeping through a tiny gap in the curtain on the theatre stage set for a sneak preview of their audience. Some of the children gave me a little wave. One little boy sat watching from his favourite upstairs bedroom space, and some were shadowed by their mums. On one occasion, a child sat alone on a front bench with his head bowed, shadowed by his family, and in another family, the child was sent out to meet me from the car.

On reaching each of my visits my car door closed, I heard the click of the door, then checked the blip of my key lock, and the flash of lights confirmed the car was secure. My heels clipped on the pavement and my strong feeling of anticipation, of wanting to see the sibling and their family, blended with a sense of relief that I had arrived after a long journey. The sounds of my footsteps were followed by my knock on the door. The door opened and the dramaturge/researcher was invited in.

On entering the field, I had tried to prepare myself for meeting the siblings and their families, and for conducting the research, but I had not anticipated the 'emotional labour' (Hochschild, 1983) that lay ahead. One of the most moving moments I encountered in the field was meeting an eight-year-old boy with his head bowed, Raff, mentioned above.[1] This moment has remained with me, and in writing about this encounter, I experienced the welling up of emotion.

MEETING RAFF (NON-CF SIBLING)
VISIT ONE OF FOUR

Raff has blond hair and is slim and pale. When I arrived, his family were all waiting outside to meet me. His parents, Neil and Alice, and his two CF sisters, Rumer (aged 13) and Bonnie (aged 10), looked happy and were smiling. I did not see Raff at first as I walked up to the front of the house, until his father pointed him out to me. I felt guilty because I had walked past him without noticing when I went up the drive to meet the family. I turned and looked to where his dad pointed. There he was, a little boy sat on his own on a bench in complete silence with his head bowed, looking really sad. 'Come and meet Amie', Neil said, but for a while the little boy did not move. Neil encouraged him further, and then informed me that Raff's sisters had told him that he was going to be adopted, and I was here to take him away.

I experienced a feeling of shock and thoughts of 'oh no'. As a researcher nothing had prepared me for this, where siblings had invented such a story, but my protective instincts prevailed as I informed Raff that I was not here to take him away, that his mum thought he might like to be involved in my research, and so I had come to see if he wanted to help me. I knew that now I would need to work through additional barriers with Raff to make him feel secure in my presence. I told him that I would only see him when his mum and dad were at home, would leave the house on my own, and would return to my own family at the end of the visit.

Raff remained shy, withdrawn, quiet and apprehensive during that first visit, but he did show that he would like to be involved in the research study by nodding his head and choosing what materials he wanted to make pictures for me during the visits. I checked at every stage of each visit that he wanted to be involved, as I was not always sure. I almost felt in a dilemma, but he confirmed that he wanted me there, and wanted to help with the study.

During my visit with Raff, I sat on the left-hand side of the sofa in the open-space lounge; Alice sat to the right of the L-shaped chair; Neil sat to the other side of the sofa; and Raff stayed near Alice. Rumer entered the room and almost sat on Raff. She pushed him out of the way and in a loud voice said 'MOVE, THAT'S WHERE I AM SITTING, THAT'S MY PLACE'. Raff did not say anything, but moved to the arm of the sofa and sat there with his head down, looking sad. Rumer remained in the place she had gained ownership of, and Raff stayed seated on the arm of the chair. Later, Neil moved out of the room, and I asked Raff if he wanted to sit next to me on the sofa, which he did.

I continued to talk to Raff, and asked if he had any friends. Raff stayed silent as his sister started giggling. She shouted, 'Friends!' as she laughed and snorted behind her hand. She continued, 'He has not got any friends', and then turned to Raff and said, 'Who would want to be your friend? Not even (name of child) wants to be your friend'. She looked back at me and said, 'He does not have any friends'.

Alice removed Rumer from the room and took her into the kitchen to stay with Neil, because she was continually acting out and responding inappropriately to my questions to Raff, but she later returned to maintain her place. She ordered Raff not to talk with the words, 'You don't talk'.

The dramaturgic scene that I witnessed above demonstrated a very powerful sibling interaction between the CF sibling (Rumer) and the non-CF sibling (Raff). It was upsetting to watch as a researcher. Raff remained inferior to Rumer as she exerted her authority over him, taking away his voice, ordering him not to speak and trying to answer on his behalf, with inappropriate words. Raff himself did not retaliate, answer back or stick up for himself. He just seem to accept the situation.

As I left that first visit, I reassured Raff that I was leaving on my own and that he was staying with his mum and dad. I got into my car and switched on the radio in readiness for my long drive home. During the journey I experienced a serendipitous moment. The ABBA song 'Chiquita' played, and its description of observing the quiet sorrow and hopelessness of another person resonated with my experience of witnessing Raff's sadness. As the words played, I felt a tear roll down my cheek because my first visit with Raff had left me feeling burdened. This was a significant moment in my research journey. Raff seemed sad, and it made me sad to see this. It was as if I had felt the transference of his emotion (see also Mannay, 2018 [this volume]). Whilst 'chiquita' normally refers to a young girl, I felt the lyrics just linked to the experience of meeting the little boy. The song provided connectedness to the family situation that I had witnessed, whilst at the same time it allowed emotional release. Even now when I hear that song, I feel the sadness of that day.

Initially, I wondered if Rumer was acting out as she had entered her teenage years and was experiencing the changes that adolescence brings, as well as living with a life-limiting condition. However, as I visited more siblings within their family homes, I began to notice a commonality in CF sibling behaviours. I realised that my study, with its focus on the non-CF siblings, was perhaps shifting the family dynamic for both the CF and non-CF siblings. This was reinforced when I visited David (aged 10).

DAVID – NON-CF SIBLING: VISIT ONE

I sat with David on the sofa in the lounge whilst talking to his mum. Suddenly David's brother who has CF (Henry, aged 5) ran into the room. It was a warm summer's day, and he was wearing only his swimming trunks, having just come out of the paddling pool. It was our first meeting, but he appeared confident. He stood directly in front of me and shouted, 'Do you want to see me? Are you here to see me?' During this time, David sat quietly on the sofa beside me, looking sullen with his head bowed.

Henry was quick to engage in conversation with me, and he had assumed that I was there specifically to see him because of his CF. He was not used to anyone coming to see his brother. When he realised that the focus was on David, he quickly jumped into his mum's arms, while remaining lively and vocal. She cuddled Henry and rocked him on her lap. David pulled a face at this point to show that he did not want Henry to have his mum's attention, and asked his mum why she was holding Henry like a baby when he was no longer a baby. Within this scene, Henry ensured that he remained the focus of attention by jumping into his mum's arms for a cuddle, while David was dismayed at Henry's need to remain the central focus.

ALTERED SIBLING EQUILIBRIUM

I realised that in conducting my study, I had altered the equilibrium of siblings' positional roles within their family. My research brought the non-CF sibling to the forefront. This was unsettling for both the CF and non-CF child, because normally people such as healthcare professionals came to see the sibling who had CF. The parents' attention was also normally focused on CF siblings due to the daily treatment interventions required to manage the disease. I became conscious that, as a researcher primarily focused on exploring the experience of the non-CF sibling, I was making the familiar strange for both non-CF and CF siblings (Mannay, 2010).

The altered sibling equilibrium was reflected in the socially interactive performances of CF siblings, as they drew attention to themselves and made their presence known to me as the researcher. Reflecting back, it was almost as if CF siblings were pleading with me to not take the focus away from them. Their positional co-constructed place of centrality within the family provided them with an element of security, reassurance and validation. My presence threatened this status.

My dramaturgical lens led to a reflective comparison. The CF sibling reaction reminded me of a key actor pleading with the director for the main part in a new play, because they have always had the starring role in previous performances. However, on this occasion the director/researcher has chosen the understudy because s/he wants to bring a new dimension to the show and attract a new audience.

The CF siblings competed for attention, but it was a rivalry with oneself (as much as the sibling) that was linked to the new situation they found themselves in. The non-CF sibling did not compete back, but maintained a passive stance. They were on the familiar stage set of home, but in a strange situation. The CF siblings' performances of acting out, whether long or brief, were powerful and left an impact on me. Becoming aware of my role in this changed situation provided me with greater understanding of the sibling relationships, family dynamics and positionality but I also felt a strong sense of guilt and responsibility for unbalancing their equilibrium.

However, I was also mindful that as a researcher, I chose to just let social interactions unfold when I visited the families. Even though my study focused on the non-CF siblings, I did not ask for CF siblings or family members to be absent during any of my visits. When parents or CF siblings wanted to chat to me, they could, and if they asked to do a picture I provided the material for them, so as not to leave anyone out. I was aware that I had not consciously segregated the siblings, but their relationships played out during my presence.

THE TRANSITION

As my research progressed over the four visits, I witnessed a remarkable transition in family life in terms of the CF sibling's acceptance of my presence and the attention given to their non-CF siblings. I observed changes in their behaviour, overall demeanour, and social interactions with the non-CF sibling, parents and myself. The most striking and significant transformation was in Rumer (Raff's sister). The account here is taken from my fourth and final visit as I was preparing to leave the field.

RAFF AND RUMER: VISIT FOUR

Before my final visit with Raff, I knew that the family had been on holiday over the summer, and so I suggested to his mum Alice that it might be useful to look at the photos with him. Raff was sometimes silent, and I thought this might help. Our visit took place in the study because their holiday photos had been uploaded onto the computer. When I arrived at the house I was greeted by Alice, and Raff stood close to her holding her hand. Rumer and Bonnie were in the hallway, and Neil was sitting in the study. Alice explained that Neil was opening the photo files. We all stayed in the hall with the study door open, and Neil was involved in our conversation too.

My previous visits had always taken place in the lounge, but Alice asked if it was okay for this visit to take place in the study. Whilst Alice talked to me, I noticed Rumer and Bonnie hovering at her side. Today, Rumer was smiling as I looked at her. I was conscious that on previous visits she had refused to answer when I asked how she was, but today I still asked. Rumer responded positively, stating that she was fine, that she had enjoyed her holiday and that today she had been to school and made a cheesecake. She looked really pleased with herself. Eventually, Neil stepped out of the study and said that the computer was ready for Raff to show me his holiday photos. I then witnessed the following short scene:

Rumer entered the study, hovered around the computer and moved a couple of things.

Neil: What are you doing?

Rumer: I am getting things ready for Raff.

Rumer moved the black chair and brought forward another to the computer so there was one for me and one for Raff. She almost invited Raff to come and sit on the chair by the desk in the study.

Raff entered the room and sat down as Rumer pushed the chair underneath him.

I was taken aback by Rumer's transformation, her sudden kindness and open stance towards myself and Raff. She prepared the stage set for Raff to enter by moving herself to one side, inviting him in and placing him in a position of focus, before leaving the room. It was as if she was giving him permission to be there. She occasionally returned to the room to see the photos. She also went to the shop. On re-entering the study, she leaned over to Raff and said, 'Mmm look what I have got for our feast later', showing Raff a packet of biscuits. Raff looked at her and smiled.

On this visit, Rumer was more positive and open in her communication and body language. She had actively prepared the research space for Raff and she skilfully placed him in a central position. When I left she said that if I ever came to stay for dinner she would make me a chocolate cheesecake. I smiled and replied, 'I look forward to that'.

CONCLUSION: TURNING TABLES

Within the research journey, I had destabilised the sibling equilibrium, but working with the siblings and their families also destabilised my world. I looked at sibling experiences and family life through a new lens. This enabled new understandings of not only those I was studying but also my own sibling relationship with a sister who is ever-present but no longer here. The shifting of the sibling dynamic within the family was significant and powerful. It highlighted the importance, particularly in childhood studies, for the researcher to consider how her presence might change family dynamics. Furthermore, it highlighted how a study design that enables the researcher to visit a child and family on several occasions may be beneficial for the family members. It is also useful in generating research findings that go beyond the impressions of the first visit. Had I only visited each sibling on one occasion, I would not have recognised the dynamic shifts in sibling positional roles.

Having four visits with each sibling and their family extended the value and contribution of this study, but most importantly it highlights my privilege in being allowed to spend quality moments of time with the families. The shifting of the family dynamic, whilst risky, was also beneficial, because this longitudinal study opened up subtle channels of communication and interactions of family life. The destabilisation of the sibling world remained and with it a positive outcome. Arguably, this added a therapeutic value to the work. The use of metaphorical expression, reflexivity and dramaturgic fantasia can enable researchers to capture their own emotional transition within such a research journey and help them to gain more nuanced understandings of family life.

NOTE

1. All of the participants in the study were assigned pseudonyms to maintain anonymity.

ACKNOWLEDGEMENTS

I would like to thank all the participants who made this study possible and my doctoral supervisors Professor Daniel Kelly and Dr Katie Featherstone. I would also like to thank The Florence Nightingale Foundation, The Brocher Foundation, The Royal College of Nursing and Cardiff University for supporting this research study.

REFERENCES

Bank, S. P., & Kahn, M. D. (1982). *The sibling bond*. New York, NY: Basic Books.
Brody, G. H. (1998). Sibling relationship quality: Its causes and consequences. *Annual Review of Psychology, 49*(1), 1–24.
Buss, A. H., & Briggs, S. R. (1984). Drama and the self in social interaction. *Journal of Personality and Social Psychology, 47*(6), 1310–1324.
Cresswell, J. (2014). *Research design: Qualitative, quantitative and mixed method approaches* (4th ed.). London: SAGE.
Durant-Law, G. (2005). Soft systems methodology and grounded theory combined: A knowledge management research approach. *Online Journal of Knowledge Management, 2*(1), 13–23.
Edwards, R., Hadfield, L., Lucey, H., & Mauthner, M. (2006). *Sibling identities and relationships: Sisters*. London: Routledge.

Fineman, S. (1993). *Emotion in organisations.* London: SAGE.

Goffman, E. (1959). *The presentation of self in everyday life.* Garden City, NY: Doubleday.

Goffman, E. (1969). *Where the action is. Three essays.* London: Allen Lane.

Hochschild, A. (1983). *The managed heart: Commercialization of human feeling.* Berkeley, CA: University of California Press.

Hodges, A. S. (2016). *The family centred experiences of siblings in the context of cystic fibrosis. A dramaturgical exploration.* Ph.D. thesis. Cardiff School of Healthcare Sciences.

Hollway, W., & Jefferson, T. (2000). *Doing qualitative research differently.* London: SAGE.

James, W. (1980). *The principles of psychology* (Vol. 1). New York, NY: Holt.

Klett-Davies, M. (2008). *Putting sibling relationships on the map: A multi-disciplinary perspective.* London: Family and Parenting Institute.

Knecht, C., Hellmars, C., & Metzing, S. (2015). The perspectives of siblings of children with chronic illness. A literature review. *Journal of Pediatric Nursing, 30*, 102–116.

Kuo, D. Z., Mac Bird, T., & Tilford, J. M. (2011). Associations of family-centred care with health care outcomes for children with special health care needs. *Maternal and Child Health Journal, 15*(6), 794–805.

Mannay, D. (2010). Making the familiar strange: Can visual research methods render the familiar setting more perceptible? *Qualitative Research, 4*(3), 361–382.

Mannay, D. (2018). 'You just get on with it': Negotiating the telling and silencing of trauma and its emotional impacts in interviews with marginalised mothers. In T. Loughran & D. Mannay (Eds.), *Emotion and the researcher: Sites, subjectivities and relationships* (Vol. 16). Studies in Qualitative Methodology (pp. 81–94). Bingley: Emerald.

Mason, J. (2002). *Qualitative researching* (2nd ed.). London: SAGE.

McGuire, S., Manke, B., Eftekhari, A., & Dunn, J. (2000). Children's perceptions of sibling conflict during middle childhood: Issues and sibling (dis)similiarity. *Social Development, 9*(2), 173–190.

O'Brien, I., Duffy, A., & Nicholl, H. (2009). The impact of childhood chronic illnesses on siblings: A literature review. *British Journal of Nursing, 18*(22) 1358–1365.

Rowe, D. (2007). *My dearest enemy, my dangerous friend: Making and breaking sibling bonds.* London: Routledge.

Watts, L. (2009). Managing self in role: using multiple methodologies to explore self-construction and self-governance. In S. Clarke & P. Hoggett (Eds.), *Researching beneath the surface. Psycho-social research methods in practice* (pp. 215–239). London: Karnac Books.

CHAPTER 4

'IT'S NOT HISTORY. IT'S MY LIFE': RESEARCHER EMOTIONS AND THE PRODUCTION OF CRITICAL HISTORIES OF THE WOMEN'S MOVEMENT

Kate Mahoney

ABSTRACT

Purpose – *This chapter explores the significance of emotional exchanges between historians and their research participants in the production of critical histories of the late twentieth-century British women's movement. It argues for the importance of exploring the ways in which positive emotions, including feelings of excitement, reverence and commonality, influence the research process and potentially complicate historians' capacity to produce histories that critically assess popular narratives of the development of the women's movement.*

Methodology/Approach – *This chapter draws on qualitative assessments of my own experiences carrying out oral history interviews with women's movement members to explore the emotional exchanges that take place*

Emotion and the Researcher: Sites, Subjectivities, and Relationships
Studies in Qualitative Methodology, Volume 16, 65–80
ISSN: 1042-3192/doi:10.1108/S1042-319220180000016005

during the research process. It utilises several historiographical concepts, including being a 'fan of feminism', discussions about historical subjectivity and oral history debates about empathy, to reflect on my emotional responses whilst carrying out research.

Findings – *This chapter demonstrates that positive emotional exchanges between historians and their research participants influence the production of critical histories of the women's movement. It highlights how historians' personal identifications with their areas of study impact on their emotional engagement with research participants, potentially complicating or contravening their wider historical aims.*

Originality/Value – *Several historians have explored how negative emotional exchanges with research participants influenced their production of critical histories of the women's movement. By focusing on the influence of positive emotional exchanges, this chapter provides an original contribution to this area of reflexive discussion, as well as wider assessments of historical subjectivity and researcher empathy.*

Keywords: Women's movement; feminism; activism; oral history; experience; narratives; subjectivity

INTRODUCTION

In recent years, histories produced by researchers who did not participate in feminist activism between the 1970s and 1990s have proliferated. Many of these historical accounts offer a critical perspective on the development of the women's movement, challenging dominant narratives that focus predominantly on the experiences of white, middle-class, socialist feminist activists (Rees, 2010b; Thomlinson, 2016). These critical histories destabilise the historiographical assumption that the British women's movement entered a period of decline after 1978 due to significant debates surrounding race, class and sexuality (Byrne, 1997, p. 110; Griffin, 1995; Segal, 1999, p. 9). In doing so, they also problematise the generational model that is often used to frame histories of the women's movement.

The emergence of critical histories of the women's movement has influenced emotional exchanges between historians and the feminist activists who have become their historical subjects. Early on in my doctoral research, I attended a conference on the history of the Women's Liberation

Movement (WLM) in Britain. One panel discussion, led by doctoral and early career researchers, resulted in a heated exchange about the representation of activists' lives in more recent histories of the WLM. A conference attendee, who was also a member of the WLM, angrily exclaimed, 'It's not history. It's my life!' My strong sense of trepidation in response to this statement heightened my awareness of my subjectivity and accountability as a historian who analyses the lives of WLM activists. The anger expressed by this conference attendee prompted my reflection on WLM members' emotional responses to becoming the subjects of popular and academic historical works, and the extent to which I negotiated comparable emotions in my own interactions with my research participants, particularly during oral history interviews.

A number of historians highlight the difficult, and sometimes negative, emotional exchanges that they have encountered while seeking to produce critical histories of the British women's movement, particularly when employing oral history approaches (Rees, 2010a; Thomlinson, 2016). However, when carrying out oral history interviews for my doctoral research on women's movement members' interactions with psychological and psychotherapeutic discourses, I deemed my emotional exchanges with my research participants to be largely positive. The conversations that I shared with my interviewees were friendly, and I was highly appreciative of their hospitality and support for my research. I also relished the opportunity to interview women who I greatly admired due to their contribution to new understandings of women's mental health care, and their activism within therapeutic and charitable organisations.

This chapter examines how positive emotional exchanges between historians and their research participants also influence the production of critical histories of the women's movement, both before and during the oral history interview, and in the subsequent processes of data analysis and writing up. First, I show why the emergence of critical histories of the women's movement necessitates increasing analysis of emotional exchanges between historians and their historical subjects. Second, I draw on my own experiences to explore how emotions experienced when interviewing prominent women's movement members, such as admiration and nervousness, influence the production of critical histories of the women's movement. Third, employing Grant's concept of being a 'fan of feminism', I explore how the development of my interest in feminist history, which predated my position as an academic scholar, influenced my emotional engagement with my research participants' expressions of nostalgia for their past political achievements.

I seek to understand how these emotional exchanges influenced the power dynamics inherent in the oral history process, and my own feelings of accountability when representing my research participants' lives. I argue that failing to recognise positive emotional exchanges between historians and their research subjects potentially complicates or contravenes the critical status of histories of the women's movement. A researcher's admiration for the achievements of her research participants, for example, can potentially slip into a reverence that valorises rather than critically assesses their activism. This valorisation bolsters the foregrounding of feminist 'figureheads' and specific activists' narratives in generational histories of the British women's movement (Chamberlain, 2017, p. 4). This chapter, therefore, argues that historians must examine their emotional exchanges with their research participants more closely.

EMOTIONAL EXCHANGES IN THE PRODUCTION OF CRITICAL HISTORIES OF THE WOMEN'S MOVEMENT

Over the past 15 years, historians have expanded histories of the women's movement in Britain beyond the prominent academic and autobiographical accounts produced by activists who participated in the movement (Alexander, 1994; Coote & Campbell, 1982; Rowbotham, 1972, 2000; Sebestyen, 1988; Segal, 1999, 2007; Wandor, 1990). Thomlinson (2016, pp. 9–10) argues that the voices in these accounts often constituted the 'white, middle-class mainstream' of the women's movement. Rees (2010a) also highlights the predominance of socialist feminist perspectives in these historical narratives. Newer histories incorporate the experiences of Black, working class, radical and revolutionary feminists, critically assessing debates within the movement around members' exclusion based on class and race (Rees, 2010a; Thomlinson, 2012).

The development of increasingly critical histories has generated strong emotional responses amongst some women who were committed participants in the WLM during the 1960s and 1970s. In her historical study on race and ethnicity in the late twentieth-century British women's movement, Thomlinson (2016, p. 198) describes how she was unprepared for the extent to which the 'emotional content' of debates between Black and white feminists in the 1970s and 1980s influenced her interactions with oral history participants, stating that it was 'very difficult for white interviewees to talk about their involvement in these debates'. She asserts that the 'obvious pain that these debates provoked does pose ethical questions about the use of such material' (Thomlinson, 2016, p. 198). Recalling her experience carrying out oral history interviews for her doctoral thesis on revolutionary feminism, Rees (2010b, p. 177) highlights the 'difficulties in intergenerational communication between myself and some of the women whose stories I wished to access and use in my work'. She describes how some oral history participants were 'distrustful' of her motives as a historian without lived experience of the women's movement that she was studying (Rees, 2010b, p. 177 and 85). These accounts highlight how potentially difficult emotional exchanges between historian and oral history participants can influence the production of critical histories of the late twentieth-century women's movement.

My own research contributes to this emergent critical historiography. By examining the proliferation of women's movement activism around mental health concerns in the 1980s and 1990s, I aim to destabilise historiographical assumptions concerning the ascendancy of feminist activism between the late 1960s and the mid-1970s, and its subsequent decline from 1978 onwards (Byrne, 1997, p. 110; Griffin, 1995; Segal, 1999, p. 9). The period of feminist activism from the late 1960s until the late 1970s has typically been defined as 'second-wave' feminism (Byrne, 1997, p. 110; Segal, 1999, p. 9). I argue that demarcating the late twentieth-century British women's movement into waves does not reflect the experiences of feminist activists who continued to operate in the 1980s (Mahoney, 2016, p. 1006). Several of my oral history participants felt that their trajectories as activists did not comply with definitions of the 'second wave' in histories of British feminism, arguing that their identification with and participation in the WLM did not stop in the late 1970s.

The wave model also distinguishes between the politics and approaches of feminist activists who operated in the 1970s (the 'second wave'), and those who were active in the 1990s (the 'third wave') (Gillis, Howie, & Munford, 2007; Walker, 1995). Several theorists have highlighted the emotional implications of this generational distinction. Bailey (1997, p. 18) explores how dialogue between second- and third-wave feminists is often enshrined in a 'mother/daughter' framework. The familial associations of this framework produce intense emotion, conflict and resistance in feminist debates (Gillis et al., 2007, p. xxx; Siegel, 1997, p. 66). The equation of the wave model with generations has therefore resulted in ideological and emotional conflicts between feminist activists.

In my view, the increased production of histories by researchers too young to have participated in feminist activism before the 2000s has led these intergenerational interactions and debates to be replicated within the research process itself. Many historians of the women's movement utilise oral history approaches and therefore directly engage with their research participants at a personal level. Several of my oral history interviewees remarked that I was from a different generation, and commented on the feminist politics that they associated with 'younger' activists like myself. These comments highlight how the interactions between historians and their research participants can reinforce the generational model enacted in histories of feminist activism. Unpacking emotional exchanges between historians and their research participants, therefore, highlights not only how generational differences and tensions are replicated in the research relationship, but also how they can be effectively negotiated.

NEGOTIATING EMOTIONS WHEN INTERVIEWING PROMINENT WOMEN'S MOVEMENT MEMBERS

While carrying out oral history interviews, I was aware of my admiration for my research participants and their political achievements. This admiration was also influenced by my identification as a feminist who is committed to enacting political change through awareness and activism. Oral history practitioners have documented the 'heady experience' of interviewing significant historical figures (Ritchie, 2015, p. 118). Ritchie (2015, p. 118) argues that oral historians 'must not let personal admiration keep them from weighing the evidence dispassionately' when producing convincing accounts of the past. I became aware of the extent to which my admiration might influence my engagement with my research participants, both within the oral history setting and in my subsequent analysis of their narratives. This influence was particularly marked when I compared my contrasting emotional responses to interviewing famous feminist activists and WLM members who are less prominent in existing historical accounts. Exploring how this admiration was enacted in my interviews highlights wider issues about how historians engage with perceptions of the past and personal politics in their histories. I therefore argue that we should not simply seek to overcome emotions such as personal admiration, but that we must examine the influence of the researcher's positive emotions in the production of critical histories of the women's movement. In this way, we can align discussions of historians' subjectivity, sentimentality and nostalgia with the positioning of feminist fandom and empathy in the oral history setting (Blee, 2006; Grant, 2011; Hamilton, 2008; Harding, 2010; Phillips, 2008).

During my doctoral research, I interviewed Susie Orbach, a prominent WLM member and psychotherapist who contributed to the development of feminist therapy in the 1970s. I conducted the interview partly to establish why her narrative had come to be foregrounded in histories of feminist therapy. My aim was to create a history that recognised the previously unheard voices of WLM members who I felt also played a significant role in the development of this therapeutic approach. I was struck by how nervous I felt during the interview. Ritchie (2015, p. 118) asserts that researchers' emotional responses when interviewing significant historical figures might lead to a 'false sense of intimacy that can diminish scholarly distance and detachment'. My awareness of Orbach's public position did not lead to false intimacy. Rather, my nervousness affected the clarity of both my questions and my reflections on her answers, factors that disrupted the research relationship I wanted to develop with my interviewee.

Describing her experience of interviewing Irish nuns living in England, McKenna (2003, p. 65 and 68) recalls her feelings of nervousness and intimidation when carrying out interviews. She argues that her feelings indicated the complex power relations inherent in the oral history interviewer–interviewee relationship. Whilst McKenna entered the interview with a strong awareness of her own subjectivity and the potential power she wielded over her participants, she later felt that her nervousness and intimidation actually reflected her powerlessness as a researcher. McKenna attributed this powerlessness to her interviewing 'older, more experienced women' and her concern about what her interviewees thought about her (McKenna, 2003, p. 69).

Like McKenna, I equated the nervousness and intimidation that I felt in my oral history interview with powerlessness. Given Orbach's perceived political successes and my own identification as a feminist, I questioned whether she thought that I was a 'good' feminist activist and researcher. This concern ran counter to the general aim of my research, which was to explore why her narrative dominated histories of feminist therapy. In the interview itself, I felt that I was responding to her answers with nervous reverence rather than critical reflection. I became increasingly aware of how this reverence might influence the interview process and subsequent data analysis when I compared my feelings in that interview with my emotional responses when speaking to women less prominent in existing histories of the women's movement. Whilst approaching these interviews with some trepidation, I felt significantly more at ease during the interview process. Did the reverence that I displayed towards Orbach bolster her position as a 'figurehead' feminist, therefore reinforcing the significance of her narrative in histories of the women's movement? When subsequently analysing my oral history interviews, I sought to attribute comparable significance to each account, therefore aiding my production of an expansive history of feminist therapy that recognises numerous voices and experiences.

This critical response to contrasting emotional exchanges at the data analysis stage ensures the dispassionate analysis that Ritchie (2015, p. 118) argues is vital for researchers speaking to individuals that they personally admire. However, exploring the nature of my nervousness when interviewing Orbach also highlights how both researchers and research participants produce and reinforce popular narratives of the women's movement throughout the oral history process. Roper (2003, 2014, p. 175) uses the psychotherapeutic tenets of transference and counter-transference to explore the 'emotional force of communication' that occurs between historians and their research subjects. In the context of oral history, transference refers to the 'narrator's placing of the interviewer in a relationship familiar to him or her' (Yow, 2005, p. 168), whilst counter-transference describes the 'emotional impulses' provoked in the researcher by the interviewee (Roper, 2014, p. 175).

There were several occasions throughout my interview with Orbach in which she explicitly or implicitly alluded to her contribution to the development of feminist therapy and her prominence within the history of the women's movement. She explicitly referred to the influence of her publications when I asked her how she negotiated her position as a community-based psychotherapist and an increasingly public figure, stating that she did so 'with tremendous difficulty...I wrote a book and it happened to be really successful and that was really weird'. At other points, Orbach implied that she had already contributed to the history of the women's movement as both a historical actor and research participant. Comments such as, 'I'm sure I've already said this in the other oral history project' suggested the regularity with which she had recalled her version of events. On listening back to the recording of this comment, it appears that she was simply qualifying that she might be repeating material contained in an oral history project that I had already listened to. However, in the interview itself, I became immediately concerned that I was asking her questions that she found repetitive or unoriginal. Orbach's comment represented the transference of her awareness that she was a significant member of the WLM who already featured in its history. My emotional response to this comment, which can be perceived as a form of counter-transference, reiterated my own perception of her prominence within histories of the women's movement.

This exchange highlights the importance of acknowledging emotions in the production of critical histories of the British women's movement. My aim of exploring Orbach's predominance in existing histories was complicated by the nervousness and intimidation that I felt when I met her. Assessing the source of this nervousness, I have been able to attribute it to my interviewee's public position, as well as my reverence for her political achievements as a long-standing feminist activist. I felt as though Orbach augmented her prominence, and my emotional responses to it, by alluding to her reputation and previous contribution to histories of the women's movement. Therefore, our emotional exchange during the interview reiterated the generational model that I seek to problematise in my own research. Analysis of this interview, therefore, highlights the need for historians to acknowledge the significance of emotional exchanges with their research participants in order to effectively produce critical histories of the women's movement.

BEING A 'FAN OF FEMINISM' DURING THE HISTORICAL RESEARCH PROCESS

I have highlighted how I felt increasingly nervous when speaking to a well-known member of the WLM. However, when interviewing women who are less prominent in existing histories of the women's movement, I still felt a strong sense of admiration for their political and professional achievements. This admiration felt particularly marked because, through interviewing them, I aimed to better situate their contributions within the history of feminist psychology and psychotherapy in late twentieth-century Britain. Grant (2011, p. 267) uses the 'figure of the fan' to examine 'contemporary interest in second-wave feminism'. She describes how being a fan of something suggests an 'over-attachment, an excessive engagement that goes beyond the intellectual', and argues that being a 'fan of feminism' might have the negative connotations of 'obsession, of embarrassing desire, and of a loss of perspective' (Grant, 2011, p. 267).

This notion of being a 'fan of feminism' can be used to explore historians' engagement with both the history of feminism and their own feminist pasts. Grant (2011, p. 269) describes how feminist fandom elicits a 'nostalgia for a political past as represented by the late 1960s and 1970s' that blurs the researcher's roles as academic scholar and popular culture consumer. I draw on Grant's 'fan of feminism' concept to explore how my own identification with a particular feminist past strengthened the admiration that I felt for my research participants and influenced my emotional exchanges with them. Acknowledging the nature of this fandom further demonstrates how positive emotional responses, like admiration, complicate the production of critical histories of the women's movement. It also highlights how historians' personal politics and emotional investments influence their negotiation of nostalgia and sentimentality within their work.

Bornat (2010, p. 45) emphasises the importance of oral historians identifying their 'cultural habitus' when carrying out interviews. Hammersley (1997, pp. 138–139) defines cultural habitus as the 'intuitive component of qualitative research' acquired by the researcher as they carry out fieldwork and develop first-hand experience of their area of study. Identifying her own 'cultural habitus' as a PhD student in the early 1970s, Bornat (2010, p. 43 and 46) also cites the influence of her socialist-feminist politics on her oral history practice. Recognising my own 'cultural habitus' as a researcher further contextualises how my admiration for my oral history interviewees influenced my production of a critical history of the women's movement.

I first became aware of the history of feminist activism and culture as a teenager listening to Riot Grrrl bands. Riot Grrrl was an international radical feminist movement that emerged out of the West Coast American punk music scenes in the early 1990s (Marcus, 2010; Zeisler, 2016). Its members protested the assumption that the 1990s was an era of post-feminism, proclaiming the continued existence of structural gender inequality and repressive norms of femininity. The politics of Riot Grrrl were disseminated by punk bands including Bikini Kill and Bratmobile and reproduced in handmade zines (Marcus, 2010; Piemeier, 2009). The cut-and-stick quality of these Riot Grrrl publications, coupled with the grunge clothing worn by its proponents, gave the movement a particular aesthetic that readily reflected the period within which it emerged (Piepmeier, 2009; Strong, 2016, p. 110). I therefore associated my identification with Riot Grrrl not only with its music and politics but also how it looked and felt. In becoming a fan of Riot Grrrl bands, I also became a fan of this exciting feminist past.

Grant (2011, p. 267) asserts that being a fan of feminism incorporates irrational tendencies, such as obsessiveness and over-engagement. As a teenager, my interest in the history of Riot Grrrl reflected this purportedly irrational fandom. I did not simply admire the movement's proponents; I wanted to be them. My historical imagination situated me in a world that reflected the early 1990s Riot Grrrl scene, where I could be these women, live out their contemporary cultural influences and enact their political achievements. Consequently, I viewed this period of feminist history through a nostalgic lens. Ferrier (2012) argues that 1990s nostalgia is not simply 'driven by those who lived it first time around; it is also reimagined by those who didn't, for whom this decade is retro rather than remembered'. She argues that this reimagining of the 1990s is influenced by its perception as a decade of creative, cultural and political extremes (Ferrier, 2012). Certainly, my imagined world of Riot Grrrl drew on little historical evidence but was based on my desire to be part of a community within which women could raise their voices, express themselves politically and creatively and support one another.

Grant (2011, p. 267) describes how feminist fandom on the part of the researcher transcends their scholarly position. Was my admiration for my research participants partly founded on nostalgia for a feminist past that aligned with my initial engagement with women's movement activism? A central element of my admiration for my oral history interviewees was their ability to form politically influential community-based services from scratch. The women in my doctoral thesis established feminist psychology groups and therapy centres in their own homes that still exist now. Integral to my admiration was my assumption that it would be almost impossible to set up comparable organisations in the present day.

Other oral history practitioners have expressed similar disbelief at the organisational achievements of 1970s women's movement members. Interviewing Susie Orbach for the *Sisterhood and After: An Oral History of the Women's Liberation Movement* project in 2011, Polly Russell enquired about her foundation of the London-based Women's Therapy Centre (WTC) in 1976. The WTC was the first British organisation to promote feminist therapeutic services to women beyond the women's movement. In response to Orbach's description of how she and WTC co-founder Luise Eichenbaum established the organisation in the basement of her house, Russell stated, 'What, how? I mean, you can't just start these things'. Orbach responded, 'Well you could. That's the thing' (Orbach, 2011).

My oral history participants also presented the 1970s and 1980s as a period in which women's movement members had the creative and political freedom to establish new and exciting political projects. One WTC staff member, Iona Grant, who joined in the early 1980s, described how 'you could just explore and you had this group of very diverse women in terms of backgrounds, culture, education and you could just throw it into one of the meetings and get it up and running. It was great'. Recalling her excitement at being involved in the WTC, Grant was aware that she was drawing on wider narratives of nostalgia to sentimentalise her experiences. She described staff members at the WTC as 'a lot of very bright, determined, turned on women, if I can use that very sixties expression'. Elsewhere, she stated: 'I think without a doubt the early years for me personally were very, very creative…Oh dear, I'm trying not to sound too sixties but it's hard'.

Historians and cultural theorists have assessed the role that 1960s nostalgia has played in the portrayal of subsequent political activism. Pierson (2014, p. 147) argues that the 'moments of social resistance' associated with the youth counterculture movements of the 1960s often serve as 'nostalgic sites of continuity and potential political critique for present-day critics of the traditional patriarchal role for men'. By aligning her professional experiences and emotional responses at the WTC in the 1980s with nostalgia for the countercultural ideas and creative freedoms of the 1960s, Grant established continuity between the radical politics and women's movement activism enacted during the two decades. She also compared the excitement and inclusivity she associated with her work at the WTC in the early 1980s with the frustration and alienation she experienced in the late 1980s to argue that the organisation became increasingly depoliticised throughout the decade. Grant, therefore, employed a narrative of 1960s nostalgia to comment on subsequent political developments that she felt occurred at the WTC, and to lament the perceived absence of particular professional and political freedoms in the present day.

As previously highlighted, my own identification with the history of the women's movement reflected my desire as a teenager to be part of a feminist past that I felt no longer existed. Listening to my research participants' employment of sentimental narratives during the interview process fuelled my own nostalgia for their particular feminist past. In the same way that I had identified with the Riot Grrrl movement, I now found myself imagining being in my interviewees' positions as they lived out their personal politics and established community-based organisations in 1970s Britain. In her discussion on historical subjectivity, Taylor (2012, p. 205) argues that historians' 'interpretations of past subjectivities draw on our imaginative identifications, conscious and unconscious, with the people we study'. She asserts that this form of empathy is intrinsic to the production of historical studies (Taylor, 2012, p. 205). However, given my identification with the nostalgia articulated by my oral history interviewees, the 'imaginative identifications' that informed my empathy for my research participants transcended my position as an academic scholar, reflecting the personalised feminist fandom that I equated with my initial interactions with women's movement history.

My engagement with my oral history participants' nostalgic narratives influenced my capacity to produce a critical history of feminist therapy and the women's movement. Empathy is often presented as integral to feminist oral history methodologies because it equalises the interviewer–interviewee relationship and destabilises assumptions about researcher objectivity (Oakley, 1981; Stacey, 1991, p. 109). Historians, however, have increasingly queried this emphasis on empathy (Blee, 2006; Hamilton, 2008). Roper (2014, p. 175) argues that whilst empathy can be a 'creative force', its 'affective "stickiness"' places pressure on historians as they conduct their research. He draws on Loewenberg's account of the 'distorted perceptions' that occur in historical work to argue that empathy can result in historians 'skating over…the complexity and ambiguity of actions and emotional states', leading to the development of 'historical blind spots' (Loewenberg, 1996, p. 6; Roper, 2014, p. 175).

This danger resonates with my own experiences, especially as it concerns the need to acknowledge the limitations of the WLM's political achievements. The WTC, for example, successfully popularised ideas surrounding feminist therapy in the 1980s, but debates about accessibility and inclusivity existed within the organisation into the 1990s. Black feminist psychotherapists called out its absence of support for women who were not white, and championed the importance of expanding its services and making them more accessible (Alleyne, 1998). These critical elements of the WTC's development were not foregrounded within my oral history participants' nostalgic accounts. If I had not unpacked my emotional engagement with their nostalgia, and its propensity to fuel my historical imagination, I may have produced a history of feminist therapy that overlooked these critical areas of debate.

Phillips (2008, pp. 52–53) argues for the importance of sentimentality as a historical tool in 'not just acknowledging the importance of the emotions, but also recognising their central role in social communication and moral judgement'. Recognising and assessing my own sentimentality highlights that this nostalgia was connected to my teenage fandom of a particular feminist past. Acknowledging the roots of my personal association with feminist history demonstrates how it played out in the emotional exchanges between myself and my research participants, potentially contravening my capacity to produce a critical historical study of the women's movement.

CONCLUSION

Drawing on my own experience of conducting oral history interviews with women involved in the development of feminist therapy in 1970s and 1980s Britain, this chapter has examined some of the emotional exchanges that can occur between historians and their research participants. I have demonstrated the importance of analysing how positive emotions such as admiration and excitement influence the production of critical histories of the women's movement. Failing to assess the influence of positive emotional exchanges in the research process reinforces the assumptions found in existing histories of the women's movement.

Some oral historians have asserted that researchers should repress their personal admiration for their interviewees in order to produce dispassionate historical studies. However, exploring the ways in which admiration is enacted in the emotional exchange between the historian and their research participants highlights its role in reinforcing popular women's movement narratives, such as the dominance attributed to specific 'figurehead' feminists. Assessing the emotional exchange that took place between myself and Susie Orbach demonstrates her role in reiterating her prominence, both explicitly and implicitly, during the interview process. Assessing my own emotional responses to Orbach's comments highlights the ways in which they complicated my desire to produce a history of feminist therapy that critically assessed the predominance of her narrative.

This chapter has also explored how my personal admiration played out in interviews with women who were less prominent in existing histories of the women's movement. Although I felt less nervous before these interviews, I still found myself responding to these women's narratives with a strong level of excitement, reverence and identification with their experiences. My own initial engagement with the history of feminism, grounded in my fandom for the political culture of the 1990s Riot Grrrl movement, influenced my historical imagination as I engaged with my oral history participants. Assessing the extent to which my own historical imagination was grounded in a fandom that transcended my position as an academic scholar demonstrates the need for historians to critically assess their emotional identifications with their subjects and sources. Doing so provides greater insight into the ways in which historical studies are researched and produced, acknowledging the influence of historians' personal lives and politics, and their contemporary engagement with particular perceptions of the past.

REFERENCES

Alexander, S. (1990). *Becoming a woman and other essays in 19th and 20th century feminist history*. London: Virago.

Alleyne, A. (1998). Which women? What feminism? In I. B. Seu & M. C. Heenan (Eds.), *Feminism and psychotherapy: Reflections on contemporary theories and practices*. London: SAGE.

Bailey, C. (1997). Making waves and drawing lines: The politics of defining the vicissitudes of feminism. *Hypatia, 12*(3), 17–28.

Blee, K. (2006). Evidence, empathy and ethics: Lessons from oral histories of the Klan. In R. Perks & A. Thompson (Eds.), *The oral history reader* (2nd ed., pp. 322–331). London: Routledge.

Bornat, J. (2010). Remembering and reworking emotions: The reanalysis of emotion in an interview. *Oral History, 38*(2), 43–52.

Byrne, P. (1997). *Social movements in Britain*. London: Routledge.

Chamberlain, P. (2017). *The feminist fourth wave: Affective temporality*. Basingstoke: Palgrave Macmillan.

Chaplin, J. (1988). Feminist therapy. In J. Rowan & W. Dryden (Eds.), *Innovative therapy in Britain* (pp. 39–60). Milton Keynes: Open University Press.

Coote, A., & Campbell, C. (1982). *Sweet freedom: The struggle for women's liberation*. London: Picador.

Ferrier, M. (2012). Stone Roses, Trainspotting and the grunge look: The 90s revival is here. *Guardian*, February 12. Retrieved from https://www.theguardian.com/culture/2012/feb/11/90s-revival-music-culture. Accessed on June 3, 2017.

Gillis, S., Howie, G., & Munford, R. (2007). Introduction. In S. Gillis, G. Howie, & R. Munford (Eds.), *Third wave feminism: A critical exploration* (pp. xxi–xxxiv). Basingstoke: Palgrave Macmillan.

Grant, C. (2011). Fans of feminism: Re-writing histories of second-wave feminism in contemporary art. *Oxford Art Journal*, *34*(2), 265–286.

Griffin, G. (1995). Introduction. In G. Griffin (Ed.), *Feminist activism in the 1990s* (pp. 1–10). London: Taylor & Francis.

Hammersley, M. (1997). Qualitative data archiving: Some reflections on its prospects and problems. *Sociology*, *31*(1), 131–142.

Hamilton, C. (2008). On being a 'good' interviewer: Empathy, ethics and the politics of history. *Oral History*, *36*(2), 35–43.

Harding, J. (2010). Talk about care: Emotions, culture and oral history. *Oral History*, *38*(2), 33–42.

Loewenberg, P. (1996). *Decoding the past: The psychohistorical approach* (2nd ed.). Piscataway: Transaction Publishers.

Mahoney, K. (2016). Historicising the 'third wave': Narratives of contemporary feminism. *Women's History Review*, *25*(6), 1006–1013.

Marcus, S. (2010). *Girls to the front: The true story of the Riot Grrrl Revolution*. New York, NY: Harper Perennial.

McKenna, Y. (2003). Sisterhood? Exploring power relations in the collection of oral history. *Oral History*, *31*(1), 65–72.

Oakley, A. (1981). Interviewing women: A contradiction in terms? In H. Roberts (Ed.), *Doing feminist research* (pp. 30–61). London: Routledge.

Orbach, S., in an interview recorded by P. Russell, 6 June 2011, 10 June 2011, 4 July 2011, 15 August 2011, 6 October 2011, 29 November 2011. London. *Sisterhood and after: An oral history project of Women's Liberation*, British Library.

Phillips, M. S. (2008). On the advantage and disadvantage of sentimental history for life. *History Workshop Journal*, *65*, 49–64.

Piepmeier, A. (2009). *Girl zines: Making media, doing feminism*. New York, NY: New York University Press.

Pierson, D. (2014). AMC's mad men and the politics of nostalgia. In K. Niemeyer (Ed.), *Media and nostalgia: Yearning for the past, present and future* (pp. 139–151). Basingstoke: Palgrave Macmillan.

Rees, J. (2010a). A look back at anger: The Women's Liberation Movement in 1978. *Women's History Review*, *19*(10), 337–356.

Rees, J. (2010b). 'Are you a lesbian?' Challenges in recording and analysing the Women's Liberation Movement in England. *History Workshop Journal*, *69*, 177–187.

Ritchie, D. (2015). *Doing oral history* (3rd ed.). Oxford: Oxford University Press.

Roper, M. (2003). Analysing the analysed: Transference and counter-transference in the oral history encounter. *Oral History, 31*(2), 20–32.

Roper, M. (2014). The unconscious work of history. *Cultural and Social History, 11*(2), 169–193.

Rowbotham, S. (1972). The beginnings of Women's Liberation in Britain. In M. Wandor (Ed.), *The body politic: Women's Liberation in Britain 1969–1972* (pp. 91–102). London: Stage 1.

Rowbotham, S. (2000). *Promise of a dream: Remembering the sixties*. London: Allen Lane.

Sebestyen, A. (Ed.). (1998). *'68, '78, '88: From women's liberation to feminism*. Bridport: Prism Press.

Segal, L. (2007). *Making trouble: Life and politics*. London: Serpent's Tail.

Segal, L. (1999). *Why feminism? Gender, psychology, politics*. Cambridge: Polity.

Siegel, D. L. (1997). The legacy of the personal: Generating theory in feminism's third wave. *Hypatia, 12*(3), 46–75.

Strong, C. (2016). *Grunge: Music and memory*. Abingdon, Oxon: Routledge.

Taylor, B. (2012). Historical subjectivity. In S. Alexander & B. Taylor (Eds.), *Psyche and history: Culture, psychoanalysis and the past* (pp. 195–110). Basingstoke: Palgrave Macmillan.

Thomlinson, N. (2016). *Race, ethnicity and the women's movement in England*. Basingstoke: Palgrave Macmillan.

Walker, R. (Ed.). (1995). *To be real: Telling the truth and the changing the face of feminism*. New York, NY: Anchor.

Wandor, M. (Ed.). (1990). *Once a feminist: Stories of a generation*. London: Virago.

Yow, V. R. (2005). *Recording oral history: A guide for the humanities and the social sciences* (2nd ed.). Oxford: AltaMira Press.

CHAPTER 5

'YOU JUST GET ON WITH IT': NEGOTIATING THE TELLING AND SILENCING OF TRAUMA AND ITS EMOTIONAL IMPACTS IN INTERVIEWS WITH MARGINALISED MOTHERS

Dawn Mannay

ABSTRACT

Purpose – This chapter explores the relational and emotional lifeworlds of qualitative interviews. The chapter documents the ways in which I have negotiated the sharing of traumatic accounts without being able to fix or repair their causes, and how I struggled to listen to recollections without trying to appropriate, accentuate or ameliorate their affective resonances.

Methodology/Approach – The chapter focuses on one case from a four-year study with mothers and their daughters in a marginalised area of South Wales, UK. The study drew on visual and creative methods of data production, including mapping, collage, photoelicitation and timelines, which were accompanied by in-depth elicitation interviews.

Emotion and the Researcher: Sites, Subjectivities, and Relationships
Studies in Qualitative Methodology, Volume 16, 81–94
ISSN: 1042-3192/doi:10.1108/S1042-319220180000016006

Findings – The chapter illustrates the usefulness of reflecting on emotions to understand the communication of trauma, and its emotional impacts on research relationships both within and beyond the field.

Originality/Value – The chapter builds on earlier work that has attempted to consider in detail the nature of the interaction between researchers and participants. It argues that psychoanalytically informed frames of analysis can engender a more nuanced understanding of the relationality and emotionality of qualitative research; particularly when topics are hard to speak of and hard to bear.

Keywords: Emotion; defended subject; helplessness; psychoanalytically informed approaches; qualitative research; relationality

INTRODUCTION

As Gabb (2008) argues, in empirical qualitative studies of family life, the researcher inevitably becomes embedded in the personal worlds of those being researched. These worlds are emotional, embodied and affective, and they deny the premise of the objective, detached social researcher. Accordingly, fieldwork is not simply an exercise in data collection but an active process of production, which shapes and constructs identities, intimate relations, an emotional self and a physical self (Coffey, 1999), for both researchers and participants. Arguably, then, psychoanalytically informed approaches can be useful in exploring the affective elements of research relationships and the value of emotion in the activities of research. However, it is important to note that there have been strong objections to taking psychoanalysis outside the clinical situation of the 'consulting room' (Frosh, 2010; Frosh & Emerson, 2005; Midgley, 2006). In these critiques, psychoanalysis is positioned as an undemocratic dialogue in which taking a psychoanalytical style of inquiry outside the clinic to the research setting imports power inequalities.

Yet psychoanalytically informed work can, and often does, take a democratising and dialogical stance (see Hoggett, Beedell, Jimenez, Mayo, & Miller, 2010; Morgan, 2015). Utilising this approach, Hollway and Jefferson (2013) contend that traditional interviews based on the question-answer method are thin, rationally driven accounts that omit more than they reveal of human subjects. In their own psychoanalytically informed work, employing free association narrative interviews, they emphasise the importance of biography and the usefulness of open-ended questions which are understood through participants' meaning-frames and not predetermined by the researcher. This approach engenders:

> a largely uninterrupted flow of talk with an attentive listener whose role it is to try and understand what is being said; opening up opportunities to gain a more nuanced understanding of participants' lived subjectivities. (Mannay, 2016, p. 111)

Two key concepts in psychoanalytically informed approaches are 'transference' and 'counter-transference'. In a clinical setting, transference is understood as unconscious images from the patient's past being imposed on the analyst, while counter-transference represents the analyst's unconscious response to the patient or the patient's transference itself (Walkerdine, Lucey, & Melody, 2001). Within social research, these concepts have been utilised to deepen understandings of the research relationship and engender the reflexivity to appreciate the researcher's somatic responses to the participant as affective ways of knowing (Lucey, Melody, & Walkerdine, 2003). In this way, the relational aspect of the qualitative research parallels the experience of psychotherapists in reacting to their clients' concerns and narrations.

For example, Walkerdine et al. (2001) developed a psychosocial research method of engagement that considered the psychoanalytic concepts of desire, anxiety and defences to think through the effects of unconscious processes and social constraints in the lives of working-class girls. Working with emotions, they cautiously used their own subjectivity as a tool and explored their own defences as researchers in relation to the interview encounter and data produced. In one case, they noted how 'too close a correspondence' between interviewees (the working-class parents who could not envisage their daughter moving away), and the researcher (the working-class daughter who would have felt trapped if she had stayed), impacted on the understandings produced about the data (see Lucey et al., 2003). Accordingly, the boundaries of objective researcher and researched were breached to consider issues of affect, which provided insights into complex negotiations and emotional struggles and illuminated the role that these play in both creating and analysing data (Walkerdine et al., 2001).

The importance of recognising unconscious feelings has also been explored by Gemignani (2011) in a study with refugees. The tension between involvement and detachment has important implications for qualitative fieldwork, and in this study, the researcher took an autoethnographic approach to understand the emotional life of the interview. For Gemignani, the distance between forced and chosen emigration, and the closeness invoked in the everyday inevitable difficulties of the migratory experience, were key factors in unpicking the liminal spaces between the subjectivities of the researcher and participants in both fieldwork and data analysis. Importantly, this approach not only positions the participant as a defended subject, but also accepts that as researchers we habitually defend ourselves from threats to the self which create anxiety both consciously and unconsciously (Hollway & Jefferson, 2013).

These relational aspects of the research process have also been explored in the field of oral history. In relation to transference, here authors have explored how narrators position the researcher in a relationship familiar to them, whilst counter-transference represents the ways in which the interviewee provokes particular emotions in the researcher (see Mahoney, 2018 [this volume]). The idea of 'familiar to them' is also central in discourses of appropriation, and Rose (2010) has documented the ways in which the audiencing of traumatic accounts often creates a deceitful form of empathy, where the capacity to care exists only where the viewer can see the subject as 'like them'. This chapter builds on these and earlier works to illustrate how researchers' emotional reactions become an important source of reflexivity in negotiating the telling and silencing of trauma.

THE STUDY

The data discussed here were drawn from an Economic and Social Research Council-funded study that focused on the everyday lives of mothers and daughters residing in a marginalised area in urban South Wales, UK. The research was interested in the stigma of place, barriers to education, gendered inequalities and the role of social class (Mannay, 2013a, 2014). Visual images are widely recognised as having the potential to evoke empathetic understandings of the ways in which other people experience their worlds (Belin, 2005; Fink, 2012; Gabb & Fink, 2015; Liveng et al., 2017; Rose, 2001). The experiential accounts of participants were facilitated by creative visual and narrative activities (Mannay, 2010, 2016) and repeat elicitation interviews, which allowed participants to reflect in detail on the micro-interactions of their lives in the past, present and their imagined futures. Therefore, although the study did not adopt a classic psychosocial interview approach, introducing visual and creative aspects moved beyond the sanitised form of accounts that are often associated with standard interview-based research (Hollway, 2015).

It is important to note that this research was indigenous, in that I had a high level of familiarity with the research site, and to differing extents, the participants. The notion of being an insider or an outsider is inadequate in an absolute sense, and the complex and multifaceted nature of lived experiences positions researchers as neither total 'insiders' nor 'outsiders' in relation to the individuals they interview (Hammersley & Atkinson, 2007; Mannay & Creaghan, 2015; Song & Parker, 1995; see also Latchem-Hastings, 2018; Roberts, 2018; Sheppard, 2018; van den Scott, 2018 [this volume]). However, the overlap in our geographies, histories and experiences built emotional connections with participants and engendered a high level of affinity and empathetic understanding. We have agency over our own interpretations of events and are not victims of our own biographies (Iantaffi, 2011), yet the 'specifity of place and politics has to be reckoned with in making an account of anybody's life, and their use of their own past' (Steedman, 1986, p. 6). Therefore, reflecting on the emotional lifeworld of the research encounter can be particularly useful for exploring the intricacies of shared meanings and moving beyond the narrowness of what we might expect to know or find.

Reflecting further on place, the research site was a marginalised locale, and discourses of shame often form a symbolic nexus from which working-class women struggle to disassociate (Aaron, 1994; Davidoff, 1976; Evans, 2007; Skeggs, 2009; Tyler, 2008). Consequently, investments in working-class respectable femininity have been built as a resistance to stories of working-class lack (Gillies, 2007; Walkerdine, 1997). In presenting data from this study with working-class women, I do not want to further stigmatise the participants or situate their home as a 'spatial folk devil' (Mannay, 2014, p.19), but neither do I want to represent them as 'working-class heroes'. This is not simply because I share classed and spatial biographies, and this attaches some form of solidarity or familiarity, but because it needs to be acknowledged that trauma is not a working-class phenomenon. Trauma exists across class. Those without access to capital may find it harder to negotiate liveable lives, but the women I worked with were individuals, with their own agency, biographies and subjective realities. They were not simply research 'subjects'; rather they entered into relational conversations that produced the interview accounts. The following section focuses on one such relational encounter, reflecting on the sharing of trauma, appropriation, amelioration, silencing and helplessness.

RESEARCH REFLECTIONS – GRACE

As de Beauvoir (1949) argues, for women, the future is often haunted by phantoms of the past, which impact upon the present, and my interviews with mothers and their daughters were permeated with biographical reflections. Violence was not the initial research focus; nonetheless, as Rock (2007, p. 30) contends, there is a 'need to remain open to the features that cannot be listed in advance of the study', and family troubles were an invasive element in the accounts (see Mannay, 2013b). Male violence was often central in participants' biographies and traumatic events were normalised and naturalised. This was the case for Grace, who, at the time of the research, was a single mother to two children, who had previously experienced both familial and domestic abuse and was living on a low income, as a full-time mother in a marginalised and stigmatised housing estate.

In Grace's extract below the 12 years of physical, mental and, later, sexual abuse from her stepfather were centralised in recollections of her past, as well as in her present-day relationship with her mother.

Grace: As I got older it got worse anyway you know really he should have been (pause) me and there's a... a... a..., another female on his side that would be, I suppose a cousin, and we should have gone to court and got him done.

Dawn: Mmm.

Grace: Years ago for the stuff that he done (pause) cause he changed (pause) it wasn't just physical abuse in the end with him you know it really wasn't, so we should of (pause) both of us a long time ago gone.

Dawn: Mmm.

Grace: But I just didn't have the strength to face him in court cause they were very clever so there was never a lot of evidence, and because when social services come round as well, ah, they interviewed me with them right next door, but it wasn't a solid wall it was a door.

Dawn: So they knew they were listening.

Grace: Yeah, but there was no way I was goanna say nothing, so because of that social services just didn't take it any further, like I mean I never got a visit ever again (pause) you know (pause) and that was because the school obviously reported him, cause I can remember one day crying and they seen the marks and that, and I said to them 'no I fell' (laughs).

Dawn: Ahh.

Grace: And back then they accepted it (laughs) you know (laughs) but you know he just, and she just, I think that was the worse thing knowing that your own mother did nothing you know, even now question her and she'll go I wasn't aware of nothing.

Dawn: And did he used to hit her an all then.

Grace: No he never touched my mother (pause) it's the one thing he didn't do, I got it all, he never touched my mother, never touched her at all.

Dawn: But d'you think she was scared of him psychologically then.

Grace: I don't know, I don't know because he never threatened her, he never hit her (pause) and years ago she actually left him for two weeks and she's the one that went back (pause) he never harassed her or hounded her once you know.

Dawn: Mmm.

Grace: There was nothing, he didn't chase her at all (pause) she was going to the pay-phone-boxes and ringing him and getting him to come down and all stuff like that so you know, I was, I would say she would have to accept the responsibility as well there (pause) she just don't (laughs) (both laugh).

In everyday interactions, including qualitative research, emotions constantly pass between people; and when projection is used as a defence to get rid of painful feelings by putting them into someone else, they can be experienced by the other through empathy (Hollway & Jefferson, 2000). In this interaction, I was confronted with an overwhelming feeling of helplessness. This emotion, which I initially interpreted as belonging to me, was provoked in me through my discussion with Grace. I understood it in relation to a 'hangover from beliefs about scientific objectivity' (Hollway, 2001, p. 16); as a rationalisation of the limitations of the research project and its inability to make anything right in relation to the reflexive account of an adult, which cannot be attended to in the same way as safeguarding issues raised by children.

Across our two interviews, Grace appeared strong and capable. Her creative activities and the related interview accounts described how she has negotiated both a childhood characterised by abuse and an early adulthood fraught with further violence, trauma and insecurity. Now, as a mother to her own children, despite her lack of nurturing she demonstrates her own capacity to care (Hollway, 2006). In this way, any sense of a 'spoiled identity' (May, 2008, p. 470) is challenged by a narrative of resilience rather than one that centralises feelings of helplessness. As Richardson (1997, p.1) argues, researchers routinely turn their gaze to the lives of others, but 'they are less prone to see themselves as social and cultural products, producing social and cultural products'. It is important then to explore the origins of this overwhelming helplessness that I experienced.

My initial reflections focused on the inability of the researcher to change the past or put things right. There was also the possibility that I was evoking a passive ideal of empathy, constructed from caring based on similarity (Rose, 2010). Through transference, Grace may have positioned me in a relationship familiar to her, and I also understood and felt a sense of familiarity, which was evoked affectively as an aspect of counter-transference. Although our childhood biographies are different, Grace and I shared similar geographies and have experienced poverty, motherhood and housing instability. There are similarities in the present, but arguably my emotional responses were resonant of a crude empathy, which comes 'dangerously close to the appropriation of someone else's experience because we feel for another only insofar as we are positioned as being like that other' (Rose, 2010, p. 113).

These inherently selfish responses to the accounts of this unliveable, yet lived, life might have contributed to the emotions experienced, but they are insufficient to explain the weight of these emotions.

In considering the associated concepts of projection and denial, there are different ways to understand the emotionality of helplessness. The dynamic unconscious defends against anxiety, and although the account was presented as matter of fact, a straightforward recollection of the past, arguably these memories were not simply processes of factual recall but evidence of an emotional lifeworld. In psychoanalytic theory, threats to the self create anxiety. Defences against such anxiety are mobilised at a largely unconscious level so that when 'memories of events are too anxiety-provoking, they will be either forgotten or recalled in a modified, more acceptable fashion' (Hollway & Jefferson, 2009, p. 300). Positioning Grace as a defended subject requires an understanding of how pain needs to be projected to guard against anxiety. The performed denial of the helplessness experienced by the child Grace perhaps allows Grace to access to a 'dimension through which human beings create themselves anew' (Elliott, 1992, p. 4).

The adult Grace appears contained and confident. The affective life of the interview, even in her paralanguage, did not communicate any distress. The accompanying laughter, to things that are not humorous, acted as a denial of the pain associated with recollection. However, my reaction to Grace's talk was a palpable feeling of helplessness, which stayed with me long after the interview. This helplessness was only a faint trace of the helplessness of the child Grace, but it helped me to look at the data again and explore the weight of the everyday negotiation of abuse, where the usual agents of help – mother, teachers and social workers – did not assist.

The account is situated in childhood but as Berger (1972, p. 370) contends:

> The present tense of the verb to be refers only to the present: but nevertheless with the first person singular in front of it, it absorbs the past, which is inseparable from it. 'I am' includes all that has made me so. It is more than a statement of immediate fact: it is already biographical.

Grace, at least outwardly, has been able to produce a liveable sense of self, an 'I am' that has not just survived but thrived; a maternal self that has created a successful family unit. However, in rationalising the childhood past in a present adulthood, Grace was still confronted by what she calls the 'worse thing', 'knowing that your own mother did nothing, you know, even now question her and she'll go I wasn't aware of nothing'. Grace, as a mother, and as a woman aware of wider discourses of what mothers can and should be (Aaron & Rees, 1994; Gillies, 2007; May, 2008), was still confronted by complete denial from her mother. This denial may be the only liveable option for Grace's mother, and maternal subjects can adopt the defences of repression, denial and splitting as a protection of 'self as mother' (Hollway & Jefferson, 2001), but this means that for Grace there is a denial of recognition, legitimisation and responsibility.

In a psychosocial qualitative approach, it is important that the researcher attempts to contain the pain communicated in the interview so that it can be returned detoxified and faced as an aspect of reality (Hollway & Jefferson, 2000). When the experience is too painful, this pain can be returned too quickly, acting to deny painfulness and offering reassurance and rationalisation. In my own responses to the interview as a whole, initially there was a sense of containment (Winnicott, 1965). Later, there were attempts to make excuses and to provide justifications, which could make the account easier to bear – easier for the researcher, because for the participant it is already biographical. I offered the inadequate, 'did he used to hit her' and 'd'you think she was scared of him'.

My interruptions only served to accentuate, not ameliorate. Grace does not remember any forms of domestic abuse towards her mother. She has experienced, and had previously discussed, domestic violence and psychological attacks in her own adult life, which suggest that she can read these signs effectively. My attempts to provide reassurance and a rationale were not met with the possibilities of any rationalisation. They only accentuated a darker remembering. My own experience of being a mother, an experience shared by Grace, acted to raise further questions, silently to myself, about the absence of care, then and now. In the last line of the extract, the effects of the past in the present, and their lack of resolution, were restated: 'I would say she would have to accept the responsibility as well there (pause) she just don't (laughs) (both laugh)'. In this exchange, Grace laughed, and I also laughed, we both laughed. The laughter is resonant of the colloquial 'don't know whether to laugh or cry', as we were laughing but nothing was funny. It was a response to the lived trauma Grace shared. I had given up on any attempts to contain the pain so that it can be faced as an aspect of reality (Hollway & Jefferson, 2000). Instead, I denied the pain and linked on to the release of laughing, choosing to laugh and not cry. The laughter normalised the situation and somehow it helped. Crying would, for me, have been a disrespectful appropriation of someone else's experience (Rose, 2010).

In the research process, reflecting on emotions can provide a more nuanced understanding of what is said, and what is silenced. Emotions offer a way to move beyond a simple question–answer analysis, which can leave out more than it allows of human subjects (Hollway & Jefferson, 2013). Focusing on what was felt enables an appreciation of the weight of Grace's account, the lived trauma of the child Grace, as well as the continual psychosocial work that is needed to maintain a defended subject in respect to the ongoing relational maternal denial. It also opens up the shared social worlds of the interview and provides an opportunity to reflect on not just how, but why researchers interrupt and reassure – to deflect, deny and return difficult emotions too quickly.

Returning again to the overwhelming feeling of helplessness felt in the interview, importantly this did not disappear as I moved from the situatedness of the interview space. Liveng et al. (2017, p. 166) have reported how the emotional states that the images and talk of their research activities produced in them continued beyond the fieldwork in the form of 'dreams and feelings'. Grace's account, and others that featured relational trauma, stayed with me not simply because they were traumatic, moving and difficult to hear and bear (although claiming that simply listening to an account that someone else has lived is 'difficult for me' seems discourteous). The additional issue with these accounts was my indigenous connection with people and place.

Lisiak and Krzyżowski (2018 [this volume]) discuss being stripped of their right and duty to speak up, and this was also an inevitable aspect of my insider research, knowing others who were spoken about but remaining silent. I have explored the weight of knowing unconsenting others who are storied in participants' accounts elsewhere (Mannay, 2011), but in returning to this account in particular, and reflecting on helplessness, its ownership, projection, defence and transference, it may well be that I was the defended subject, afraid of knowing and what this knowledge would mean for me. As a researcher, I can listen and I can speak, within the interview, but I cannot speak outside it, not to others in the participants' accounts, the unknowing and the unconsenting, those positioned as abusers and abusive. These stories are not owned by me, the biographies are not my own and the decisions not to report or address are not mine. I keep quiet, and I maintain confidentiality. I have realised, eventually, that my own need, or want, to speak and challenge and seek justice, is insignificant, and that although silence may feel helpless, I should in fact be grateful that participants felt able to share the emotionality of their lived realities and the pathways they have negotiated to reach the present.

CONCLUDING REMARKS

'Unsettling stories on emotional social worlds redefine our understandings of harm and distress and reconfigure ideas of responsible knowing' (Gabb, 2010, p. 461); therefore, there is an important responsibility for researchers to reflexively consider the emotional weight of relational encounters in the field. Women living on the margins are already pathologised, so to act as if we are objective researchers, ignoring our own subjectivities, emotions and their effects on and in the fieldwork is a disservice to our participants, othering them as research objects. Reflecting on interviews and drawing on their relationality and affect centralises the emotional life of interviewing, and the inherent value of recognising not only what is said but also what is felt. In the telling and silencing of trauma, the emotions that pass between researchers and participants are key mechanisms for analysing, questioning, exploring and achieving some forms of understanding.

As Froggett, Conroy, Manley, and Roy (2014) argue, it is difficult to relay multisensory experiences and their emotional content into words as this "'thins-out" the experience, or abstracts those elements that can be verbalised giving an overtly discursive view, so that…emotional processes…become difficult to see'. However, despite these difficulties, it is important to attempt to communicate the emotionality and relationality of the research process, rather than hold on to the ideology of the objective, disconnected researcher, devoid of any feelings that could contaminate the integrity of the data. Emotions help to inform us about the research process itself and, in the example presented, they also enable insights into the complexities, defences and psychological work needed to negotiate trauma and enable spaces where 'you just get on with it'.

REFERENCES

Aaron, J. (1991). Finding a voice in two tongues: Gender and colonization. In J. Aaron, T. Rees, S. Betts, & M. Vincentelli (Eds.), *Our sisters' land: The changing identities of women in Wales* (pp. 183–198). Cardiff: University of Wales Press.

Aaron, J., Rees, T., Betts, S. & Vincentelli, M. (Eds.) (1994). *Our sisters' land: The changing identities of women in Wales*. Cardiff: University of Wales Press.

Belin, R. (2005). Photo-elicitation and the agricultural landscape: 'Seeing' and 'telling' about farming, community and place. *Visual Studies, 20*(1), 56–68.

Berger, J. (1972). *About looking: Writers and readers*. London: Penguin.

Coffey, A. (1999). *The ethnographic self, fieldwork and the representation of identity*. London: SAGE.

Davidoff, L. (1976). The rationalisation of housework. In D. Barker Leonard & S. Allen (Eds.), *Dependence and exploitation in work and marriage* (pp. 121–151). London: Longman.

de Beauvoir, S. (1949). *The second sex*. London: Penguin.

Elliott, A. (1992). *Social theory and psychoanalysis in transition: Self and society from Freud to Kristeva*. Cabridge: Polity Press.

Evans, G. (2007). *Educational failure and working class white children in Britain*. London: Palgrave Macmillan.

Fink, J. (2012). Walking the neighbourhood, seeing the small details of community life: Reflections from a photography walking tour. *Critical Social Policy*, *32*(1), 31–50.

Froggett, L., Conroy, M., Manley, J., & Roy, A. (2014). Between art and social sciences: Scenic composition as a methodological device. *Forum: Qualitative Research*, *15*(3), September 2014. Retrieved from http://www.qualitative-research.net/index.php/fqs/article/view/2143/3685 Accessed on August 6, 2017.

Frosh, S. (2010). *Psychoanalysis outside the clinic: Interventions in psychosocial studies*. Basingstoke: Macmillan.

Frosh, S., & Emerson, P. (2005). Interpretation and over-interpretation: Disrupting the meaning of texts. *Qualitative Research*, *5*(5), 307–324.

Gabb, J. (2008). *Researching intimacy in families*. Basingstoke: Palgrave Macmillan.

Gabb, J. (2010). Home truths: Ethical issues in family research. *Qualitative Research*, *10*(4), 461–478.

Gabb, J., & Fink, J. (2015). *Couple relationships in the 21st century*. London: Palgrave Macmillan.

Gemignani, M. (2011). Between researcher and researched: An introduction to countertransference in qualitative inquiry. *Qualitative Inquiry*, *17*(8), 701–708.

Gillies, V. (2007). *Marginalised mothers: Exploring working class parenting*. Abingdon, Oxon: Routledge.

Hoggett, P., Beedell, S., Jimenez, L., Mayo, M., & Miller, C. (2010). Working psychosocially and dialogically in research. *Psychoanalysis, Culture and Society*, *15*(2), 173–188.

Hollway, W. (2001). The psycho-social subject in evidence-based practice. *Journal of Social Work Practice*, *15*, 9–22.

Hollway, W. (2006). *The capacity to care: Gender and ethical subjectivity*. London: Routledge.

Hollway, W. (2015). *Knowing mothers*. London: Palgrave Macmillan.

Hollway, W., & Jefferson, T. (2000). *Doing qualitative research differently*. London: SAGE.

Hollway, W., & Jefferson, T. (2001). Free association, narrative analysis and the defended subject: The case of Ivy. *Narrative Inquiry*, *11*(1), 103–122.

Hollway, W., & Jefferson, T. (2009). Researching defended subjects with the free association narrative interviewing method. In H. J. Cook, S. Bhattacharya, & A. Hardy (Eds.), *History of the social determinants of health: Global histories, contemporary debates* (pp. 296–315). Hyderabad: Orient Black Swan.

Hollway, W., & Jefferson, T. (2013). *Doing qualitative research differently: Free association, narrative and the interview method* (2nd ed.). London: SAGE.

Latchem-Hastings, G. (2018). The emotion of 'doing ethics' in healthcare research: A researcher's reflexive account. In T. Loughran & D. Mannay (Eds.), *Emotion and the researcher: Sites, subjectivities and relationships* (Vol. 16). Studies in Qualitative Methodology (pp. 213–228). Bingley: Emerald.

Lisiak, A., & Krzyżowski, L. (2018). With a little help from my colleagues: Notes on emotional support in a qualitative longitudinal research project. In T. Loughran & D. Mannay (Eds.), *Emotion and the researcher: Sites, subjectivities and relationships* (Vol. 16). Studies in Qualitative Methodology (pp. 33–48). Bingley: Emerald.

Liveng, A., Ramvi, E., Froggett, L., Manley, J., Hollway, W., Lading, A., & Gripsrud, B. H. (2017). Imagining transitions in old age through the visual matrix method: Thinking about what is hard to bear. *Journal of Social Work Practice*, *31*(2), 155–170.

Lucey, H., Melody, J., & Walkerdine, V. (2003). Project 4:21 transitions to womanhood: Developing a psychosocial perspective in one longitudinal study. *International Journal of Social Research Methodology*, *6*(3), 279–284.

Mahoney, K. (2018). 'It's not history. It's my life': Researcher emotions and the production of critical histories of the women's movement. In T. Loughran & D. Mannay (Eds.),

Emotion and the researcher: Sites, subjectivities and relationships (Vol. 16). Studies in Qualitative Methodology (pp. 65–80). Bingley: Emerald.

Mannay, D. (2010). Making the familiar strange: Can visual research methods render the familiar setting more perceptible? *Qualitative Research*, *10*(1), 91–111.

Mannay, D. (2011). Taking refuge in the branches of a guava tree: The difficulty of retaining consenting and non-consenting participants' confidentiality as an indigenous researcher. *Qualitative Inquiry*, *17*(10), 962–964.

Mannay, D. (2013a). 'Keeping close and spoiling' revisited: Exploring the significance of 'home' for family relationships and educational trajectories in a marginalised estate in urban south Wales. *Gender and Education*, *25*(1), 91–107.

Mannay, D. (2013b). The permeating presence of past domestic and familial violence: 'So like I'd never let anyone hit me but I've hit them, and I shouldn't have done'. In V. Gillies, C. A. Hooper, & J. Ribbens McCarthy (Eds.), *Family troubles? Exploring changes and challenges in the family lives of children and young people* (pp. 151–162). Bristol: Policy Press.

Mannay, D. (2014). Achieving respectable motherhood? exploring the impossibility of feminist and egalitarian ideologies against the everyday realities of lived Welsh working-class femininities. *Women's Studies International Forum*, *53*, 159–166.

Mannay, D. (2015). Myths, monsters and legends: Negotiating an acceptable working class femininity in a marginalised and demonised Welsh locale. In V. E. Cree, G. Clapton, & M. Smith (Eds.) *Revisiting moral panics. Moral panics in theory and practice* (pp. 19–29). Bristol: Policy Press.

Mannay, D. (2016). *Visual, narrative and creative research methods: Application, reflection and ethics*. Abingdon, Oxon: Routledge.

Mannay, D., & Creaghan, J. (2016). Similarity and familiarity: Reflections on indigenous ethnography with mothers, daughters and school teachers on the margins of contemporary Wales. In M. Ward (Ed.), *Gender identity and research relationships*. (Vol. 14). Studies in Qualitative Methodology (pp. 85–103). Bingley: Emerald.

May, V. (2008). On being a 'good' mother: The moral presentation of self in written life stories. *Sociology*, *42*(3), 470–486.

Midgley, N. (2006). Psychoanalysis and qualitative psychology: Complementary or contradictory paradigms? *Qualitative Research in Psychology*, *3*(3), 213–231.

Morgan, M. (2015). *Class, motherhood and mature studentship: (Re)constructing and (re)negotiating subjectivity*. Ph.D. thesis, Cardiff University.

Richardson, L. (1997). *Fields of play: Constructing an academic life*. New Brunswick, NJ: Rutgers University Press.

Roberts, E. (2018). The 'transient insider': Identity and intimacy in home community research. In T. Loughran & D. Mannay (Eds.) *Emotion and the researcher: Sites, subjectivities and relationships* (Vol. 16). Studies in Qualitative Methodology (pp. 113–126). Bingley: Emerald.

Rock, P. (2007). Symbolic interactionism and ethnography. In P. Atkinson, A. Coffey, S. Delamont, J. Lofland, & L. Lofland (Eds.), *Handbook of ethnography* (pp. 26–38). London: SAGE.

Rose, G. (2001). *Visual methodologies*. London: SAGE.

Rose, G. (2010). *Doing family photography: The domestic, the public and the politics of sentiment*. London: Routledge.

Sheppard, L. (2018). 'Poor old mixed-up Wales': Entering the debate about bilingualism, multiculturalism and racism in Welsh literature and culture. In T. Loughran & D. Mannay (Eds.), *Emotion and the researcher: Sites, subjectivities and relationships* (Vol. 16). Studies in Qualitative Methodology (pp. 197–212). Bingley: Emerald.

Skeggs, B. (2009). Haunted by the spectre of judgement: Respectability, value and affect in class relations. In K. P. Sveinsson (Ed.), *Who cares about the white working class?* (pp. 36–45). London: Runnymede.

Song, M., & Parker, D. (1995). Commonality, difference and the dynamics of discourse in in-depth interviewing. *Sociology, 29*(2), 241–256.

Tyler, I. (2008). Chav mum chav scum: Class disgust in contemporary Britain. *Feminist Media Studies, 8*(1), 17–34.

van den Scott, L. K. (2018). Role transitions in the field and reflexivity: From friend to researcher. In T. Loughran & D. Mannay (Eds.), *Emotion and the researcher: Sites, subjectivities and relationships* (Vol. 16). Studies in Qualitative Methodology (pp. 19–32). Bingley: Emerald.

Walkerdine, V. (1997). *Daddy's girl: Young girls and popular culture*. London: Macmillan.

Walkerdine, V., Lucey, H., & Melody, J. (2001). *Growing up girl: Psycho-social explorations of gender and class*. Basingstoke: Palgrave.

Winnicott, D. W. (1965). *The family and individual development*. London: Tavistock Publications.

PART II
EMOTIONAL TOPOGRAPHIES
AND RESEARCH SITES

CHAPTER 6

APPROACHING BEREAVEMENT RESEARCH WITH HEARTFELT POSITIVITY

Katherine Carroll

ABSTRACT

Purpose – *This chapter critically engages with a positively oriented emotional reflexivity with the aim of improving inclusivity in bereavement research.*

Methodology/Approach – *The heartfelt positivity methodology intentionally creates positivity through the everyday practices of academic research. In this chapter, emotional reflexivity is guided by the heartfelt positivity methodology to identify and learn from collaborators' emotions. It focuses on collaborators whose involvement in the academic community falls beyond that of the immediate research team at different stages of bereavement research.*

Findings – *The emotions of collaborators involved in bereavement research have been overlooked, yet their inclusion reveals a significant potential for the sanctioning of bereaved mothers' potential participation in bereavement-focused research or breastmilk donation programmes. Key learnings that may be applied to conducting future bereavement research are*

Emotion and the Researcher: Sites, Subjectivities, and Relationships
Studies in Qualitative Methodology, Volume 16, 97–111
ISSN: 1042-3192/doi:10.1108/S1042-319220180000016007

(i) the potential for collaborators to also be bereaved parents (ii) the continued need to strive for the inclusion of bereaved parents in research and (iii) to extend the methodological principle of emotional reflexivity to include research collaborators when researching emotionally sensitive topics.

Originality/Value – *This chapter argues that bereaved mothers' knowledge and practices of thriving in hard times can either be fostered or derailed at different stages of the research cycle depending on which narratives frame human suffering. For researchers and collaborators, emotional reflexivity is crucial to inclusive research practices and knowledge translation.*

Keywords: Heartfelt positivity methodology; bereavement research; infant death; bereaved mothers; lactation; breastmilk donation; research practices; emotional reflexivity

INTRODUCTION

'What a sad topic!' This is the response I typically receive from people who inquire about my current research area. Infant death is, most definitely, sad. It is not only a devastating loss of life proximate to the anticipated joy of birth and new life, but an enforced and infinite pause on the unfolding practices of new motherhood that were intended for that particular child (Layne, 2003). One such maternal practice is breastfeeding. Although lactation is most commonly associated with mothers of living infants, some women continue to produce, express, store and donate breastmilk after infant death (Carroll & Lenne, in press; Welborn, 2012). Not only is the onset of physiologic lactation after stillbirth and neonatal death common, but lactation after loss can actually assist some bereaved mothers with grief by enabling them to feel connected with their deceased infant, help integrate the experience of perinatal loss and provide meaning in the loss through breastmilk donation (Welborn, 2012). Meanwhile, the donation of expressed breastmilk to a human milk bank can create feelings of positivity, pride, productivity and a sense of purpose among some bereaved mothers (Carroll & Lenne, in press).[1]

As part of the broader movement of taking a *positive approach* to the social sciences and healthcare (Mesman, 2011; Penttinen, 2013; Whiting, Kendell, & Wills, 2012), I choose to focus on the gifts that donated breastmilk offers preterm infants,[2] donors[3] and the health system at large[4] rather than focusing on the very real distress of preterm birth, NICU admissions, and infant death (Guyer, 2006). This positive approach to lactation after loss offers an alternative to the dominant, taken-for-granted problem-oriented approach to healthcare inquiry (Mesman, 2011) which might, for example, focus on the poor provision of services for women in non-normative circumstances of lactation (Carroll & Lenne, in press).

CULTIVATING POSITIVITY IN THE WORLD: POSTIVELY ORIENTED METHODOLOGIES

Part One: A Comparison of Positively Oriented Methodologies

Penttinen's 'heartfelt positivity' is a methodology developed for researching resilience, resourcefulness, compassion and moments of relief amid the atrocities of war (Penttinen, 2013, p. 19). Yet it offers transferable principles to other research areas of the social sciences. The heartfelt positivity methodology consists of two parts. First, it asks researchers to turn their focus away from what is wrong in the world, to what is working well (Penttinen, 2013, p. 24). This does not mean ignoring suffering, but rather, pursuing the inquiry of 'expressions of joy and well-being, moments of relief, self-healing and empowerment, even in extreme conditions' (Penttinen, 2013, p. 24). It is argued that by focusing research on illness and trauma, the dominate model of the human as inherently 'vulnerable, weak and fragile' is perpetuated while ignoring 'what makes people thrive and what makes lives meaningful' (Penttinen, 2013, p. 25).

Although it is derived from an entirely different area of scholarship, Elina Penttinen's heartfelt positivity methodology chimes with Jessica Mesman's (2011) positive approach to researching the delivery of healthcare, and with an asset-based approach to health promotion (Whiting et al., 2012). In Mesman's practice-based ethnographic approach, rather than focusing on the errors and mistakes made in healthcare (a deficit model), she advocates for focusing on the vigour of healthcare practices which ultimately deliver patient safety (Mesman, 2011, p. 74). Mesman's (2011) approach examines competencies that already exist but which may have been overlooked, forgotten or simply taken for granted (p. 74). Penttinen (2013), too, advocates for examining what is working well: 'ruminating on worst outcomes leads to disempowerment and hinders action and as such denies the already present possibilities, or what is working well, in the present moment' (p. 24). In a similar vein, rather than using a deficit model, the asset-based approach to health promotion deliberately identifies factors and 'repertoires of potentials' that can be emphasised or developed to create resilience and promote positive health and well-being at the individual, community and societal level (Whiting et al., 2012, p. 25).

Thus, through these positively oriented methodological approaches to diverse areas of scholarship, Penttinen, Mesman and Whiting et al. avoid a binary logic of positive/negative by attending to the resilience of individuals and communities within the horrors of war (Penttinen, 2013), the unintended mortalities or morbidities in the delivery of neonatal healthcare (Mesman, 2008), and the disease burden of ill health on individuals and communities (Whiting et al., 2012). These authors' methodologies involve more than an attunement to the positive; their research aims to be a deliberate intervention in the world, albeit with very different orientations to doing so.[5] In what follows, I build on my earlier work of integrating emotions generated by participation in sensitive research (Carroll, 2012; Iedema & Carroll, 2015) to conduct a positively oriented emotional reflexivity that incorporates collaborators' emotions on the topic of lactation and milk donation after infant loss. Herein I use the term collaborator to refer to the academic community beyond merely the research team and the participants to include, in this instance, peer-reviewers, audience members and stakeholders.

Part Two: Using Emotions to Produce Positively Oriented Scholarship

The second part of Penttinen's heartfelt positivity methodology is to not only include the emotions cultivated through the research process, but to emphasise how these emotions play an active role in researchers' construction of the world. She argues that researchers help to *produce* the world through their writing, teaching and scholarly relations (Penttinen, 2013, p. 22). Thus, the heartfelt positivity methodology recognises and cultivates positive emotions in the research practice (Penttinen, 2013, p. 32) to increase and expand happiness and well-being for both the researcher and society (Penttinen, 2013, p. 27).[6] To achieve this, and not unlike the care exhibited by other feminist and sensitive research approaches (see Carroll, 2012), the heartfelt positivity methodology asks researchers to attend to their own emotions and the emotional states of those they write about. In addition, however, the heartfelt positivity methodology also asks researchers to consider how emotions may subsequently shape the production of academic scholarship, and therefore one's subsequent contribution to, and impact on, society.

This requires the researcher to mindfully engage emotions as a 'thinking that takes place in the body' through attending to 'how the feelings and emotions matter in being able to analyse and translate with clarity one's research material into a readable form' (Penttinen, 2013, p. 24). An example of this may be as simple as working on how to frame a positively oriented research question, or a more lengthy and complex process of attending to emotions in order to cultivate data analysis which steers away from habituated or dominant narratives of human frailty and suffering, or disease and deficit models. Simply put, this 'witnessing of inner and outer sensations, events and circumstances' (Penttinen, 2013, p. 38) during research and writing asks the researcher to engage in intensive emotional self-reflexivity.

Emotional reflexivity is interactional and involves examining our own or others' feelings about particular circumstances and subsequently altering practices and behaviours in response to our interpretations of these emotions (Holmes, 2015). The concept of emotional reflexivity acknowledges that emotions coexist with and inform what is often framed as 'rational knowledge', and necessarily elevates their importance in research so that they may become data or a source of knowing (Carroll, 2012). Yet by focusing on how one can respond to emotions in the research context in order to positively contribute to society the heartfelt positivity methodology goes beyond merely using emotions as data to tell us something about the world. Instead, emotional reflexivity and emotions are conceptualised as interventions to create connections and support as 'agents of positive change' (Pentinnen, 2012, p. 5) among research collaborators such as students, fellow researchers, participants and readers (among others) as part of doing the research. In this sense, the heartfelt positivity methodology offers a coherent conceptual framework for emotional reflexivity as it acknowledges the primacy of emotions, deliberately learns from them and then situates emotions as interventions in terms of both the researcher's emotions and those of research collaborators throughout academic research (Penttinen, 2013). This is important as emotional reflexivity is critiqued for its focus on the researcher at the expense of recognising research participants' (and others') capacity for emotional reflexivity throughout the research process (Holmes, 2015).

By focusing on the positive orientations that lactation and milk donation can create for some women within, or alongside, the tragedy of infant death, I have already established that I practice the first part of the heartfelt positivity methodology. I now turn to the second part of the heartfelt positivity methodology. In the following section, I extend emotional reflexivity to the emotions expressed by collaborators involved in my research on lactation and milk donation after infant death. These collaborators include an academic who performed the peer review of an application for research funding; a health professional stakeholder attending a professional research meeting on milk donation after infant loss; and an audience member of an international human milk banking conference where project findings were presented and disseminated.

HEARTFELT POSITIVITY: AN INGRESS TO EMOTIONAL REFLEXIVITY

Three vignettes detail particularly emotional moments that were articulated by research collaborators while participating in my research on lactation and milk donation after infant death. These moments remain vivid in my memory and the reflexive insights I have garnered have 'become apparent only with the passage of time' (Doucet, 2008, p. 84). Yet as 'situated emotions can be fleeting, and elude recall' (Olson, Godbold, & Patulny, 2015, p. 143), the vignettes have been recreated with assistance from the research transcripts, email correspondence, and grant assessment reports. Writing the vignettes as a form of emotional reflexivity with guidance from the heartfelt positivity methodology assisted me to take stock, reflect and learn about the felt emotion expressed by collaborators about not only the research topic but the research process. Consequently, these vignettes have acted as a fodder for, as well as the expression of, emotional reflexivity, which, in turn, has created a space for analysis, learning and intervention in research regarding enhancing the inclusivity and impact of collaborators' emotions in bereavement research. In addition, in writing these vignettes, I attended to Penttinen's assertion that the heartfelt positivity methodology must also involve an emotional reflexivity as to how these writings may be received by the reader, and in this case, knowing that a reader may also be one of the collaborators represented.

The Conference Attendee: In 2016, I presented research findings on bereaved mothers' experiences of their lactation and milk donation after infant death at an international milk banking conference. During the question time at the end of my presentation an audience member gently rose to her feet and she began to cry. She recounted how, 17 years ago, she had experienced her own infant's death. She stated that, had she had the opportunity to donate her breastmilk, she would have liked to have done so. Moreover, she went on to say that she believed that she would have found it personally beneficial. After she completed her comment, I held the floor in silence and then thanked her for her courage in sharing her story. At the end of the question time, and as the Chair took the floor, rather than returning to my speaker's seat at the front of the auditorium, I walked towards the rear of the auditorium in order to sit next to the audience member. Feeling overwhelmed with compassion and an awareness of the role my presentation had in bringing forth this woman's emotions, I asked if I could give her a hug. She accepted and we went on to talk more about her experiences.

The Stakeholder: In 2011, I convened a day-long national stakeholder meeting on the topic of milk donation after infant death in Australia. It brought together representatives from neonatal intensive care units, human milk banks, researchers, and a parent advocacy group. After hearing how some bereaved donors experienced positivity through their lactation and breastmilk donation, the stakeholders debated the donation of breastmilk as a result of sustained lactation following infant death. At the heart of the debate was who should determine the length of time a bereaved mother could sustain her lactation in order to donate her breastmilk. The majority of stakeholders felt it should be the individual woman who decided the length of her own lactation and donation, and that guidelines on donation periods for bereaved donors should not differ from donors with living infants. One stakeholder strongly disagreed and had placed a limit of two weeks (post-bereavement) for mothers to donate milk to their milk bank. The stakeholder cited concerns that sustaining lactation and donation for longer than two weeks may negatively impact the grieving process. As the facilitator of the stakeholder meeting I maintained the necessary equanimity despite feeling that this position diminished bereaved women's reproductive autonomy and did not reflect the research findings presented. As the first author of the subsequently co-authored publication with the stakeholders, I engaged in substantial email correspondence and manuscript redrafting with the stakeholder to ensure the manuscript satisfactorily conveyed the variety of positions and their relative weighting within the broader group with regards to the length of time a bereaved mother might sustain her lactation in order to donate her breastmilk.

The Academic Peer Reviewer: In 2017, I received four peer review reports on a proposal for research funding to investigate the experiences of bereaved mothers and health professionals regarding lactation and milk donation after infant death. Although three peer review reports were very positive, one assessor was troubled. In particular, the assessor expressed concern over conducting interviews with bereaved mothers, particularly that their participation may cause difficult or distressing memories, and that s/he was unclear how they would be protected from emotional distress. Later in the assessment the peer reviewer disclosed that her/his baby had suffered from a life-threatening illness and that after reading the proposal s/he was confronted by his/her own distressing memories. In my rejoinder, I reiterated the proposed study's ethical safeguards and my successful track record of piloting research with bereaved mothers. I did not directly address the assessor's heartache, although my knowledge of the assessor's emotional reaction to the proposal did shape the words I chose in the scholarly reply.

Although ethical research attention is focused on the emotional care and protection of vulnerable research participants, the vignettes demonstrate that the potential for significant emotions extends to other research collaborators to include the audiences and assessors of academic work and project stakeholders. Importantly, the research collaborators in these vignettes experienced significant emotion despite not being identified in advance as 'vulnerable persons' or named as 'bereaved mothers' in human research ethics applications or study protocols. While some sensitive research methodologists suggest that emotional 'risks' should be planned for, others highlight the unpredictability of emotional dilemmas or turmoil (Evans et al., 2017, p. 2) such as the unanticipated emotion I encountered from collaborators. That researchers may encounter bereaved parents (or those who are closely engaged in assisting their suffering) at any stage of the research process reinforces the concerns of human research ethics committees and bereavement research methodologists (among others) for how mindfully and carefully researchers must engage in bereavement topics.

However, the gift of the heartfelt positivity methodology is that it emphasises the existence of two orientations to researching the experience of human hardship. The dominant logic within the social sciences, Penttinen argues, is to focus on what is wrong with the world, including a focus on human frailty and suffering. The other possible approach is to question inherent human frailty and to research 'expressions of joy and well-being, moments of relief, self-healing and empowerment, even in extreme conditions' (Penttinen, 2013, p. 24). It is through these contrasting lenses highlighted by the heartfelt positivity methodology that I can characterise how I perceived each of the collaborators' orientations to bereavement, alongside their potential impact on participation in bereavement research and bereavement breastmilk donation programmes.

The first vignette describes the tearful emotional confession of an audience member at a conference as she recollected the emotional pain of her own infant's death, and her lack of opportunity to manage her lactation in order to be able to donate her breastmilk. Despite her tears, the collaborator explained she would have liked to donate her breastmilk as a bereaved mother. Therefore, it could be presumed that she supported bereaved breastmilk donation programmes, and the broader research into lactation and donation as embodied practices that make some bereaved mothers' lives meaningful, even in the midst of grief. In contrast, the vignettes of the stakeholder and peer reviewer differ in their orientations towards the emotional vulnerability of the bereaved mother.

For example, the stakeholder expressed discomfort with both the notion of sustaining lactation to donate breastmilk after infant death, and the qualitative research results presented that found some bereaved mothers experienced pride, productivity and positivity in doing so. Meanwhile, in the assessment of a research proposal on lactation after loss, the peer reviewer wrote of how s/he had experienced emotional discomfort at reading the research proposal as it prompted recollections of her/his own experience with a critically ill, hospitalised infant, and hence strong discomfort with involving bereaved mothers in qualitative interviews. The views of the stakeholder and the peer reviewer could be said to align more closely with dominant conceptualisations of people experiencing hardship as 'inherently vulnerable, weak and fragile' (Penttinen, 2013, p. 25). As a result, they positioned the bereaved mothers as 'at-risk' with regard to their potential involvement in bereaved milk donation programmes, and in research interviewing.

When they occupy key positions as gatekeepers, collaborators' emotional experiences can have very real implications for research (Dyregrov, 2004; Hynson, Bauld & Sawyer, 2006; Payne & Field, 2004). At the front end of research, for example, where competitive funding is sought to engage bereaved mothers in research, an orientation that centres on emotional vulnerability could impact on the awarding of research funding to proposals that take a positive approach to difficult or sensitive research topics and which seek to directly include bereaved parents' lived experiences (Denzin & Giardina, 2007; Payne & Field, 2004, p. 52). Studies suggest that just because negative emotions are expressed within research engagement does not mean that research is unethical or insensitive (Hynson, Bauld & Sawyer, 2006, p. 810). Moreover, most bereaved parents who agree to participate in research interviews find the opportunity to reflect upon and discuss their experiences as painful but helpful (Payne & Field, 2004, p. 52). In one large interview study with bereaved parents, tears were shed when talking and thinking about their deceased child, yet all participants wished to continue the interview, rated their involvement as 'positive' or 'very positive', and none regretted their participation when surveyed at two-weeks post-interview (Dyregrov, 2004).

Through their recognition of bereaved research participants' strengths as well as their emotional pain, some bereavement researchers are pushing back against the 'paternalism' of gatekeepers, such as ethics boards and bereavement service providers, to actively include bereaved parents in research projects that aim to contribute to better understandings of grief and bereavement or palliative service needs (Payne & Field, 2004). By paying due attention to the intense grief and real ethical issues and methodological sensitivities required when undertaking research, knowledge can be generated by bereaved parents on the experience, meaning and understanding of survival, support and service engagements. This kind of knowledge cannot possibly be provided by others who may be considered less vulnerable (Buckle, Corbin Dwyer, &

Jackson, 2010) or perhaps through alternate methods to the research interview. In response to the concern of the peer reviewer, research shows that when done with due care, there is not necessarily any further risk in engaging bereaved parents in face-to-face research (Dyregrov, 2004). Indeed, when the study is appropriately designed and conducted by skilled staff, bereaved parents even report positive experiences of telling their story in the interview format as 'empowering', 'enriching' and 'being taken seriously' despite also experiencing difficulty, pain or distress (Dyregrov, 2004; Hynson, 2006).

Reinforcing the existence of two main orientations to human suffering that Penttinen outlines, bereavement researchers Payne and Field (2004, p. 55) also explain that there is a 'general acceptance of a medical or psychiatric model of bereavement, which tends to emphasis the individual distress and psychopathology associated with grief' at the expense of social models of bereavement which emphasise 'aspects of life transition, changes to social roles, the social consequences of loss and the importance of "narrative reconstruction"'. Together, the medical model of bereavement and the dominant problem-oriented approach of the social sciences (Penttinen, 2013, p. 19) influence the way bereaved parents are frequently characterised as too vulnerable for inclusion in studies using qualitative, and particularly face-to-face, research methods.

Collaborators' emotional experiences with infant death (the audience member), with bereaved mothers (the stakeholder), and with a critically ill infant (the peer reviewer), significantly informed their emotional engagement with the research and, in turn, how they perceived the suitability of bereaved mothers' participation in breastmilk donation programmes or in bereavement research. The vignettes suggest that harbouring certain orientations to bereavement and emotional vulnerability could either limit or expand which lactation options and breastmilk donation practices are made available to bereaved mothers, which research is funded, and which findings are implemented in policy and practice.

Despite good progress being made for the deliberate and sensitive inclusion of bereaved parents in research projects, there is a need to continue to strive for their ethical and sensitive inclusion (Denzin & Giardina, 2007). One way of achieving this is through emotional reflexivity during any gatekeeping work associated with bereavement research. While there is much focus on researcher and participant emotional reflexivity in doing qualitative and sensitive research, chief gatekeepers or content experts may also need to engage in emotional reflexivity in their analysis of research proposals or in their application and assessment of research findings. Notably, in the vignettes recounted above, it was by engaging collaborators' emotions in emotional

reflexivity that important parallels emerged between the sanctioned participation of bereaved mothers' participation in qualitative face-to-face interviewing as part of broader bereavement research, and their participation in
bereaved breastmilk donation programmes as a result of sustaining their lactation. Therefore, emotional reflexivity, it could be said, is particularly important for research that takes a positive approach to what provides meaning
in the lives of people living in difficult or extreme circumstances; for if this
research is not completed or its results not translated into practice, as a society we risk lagging behind in the creation of new knowledge on how to build
practices and services that will increase well-being and self-healing.

CONCLUSION

In her analysis of North American rituals of pregnancy loss and bereavement, Linda Layne states that the women's health movement has unintentionally 'systematically minimised and marginalised negative reproductive
outcomes' as a result of its challenge to the pathologisation of pregnancy
and birth (Layne, 2003, p. 239). Layne argues for the need to develop bereavement rituals which focus on the bereaved mother and her needs for support, connection to others, and a sense of belonging and identity. Moreover,
bereaved mothers need not only to receive support but also be given opportunities for demonstrating competence and their ability to give (Layne, 2003,
pp. 247–248).

Arguably, the heartfelt positivity methodology is an approach that can be
relied upon by bereavement researchers to help them shape a research study
and research practices that identify competence and capacity to survive,
thrive and contribute, while also honouring the emotional experiences of suffering and grief from the loss of a loved one. Moreover, the heartfelt positivity methodology asks researchers to be emotionally reflexive throughout
the research process to enhance the emotional clarity of their analysis, writing and interactions and their positive contribution to society. However, this
emotional reflexivity, I would contend, needs to extend beyond the researcher
and participants to include research collaborators, some of whom may also
occupy key gatekeeping positions in terms of research funding and participant recruitment, the translation of research-generated knowledge into policy, and knowledge dissemination.

The application of emotional reflexivity through the three vignettes reveals
that just as there is concern over bereaved mothers' emotions and emotional
health with regard to continuing their lactation or donating their milk after

infant loss, there is also equal concern for bereaved mothers with regards to research participation in face-to-face or interview-based research. Perhaps we (researchers and research collaborators) are not especially comfortable with the emotional expression of discomfort or emotional pain by potential or actual participants (Mannay, 2018 [this volume]) even if this emotional discomfort was anticipated by the participants themselves (Payne & Field, 2004). Thus, sanctioning exclusion from participation through a framework of concern for vulnerability may be a strategy when confronted with painful stories that one can do nothing to address (Mannay, 2018 [this volume]). Therefore, in our role as bereavement-related researchers, peer reviewers, audience members, stakeholders, and service providers it is not only bereaved mothers' emotions that should be of concern but also our own:

> None of us 'like death' and all of us would prefer to be surrounded by 'good things and positive energy' ... Grief for a dead loved one may be both inevitable and necessary, but the additional hurt that bereaved parents feel when their losses are diminished or diminished by others is needless and cruel. (Layne, 2004, p. 249)

Through the process of doing research *and* as a result of it, emotions can be heeded, highlighted and analysed to enhance sensitive methodological practices *and* positive outcomes for bereaved parents in society. Like researchers, research collaborators, including peer reviewers from funding bodies, representatives from health services and bereavement support organisations, have the power to grant *who* it is that has something to give as well as receive in bereavement. Through participating in research and telling one's story, bereaved parents are provided with the opportunity to give to themselves and society, or to engage in, contest, nuance or launch from shared agendas with researchers, policymakers or practitioners. Similarly, through the donation of breastmilk bereaved mothers are able to contribute better health to hospitalised preterm infants and construct new narratives and identities (Carroll & Lenne, in press; Welborn, 2012). In both cases, it is through their inclusion that bereaved mothers are able to display competence (not just receive help), while concurrently acknowledging their loss and the life of the baby (rather than suffering in silence), and constructing new identities by connecting with others, for example, through narrative as a research participant or through lactation practices as a breastmilk donor.

Without ignoring suffering, the heartfelt positivity methodology asks researchers to turn their focus away from what is wrong in the world, to what is working well (Penttinen, 2013, p. 24). My use of the heartfelt positivity methodology to guide emotional reflexivity yielded analytical openings which enabled more learning about bereavement research on the topic of lactation and milk donation after loss. Importantly, rather than turning to a critique of paternalism and gatekeeping (see e.g., Denzin & Giardina, 2007), as a form of 'ruminating on worst outcomes' and hindering action through ignoring the potential of what is working well (Penttinen, 2013, p. 24), I chose to focus on the competence of some bereaved parents, as displayed in their finding positivity, well-being or fulfilment in either research participation or in breastmilk donation.

I engaged the heartfelt positivity methodology to guide emotional reflexivity as a research practice and as a framework that would include research collaborators' emotions throughout the research lifecycle for analysis. This created insight into orientations to emotional vulnerability in bereavement which potentially impact on inclusivity in both bereavement research and breastmilk donation programmes. The chapter has examined how the heartfelt positivity methodology can be used to assist researchers to use emotion to drive an engaged positively oriented sociology. It reveals that public displays of emotion can be drawn upon to provide tailored insights into bereavement research as well as what is required of researchers and collaborators who engage in positive approaches to bereavement research or other sensitive, highly emotional topics.

NOTES

1. For other bereaved mothers, however, the immediate suppression of lactation is necessary in order to focus on grieving for their infant (Carroll & Lenne, in press).

2. When hospitalised, very premature infants are unable to receive their mothers' own breastmilk and are fed donated breastmilk (in place of infant formula) it significantly reduces the incidence of the severe, sometimes fatal gastrointestinal disease called necrotising enterocolitis (Boyd, Quigley, & Brocklehurst, 2007).

3. Mothers who provide their breastmilk to human milk banks have an opportunity to honour the substance of breastmilk, their labour in producing it and expressing it, and prevent it from going to waste if the expressed breastmilk ends up being surplus to their baby's needs (Arnold & Lockhardt Borman, 1996; Carroll, 2016). Donors also have their motherhood affirmed through the dominant cultural logics of intensive motherhood, of which breastfeeding or the provision of breastmilk features prominently (Gernstein Pineau, 2013).

4. Donor milk has the potential to save the health system thousands of dollars in the prevention and treatment of necrotising enterocolitis and the chronic conditions that arise from it (Carroll & Herrmann, 2012).

5. Whitting et al.'s (2012, p. 28) asset-based approach to health promotion, for instance, stresses the importance of the 'involvement of people in decisions and process that have the potential to impact on them'. Meanwhile, Mesman (2011) herself

practices an interventionist ethnography with clinician-participants in order to continuously and collaboratively intervene in, and improve, patient safety in neonatal intensive care.

6. It would be tempting to think that the heartfelt methodology is about forcing positivity or eliminating negativity. It is not. Nor is it about designating positive emotions as 'good' and negative emotions as 'bad'. Rather, it is a methodology that assists researchers to be open to 'feeling and sensing the inner body' (Penttinen, 2013, p. 40) while encountering experiences of hardship during research. Such an approach may assist the researcher to refocus away from an 'ontology of constriction, separation, competition and struggle' (Penttinen, 2013, p. 32).

REFERENCES

Arnold, L., & Lockhardt Borman, L. (1996). What are the characteristics of an ideal milk donor? *Journal of Human Lactation, 12*(2), 143–145.

Boyd, C., Quigley, M., & Brocklehurst, P. (2007). Donor breast milk versus infant formula for preterm infants: Systematic review and meta-analysis. *Archives of Disease in Childhood, 92*(3), F169–F175.

Buckle, J., Corbin Dwyer, S., & Jackson, M. (2010). Qualitative bereavement research: Incongruity between the perspectives of participants and research ethics boards. *International Journal of Social Research Methodology, 12*(2), 111–125.

Carroll, K. (2012). Infertile? The emotional labour of sensitive and feminist research methodologies. *Qualitative Research, 13*(5), 546–561.

Carroll, K. (2016). The milk of human kinship. In C. Kroløkke, L. Myong, S. Adrian, & T. Tjørnhøj-Thomsen (Eds.), *Critical kinship studies* (pp. 13–32). London: Rowman and Littlefield International.

Carroll, K., & Herrmann, K. (2012). The cost of using donor human milk in the NICU to achieve exclusively human milk feeding through 32 weeks postmenstrual age. *Breastfeeding Medicine, 8*(3), 286–290.

Carroll, K., & Lenne, B. (in press). Suppress and express: Breast milk donation after neonatal death. In C. Beyer & A. Robertson (Eds.), *Mothers without children*. Ontario: Demeter Press.

Denzin, N., & Giardina, M. (2007). Introduction. In. N. Denzin & M. Giardina (Eds.). *Ethical futures in qualitative research* (pp. 9–44). Walnut Creek, CA: Left Coast Press.

Doucet, A. (2008). 'From her side of the Gossamer Wall(s)': Reflexivity and relational knowing. *Qualitative Sociology, 31*, 73–87.

Dyregrov, K. (2004) Bereaved parents' experience of research participation. *Social Science & Medicine, 58*, 391–400.

Evans, R., Ribbens McCarthy, J., Bowlby, S., Wouango, J., & Kebe, F. (2017). Producing emotionally sensed knowledge? Reflexivity and emotions in researching responses to death. *International Journal of Social Research Methodology, 20*(6), 585–598.

Gernstein Pieneau, M. (2013). Giving milk, buying milk: The influence of mothering ideologies and social class in donor milk banking. In T. Cassidy (Ed.), *Breastfeeding: Global practices, challenges, maternal and infant health outcomes* (pp. 61–76). New York, NY: Nova Publishers.

Guyer, R. (2006). *Baby at risk.* Sterling, VA: Capital Books.

Holmes, M. (2015). Researching emotional reflexivity. *Emotion Review, 7*(1), 61–66.

Hynson, J. L., Bauld, C., & Sawyer, S. M. (2006). Research with bereaved parents: A question of how not why. *Palliative Medicine, 20,* 805–811.

Iedema, R., & Carroll, K. (2015). Research as affect-sphere: Toward sphereogenics. *Emotion Review, 7*(1), 67–72.

Layne, L. (2003). *Motherhood lost.* New York, NY. Routledge.

Mannay, D. (2018). 'You just get on with it': Negotiating the telling and silencing of trauma and its emotional impacts in interviews with marginalised mothers. In T. Loughran & D. Mannay (Eds.), *Emotion and the researcher: Sites, subjectivities and relationships* (Vol. x). Studies in Qualitative Methodology (pp. 81–94). Bingley: Emerald.

Mesman, J. (2008). *Uncertainty in medical innovation.* New York, NY: Palgrave Macmillan.

Mesman, J. (2011). Resources of strength: An exnovation of hidden competences to preserve patient safety. In E. Rowley & J. Waring (Eds.), *A socio-cultural perspective on patient safety* (pp. 71–91). Farnham: Ashgate.

Olson, R., Godbold, N., & Patulny, R. (2015). Introduction: Methodological innovations in the sociology of emotions part two – Methods. *Emotion Review, 7*(2), 143–144.

Payne, S., & Field, D. (2004). Undertaking bereavement research: Sensitivities and sensibilities. *Grief Matters: The Australian Journal of Grief and Bereavement, 7*(3), 52–56.

Penttinen, E. (2013). *Joy in international relations.* London: Routledge.

Welborn, J. (2012). The experience of expressing and donating breast milk following a perinatal loss. *Journal of Human Lactation, 28*(4), 506–510.

Whiting, L., Kendell, S., & Wills, W. (2012). An asset-based approach: An alternative health promotion strategy. *Community Practitioner, 85*(1), 25–28.

CHAPTER 7

THE 'TRANSIENT INSIDER': IDENTITY AND INTIMACY IN HOME COMMUNITY RESEARCH

Erin Roberts

ABSTRACT

Purpose – *This reflexive account of bilingual research on rural household energy consumption within the researcher's home community problematises her position as an insider researching 'at home'. The chapter introduces the idea of the 'transient insider' as a way of better explaining her position, before going on to consider the ways in which fieldwork becomes bound up with emotionally and intellectually taxing professional and personal dilemmas.*

Methodology/Approach – *The study involved conducting repeat in-depth interviews with 11 households (25 individuals) – both together and apart – in rural north-west Wales.*

Findings – *The chapter illustrates the importance of paying heed to one's own emotions during the research process – particularly those that may be uncomfortable – as a means of better understanding our own positionality as researchers and its role in the co-creation of interview data.*

Originality/Value – *The chapter builds on earlier work that has engaged with the role of emotion and subjectivity in shaping the research process*

Emotion and the Researcher: Sites, Subjectivities, and Relationships
Studies in Qualitative Methodology, Volume 16, 113–125
Copyright © 2018 by Emerald Publishing Limited
All rights of reproduction in any form reserved
ISSN: 1042-3192/doi:10.1108/S1042-319220180000016008

and extends these discussions by examining the complexities involved in holding the position of the 'transient insider'.

Keywords: Researching 'at home'; transient insider; positionality; emotion; reflexivity; familiarity

INTRODUCTION

Within the interpretive social sciences, the relationship between the researcher and the research setting has long been understood to be central to the research process at every stage, from accessing groups to the interpretation and representation of the data. The benefits of working on 'familiar territory' (Mannay, 2010) have been well-documented, particularly in relation to ease of access, immediate legitimacy in the field, expediency of rapport building and a nuanced perspective for observation, interpretation and representation (Chavez, 2008). The 'researcher near' (Mannay, 2010) often has an in-depth knowledge of the history, language(s) and sociocultural nuances of their chosen setting and can navigate these appropriately (Bonner & Tolhurst, 2002; Hammersley & Atkinson, 2007). Being perceived as 'one of us' could thus result in people being more willing to participate in social research (see van den Scott, 2018 [this volume]). However, as DeLyser (2001) reminds us, familiarity can signal problems too, as asking the simplest question can present great challenges. For example, overfamiliarity can often complicate or overwhelm the researcher role and can cause difficulty in recognising patterns (Chavez, 2008; Mannay, 2010; Morriss, 2016).

In recent years, however, there has been a growing recognition among scholars that absolute notions of 'insiderness' and 'outsiderness' are lacking, and in many ways impossible (Chavez, 2008; DeLyser, 2001; Hellawell, 2006; Mannay, 2010; Narayan, 1993). As Narayan (1993) reminds us, we all belong to several communities simultaneously – albeit to varying degrees – which makes us both insider and outsider at the same time. Indeed, the apparent insider can prove to be an outsider as well, as the researcher's characteristics (gender, age, class, ethnicity and education) and personal experiences might differ substantially from the people they are studying (DeLyser, 2001, p. 442). Thus insiderness, much like identity, is neither fixed nor static, but is rather a permeable social location that is experienced, expressed and negotiated relationally (Chavez, 2008). However, as Mannay (2010, p. 92) asserts, 'to ignore questions of proximity is to assume that knowledge comes from nowhere, allowing researchers to become an abstract concept rather than a site of accountability'. She goes on to argue that while the above arguments render the absolute insider/outsider dichotomy inadequate, the concept of insiderness retains its methodological usefulness.

While there is widespread appreciation of the ways in which the researcher may affect the research process, much less is *written* about the ways in which the research process may affect the researcher (Widdowfield, 2000). Doing research is an inherently affective experience, where feelings of elation, frustration, guilt and anxiety are commonplace. Where emotion work on the part of the researcher is acknowledged, Bondi (2005) argues that this is done informally – often in terms of pastoral care and support – rather than in formal publications, although this is steadily changing. Attending to the emotional dynamics of social research can provide invaluable insights not only on those being researched but also on those conducting the research (Bennett, 2004; Bondi, 2005; Jansson, 2010).

Gathering data, Bondi (2005) asserts – whether it is with texts, numerical datasets or people – draws the researcher into relationships. When those relationships involve other people, as is the case with interviewing or participant observation, issues of positionality and identity negotiations can produce an array of emotions (Jansson, 2010; see also Lisiak & Krzyżowski, 2018 [this volume]). These emotions are not only present during fieldwork but continue throughout the research process and beyond. For example, as we analyse our data we revisit the interview encounter and are frequently struck by fresh emotions. Writing up is an equally emotional experience, as it is a process that is replete with oft-conflicting feelings of excitement and anxiety as we attempt to present our data in a manner that is enlightening, whilst also doing justice to our participants' experiences.

By drawing on my experiences as a doctoral researcher doing research 'at home', this chapter contributes to this growing body of literature that attends to positionality and the emotional dynamics of research relationships through time. First, I will explore how as a novice researcher, reflecting on my experiences during the early days of my research helped me complicate my positionality as a 'native insider'. I will then go on to explore how this newfound understanding of my own positionality featured in the research process by reflecting upon key moments during fieldwork and analysis that were bound up with emotionally and intellectually taxing professional and personal dilemmas.

CONTEXT, POSITIONALITY AND EMOTION

This chapter is based upon my experiences of undertaking an Economic and Social Research Council-funded PhD studentship that sought to explore the dynamics of everyday energy consumption in rural households, both in and through time. The study took place in rural north-west Wales (UK) between November 2012 and October 2013, with 11 households, 25 individuals in all, taking part in the research. Given my interest in exploring people's experiences of change and its pertinence in terms of energy consumption, the study adopted a narrative approach to better understand participants' lived subjectivities (see Roberts, 2016). Questions were designed to make visible those taken-for-granted everyday practices that consume energy, and to create a space for reflection on how goods and services, practices and living arrangements shape domestic energy consumption in place and through time. While on the surface, this topic may not seem to be emotionally sensitive, talking to people about how they conduct their everyday lives and why they do so in specific ways is replete with moral considerations that are highly emotive. An element of my work also explores affective ties to place through the individual meanings that are ascribed to participants' rural home-places through experiences and memories, hopes for the future and the resulting emotions connected to them.

North-west Wales is a research setting that is very familiar to me. I was born and raised in a small village nestled within the borders of Snowdonia National Park (Gwynedd County) – an area of strong Welsh-language culture – to Welsh-speaking parents. While I have not resided there for almost a decade now, this is where the entirety of my familial network can be found, and, as such, it is the place I call 'home'. Perhaps unsurprisingly, this personal connection to place played a large part in my decision to focus on north-west Wales as my research setting. I then considered myself as a 'native insider' (Narayan, 1993), and in the early days of the study I felt that such a position could be beneficial to me as I went about doing the research.

While I could not ignore nor take my privileged position as a 'researcher near' for granted, my understanding of my own positionality was quickly complicated. I often felt caught between two worlds – that of home and that of academia – particularly given the long distances travelled between the research setting (north-west Wales) and my place of residence in Cardiff (south-east Wales). Over time, the notion of transience gradually grabbed my attention as it encapsulated my newfound understanding of positionality as being fluid and constantly in motion; much like myself. I came to position myself as a *transient insider*, a designation which I felt encapsulated the cultural and linguistic competencies that I shared with my participants within the research setting, whilst also being more flexible and fluid than absolute understandings of insiderness. The notion of being a transient insider had great salience for me, given that in practice, the level of 'sameness' between participants and myself varied dramatically: age, gender, household arrangement, educational experience and position in the life-course were among these many differences. As such, during interviews I would often feel myself sliding along the 'insider–outsider continuum' (Hellawell, 2006), as my positionality shifted depending on what locality I was in, who I was speaking to and the topic under discussion. In what follows, I trace how this more nuanced understanding of researcher subjectivity played out during fieldwork and analysis, whilst paying attention to the emotional dynamics of social research.

BEFORE THE INTERVIEW

Building and maintaining research relationships with participants is part and parcel of qualitative research, particularly when undertaking repeat interviews. This is a process that starts before any data collection takes place and continues well beyond the conclusion of fieldwork. Researchers are required to walk the fine line between closeness and distance as part of this process, which can be particularly difficult to manage – both practically and emotionally – when what constitutes 'field' and 'home' become blurred (see Hall, 2009). Indeed, maintaining distance when researching 'at home' has often been cited as being potentially problematic (Chavez, 2008; Hall, 2009, 2014; Mannay, 2010).

Having engaged with the various academic debates regarding positionality and its role in research relationships, as a novice researcher entering a setting with which I was already well acquainted, I was painfully aware of the need to 'make the familiar strange' (Geer, 1964). In this vein – and perhaps rather naïvely given my cultural competencies – I endeavoured to reach households that had little-to-no prior connection to me or my family, so as not to be over-familiar with my participants. However, Wales is often described as being a 'small world' (BBC, 2005), where the familiar concept of six degrees of separation, one could suggest, is more likely to be closer to two. This certainly became apparent during fieldwork, as participants were eager to 'place' me within their social networks. For example, prior to the start of an interview I was often asked questions about my personal life, particularly in relation to where I was from, who my relatives were, which schools and college I had attended and if or when I intended to return home. Even with individuals with whom I had not had previous contact, it transpired that two degrees of separation was in fact optimistic. In one instance, it emerged that Alys – who lived with her husband and two small children more than 30 miles away from my home parish – had given my sister-in-law clothes that her children had outgrown during a local swap sale.

While for some this questioning might seem intrusive, I understood it to be a common cultural practice in north-west Wales, particularly with Welsh-speakers, and regarded it as part and parcel of building rapport. Nevertheless, I often felt conflicted about this 'placing practice'. Normal as it was to me in my personal life, professionally I frequently felt fearful that participants' *placing* and *knowing* me would somehow impede my ability to do the research effectively. While I struggled to make sense of why I felt a nagging feeling about this practice at the time, hindsight has helped me to realise that in my endeavour to make the familiar strange, I was afraid of making the strange overly familiar.

Another concern of mine related to how self-disclosure on the part of the researcher – even before the interview has begun – influences relationships with participants and the material that emerges from the interview (Josselson, 2007). One of the central tenets of good research practice within the interpretive social sciences involves 'accepting the inevitable role of the researcher in the research process' (Henwood & Pidgeon, 1992, p. 106), and acknowledging that all knowledge produced within the research encounter is the fruit of collaboration between researcher and researched. Answering questions about myself – who I am, as well as other aspects of my everyday life – inevitably influenced the research material, as topics from informal chats prior to the interview found their way into them. While at first the all-too-familiar sense of anxiety that plagues all novice researchers wriggled itself into my mind during these times, I learned – upon reflection – that this was advantageous, as participants drew upon our informal chats to illustrate how their experiences were similar or different to mine. In some instances, participants asked me to elaborate on something that I had said prior to the interview to illustrate a point of similarity or difference, and in these cases I answered as openly as I saw fit (see Hall, 2009). Because of my own self-disclosure, then, the interview took on a more relaxed, conversational nature, which helped facilitate exchange and put both participant and myself at ease.

FIELDWORK: NAVIGATING THE EMOTIONAL TERRAIN

Any form of communication is a relational act, and the research interview is by no means an exception. Josselson (2013) usefully describes the interview situation as an 'intersubjective dance' between interviewer and interviewee. She argues that the people in the interview situation are observing one another, 'forming pictures of the other' (p. 33). Just as the researcher makes judgements about who the interviewee is, so too do interviewees make judgements about the researcher's identity, all of which may or may not correspond with who each person thinks themselves to be. In some ways then, the researcher can become the researched (Al-Natour, 2011). It is to this intricate dance between researcher and researched that I now turn, as I discuss how the judgements and observations of both parties may not necessarily align with their self-perceptions. To do this, I will draw on my experience of interviewing Lowri, a young woman with whom – in my view – I shared many commonalities.

From the pre-interview chat with Lowri, it became clear that many of our demographic characteristics and worldviews were similar: like me, Lowri had been born and raised in the same area (while we *knew of* each other prior to the interview, we did not *know* each other); and we were of a similar age, had similar interests, and had gone off to university to study similar things. We also had some points of difference, particularly in relation to our backgrounds; born to English parents, Lowri described herself as being 'first-generation Welsh', and while she spoke Welsh to her friends, she spoke English at home and the interview was conducted in this language. The informal chat thus not only made me aware of the similarities and differences between us (from my perspective, we had much more in common than not) but also enabled me to quickly establish a rapport with Lowri, setting us both at ease before the interview began. However, as Lowri discussed her background and sense of belonging to the area and local community during the initial stage of the inter-view, this sense of ease – for me at least – gave way to a feeling of discomfort as Lowri began to build her narrative of who she is in relation to me:

Erin: Going back to community and place – do you feel that there's a strong sense of community in this area?

Lowri: Yeah I think one of the strongest I've ever come across in Britain at least – definitely, and that's really important to me.

Erin: Do you feel like you belong to not only the place but to the community as well?

Lowri: Yeah, you know, it's a strange one because I've got English parents and I think there are like different sub-groups in any community aren't there?

Erin: Yeah, communities of communities...

Lowri: Yeah, exactly. And one of those sub-groups is, like – sort of – hippies if you like, and I think I've definitely belonged to that, but at the same time that community isn't as strong as it was, say when I was in primary school. But I don't know, like I just developed very young like a real – I don't really like the word nationalist, because it feels like it devalues any other nationality in the world – but I have a really like strong like 'gwladgarwch' [Welsh: patriotism] you know? And I don't understand why that's happened because obviously, my parents have never instilled that in me. They've always really valued the Welsh language and culture and they've taken the approach not to say 'oh, you know, it's difficult for English people 'cause they can't get a job' you know? They've taken the approach of like 'we're here, so let's value it'... And in school and stuff, like in secondary... I used to write a lot of poetry in Welsh, like I won a chair in one of the local Eisteddfods, and I've always really been into the rugby. But at the same time, like, I know I'm not as Welsh as like [name redacted], or someone, or you [laughs]. You know, and so I feel like my whole life I've been like in the middle, like on the edge. Like I've got really close Welsh friends but then I identify with different people. And I did things as a child, and now, that most Welsh people don't do as well. Like going to festivals and stuff when I was little, and taking regular trips to London and things like that. Even going up in the mountains and stuff, like a lot of people from around here don't really do that. So I know that I haven't fitted into either box of English or hippie or Welsh or, you know, as I've got older that's something I've actually learnt to appreciate, because I can see that it helps me empathise with different people and I've stopped kind of feeling insecure about it.

Lowri, like my other participants, positioned me as a local, with an understanding of the specificities of the sociocultural context. She begins by identifying and defining three sub-groups within the community – Welsh and English (referring to linguistic communities), and 'Hippy' (that is, a subculture associated with creativity, environmentalism and alternative lifestyles) – categorisations that are commonly used to describe the sociocultural makeup of the area from which we hail. I could identify with her position of having a foot in each community, as I too have friendships with individuals in each. As Lowri proceeded to discuss her position as being 'in the middle', things took an unexpected turn – at least, they did for me – as Lowri discussed her identity in relation to (her perception of) mine.

As previously noted, at the beginning of the interview, I unconsciously focused on the points of similarity between Lowri and myself, most likely as a means of establishing rapport and calming the nerves of both researcher and researched. Rather naïvely, however, I had not considered how our points of difference could play out during the interview. Despite her lifelong connection to the area, Welsh name, everyday use of the Welsh language, and her successes in prestigious cultural events in the medium of Welsh, Lowri somehow felt herself to be 'less Welsh' than me. As I gradually felt myself slide further away from any notion of insiderness on my imaginary continuum, I began to feel a sense of intense guilt; had something I said made her somehow feel less Welsh? Although she showed no signs of distress or being upset, I felt a strong urge to pause the interview, and to reassure her that I held no such beliefs. I fought the tension between my personal and professional identities, and continued with the interview. Instead of using this moment of discomfort to explore why she felt that way, however, I let the moment pass and the conversation drift on to the next topic. In other words, I was doing a lot of emotion work trying to suppress my emotions, rather than engage with them as a means of further exploring Lowri's sense of identity and belonging. The gift of hindsight is that it grants us the ability to think about how we would have done things differently if given the chance.

Looking back, I now realise that in my enthusiasm at our points of commonality, I had overlooked our points of difference, which were critical to understanding why Lowri chose to narrate her sense of belonging in the way that she did. In the sociocultural context of rural north-west Wales, notions of 'Welshness' are intimately bound to the language (Day, 2002). This specific and situated understanding of Welsh identity, it has been argued, developed in reaction to social change in rural Wales over the last century, and particularly in-migration from neighbouring England (Day, 2002). While Lowri spoke Welsh with native proficiency, being the daughter of in-migrants speaking to a 'local' perhaps meant she somehow felt that her claim to belonging was not as strong as mine. Given the choices I made then, however, all I can do now is speculate.

(RE)PRESENTING NARRATIVES: THE ROLE OF EMOTIONS IN ANALYSIS

There is a great responsibility in telling other people's tales, and it is the duty of the researcher to do so in a sensitive and respectful manner. While undertaking interviews is a powerful, affective experience for both researcher and researched, what happens next, as the researcher attempts to interpret and (re)present the data, is equally laden with emotion. Josselson (2013) argues that over the course of the research process, the researcher's position shifts from that of an empathic listener during the interview, to one where sharing participants' experiences through various academic avenues such as conferences and publications is the norm. She goes on to state that there is inevitably some betrayal in doing so, and researchers are bound to feel a sense of guilt as they speak about their interpretation of others' truths. Learning to come to terms with the guilt of writing about others' experiences is a journey upon which the researcher must embark.

This sense of guilt is often accompanied by uncertainty and anxiety, as there lies a tension between revealing and concealing different elements of the research encounter in our interpretations of the data (Mannay, 2016). This tension to which Mannay refers often relates to the ethics of maintaining participant anonymity, whilst retaining enough contextual information to make their account meaningful in a situated way. As such, what we choose to reveal and conceal inevitably gives form to our accounts of participants' experiences, and whilst other readers may be oblivious to this, participants who recognise themselves in the writing 'may feel that their experience was distorted or misunderstood in some important ways' (Josselson, 2013, p. 148).

Going into the field, I was aware of the potential negative consequences of in-depth qualitative inquiry on the researched community, even long after the study had concluded. For example, my home community had been subject to a study some fifty years prior to my own, and through a family friend, I had been made aware that some people in the parish felt that the descriptions and conclusions made in the book were damaging in nature. While my own reading of the research had been positive, their interpretation of the way the community had been depicted was negative, with feelings of anger lingering to my ignorance and surprise. Although the resonance of these feelings did not directly affect my fieldwork, I had a newfound awareness that whatever I would produce as 'research output' could have very real, emotional implications for those that I studied. I was, however, rather unprepared for how writing-up would affect me.

It perhaps comes as no great surprise that it was in the writing-up stage of my study that I experienced the greatest struggle. Anxiety had become a familiar feeling to me as I attempted to navigate the fine line between revealing and concealing in my accounts of participants' experiences. Despite my elation and excitement at what I was finding, I also worried about revealing too much and making participating individuals and households identifiable. Frustratingly, some of the narratives most pertinent to my research topic were those of highly identifiable people. In presenting such narratives, I had to make significant alterations to some households' details to prevent them from being recognised, which ran the risk of distorting or losing the original meaning and significance of the data. The alternative – that is, not to include their accounts – would have been equally challenging from an ethical standpoint; is not telling a person's story akin to silencing them? If so, excluding certain accounts in favour of others for practical reasons feels like a greater betrayal. In the back of my mind, I was highly aware of the need to get the balance right, both ethically and – rather selfishly – for my own sake, as I would not be able to withdraw from the research setting following the culmination of the study, nor would I be able to avoid the aftermath of getting it wrong.

This fear, anxiety and guilt culminated in a writing paralysis that lasted quite some time. Rather paradoxically, it transpired that while emotions played a large role in this paralysis, they were also integral to my understanding of the data, which ultimately enabled me to push through the quagmire. As it turns out, by engaging with these difficult emotions I began to explore and account for my subjective position and its role in the co-production of data in a more critical way (see Holland, 2009). During analysis, I kept a rough note of my feelings (that is, memories of how I felt at the time of data collection as well as how I felt about the data during analysis) in a research diary, which formed the basis of many discussions with my supervisors and colleagues. In doing so, I could later unpick these uncomfortable moments to try and discern why they were so, and what this meant in the context of my research. In some ways, this challenged assumptions that I had not realised I had, and helped make the familiar a little more strange.

CONCLUSION

In this chapter, I have sought to highlight the emotional intricacies of doing research 'at home': to demonstrate some of the tensions I encountered between my professional and personal identities as I went about conducting research for my doctorate, and how these played their part in allowing me to better understand not only the data but also my position as a transient insider. It is perhaps not surprising then that navigating research relationships – with people and with data – has been at the heart of my discussion.

The notion of transience greatly helped me to negotiate fieldwork and data analysis as it emphasised a more fluid understanding of positionality. Being a transient insider enabled me to move to and fro along the continuum of nearness and distance – something that more static conceptualisations of 'insiderness' or 'outsiderness' could not do – which bears particular significance when researchers need to make the familiar strange and the strange a little more familiar. Such a concept, however, is not without its own set of tensions, particularly when researching 'at home'. Being a transient insider necessitates a great deal of emotion work at every stage of the research process, as the researcher must negotiate their way through emotionally and intellectually taxing professional and personal dilemmas.

While interviews are the fruit of collaboration between researcher and researched, it is important to note that such a collaboration is rarely done on equal terms. Telling others' tales – be that in theses, publications or in conferences – involves interpretation on the part of the researcher, and what we ultimately produce is *our version of their tales*. This is a great responsibility, the navigation of which, once again, entails significant emotion work. While the emotional labour involved on my part was at times intense, I would not have been able to develop certain insights had I not attended to my feelings – particularly those that were uncomfortable. As such, I would urge other novice researchers to use moments of discomfort as a means of engaging with their emotions to dig deeper into the subject matter at hand.

Much of my writing may appear to be confessional, and as such, I feel it incumbent to state that the intensity of my feelings – particularly those of guilt and anxiety – have dulled down considerably following the culmination of my study. This is not to say that they have disappeared, but rather that time has given me the clarity and distance I needed to effectively reflect upon the process. As such, what once caused great anxiety now stirs up feelings of intrigue and excitement. It is my hope that my writing in this chapter demonstrates this, and enables other novice researchers to understand that paying heed to their own positionality and emotions during the research process can provide invaluable insights into their subject areas.

REFERENCES

Al-Natour, R. J. (2011). The impact of the researcher on the researched. *M/C Journal*, *14*(6). Retrieved from http://journal.media-culture.org.au/index.php/mcjournal/article/view/428. Accessed on June 12, 2017.

BBC News. (2005). Six degrees of Welsh separation. *BBC News*. Retrieved from http://news.bbc. co.uk/1/hi/wales/4141581.stm. Accessed on June 12, 2017.

Bondi, L. (2005). The place of emotions in research: From partitioning emotion and reason to the emotional dynamics of research relationships. In J. Davidson, L. Bondi, & M. Smith (Eds.), *Emotional geographies* (pp. 231–246). Ashgate: Aldershot.

Bonner, A., & Tolhurst, G. (2002). Insider–outsider perspectives of participant observation. *Nurse Researcher*, *9*(4), 7–19.

Bennett, K. (2004). Emotionally intelligent research, *Area*, *36*(4), 414–422.

Chavez, C. (2008). Conceptualizing from the inside: Advantages, complications, and demands on insider positionality. *The Qualitative Report*, *13*(2), 474–494.

Day, G. (2002). *Making sense of Wales: A sociological perspective.* Cardiff: University of Wales Press.

DeLyser, D. (2001). Do you really live here? Thoughts on insider research. *Geographical Review*, *91*(1/2), 441–453.

Geer, B. (1964). First days in the field. In P. E. Hammond (Ed.), *Sociologists at work* (pp. 372–398). New York, NY: Basic Books.

Hall, S. M. (2009). 'Private life' and 'work life': Difficulties and dilemmas when making and maintaining friendships with ethnographic participants. *Area*, *41*(3), 263–272.

Hall, S. M. (2014). Ethics of ethnography with families: A geographical perspective. *Environment and Planning A*, *46*(9), 2175–2194.

Hammersley, M., & Atkinson, P. (2007). *Ethnography: Principles in practice*. Abingdon, Oxon: Routledge.

Hellawell, D. (2006). Insider-out: Analysis of the insider–outsider concept as a heuristic device to develop reflexivity in students doing qualitative research. *Teaching in Higher Education*, *11*(4), 483–494.

Henwood, K., & Pidgeon, N. (1992). Qualitative research and psychological theorizing. *British Journal of Psychology*, *83*(1), 97–111.

Holland, J. (2009). *Emotions and research: Some general and personal thoughts*. Families and Social Capital Research Group Working Paper No. 25. Retrieved from https://www. lsbu.ac.uk/__data/assets/pdf_file/0017/9440/up-close-personal-relationships-emotions-families-research-working-paper.pdf. Accessed on June 12, 2017.

Jansson, D. (2010). The head vs. the gut: Emotions, positionality, and the challenges of fieldwork with a Southern nationalist movement. *Geoforum, 41*(1), 19–22.

Josselson, R. (2007). The ethical attitude in narrative research: Principles and practicalities. In D. J. Clandinin (Ed.), *The handbook of narrative inquiry* (pp. 537–566). London: SAGE.

Josselson, R. (2013). *Interviewing for qualitative inquiry: A relational approach.* London: The Guilford Press.

Lisiak, A., & Krzyżowski, L. (2018). With a little help from my colleagues: Notes on emotional support in a qualitative longitudinal research project. In T. Loughran & D. Mannay (Eds.), *Emotion and the researcher: Sites, subjectivities and relationships* (Vol. 16). Studies in Qualitative Methodology (pp. 33–48). Bingley: Emerald.

Mannay, D. (2010). Making the familiar strange: can visual research methods render the familiar setting more perceptible? *Qualitative Research, 10*(1), 91–111.

Mannay, D. (2016). *Visual, narrative and creative research methods: Application, reflection and ethics.* Abingdon, Oxon: Routledge.

Morriss, L. (2016). Dirty secrets and being 'strange': Using ethnomethodology to fight familiarity. *Qualitative Research, 16*(5), 526–540.

Narayan, K. (1993). How native is a 'native' anthropologist? *American Anthropologist, 95*(3), 671–686.

Roberts, E. (2016). *Reducing energy consumption in everyday life: A study of landscapes of energy consumption in rural households and communities in North Wales.* Ph.D. thesis, Cardiff University.

van den Scott, L. K. (2018). Role transitions in the field and reflexivity: From friend to researcher. In T. Loughran & D. Mannay (Eds.), *Emotion and the researcher: Sites, subjectivities and relationships* (Vol. 16). Studies in Qualitative Methodology (pp. 19–32). Bingley: Emerald.

Widdowfield, R. (2000). The place of emotions in academic research. *Area, 32*(2), 199–208.

CHAPTER 8

EMOTIONS, DISCLOSURES AND REFLEXIVITY: REFLECTIONS ON INTERVIEWING YOUNG PEOPLE IN ZAMBIA AND WOMEN IN MIDLIFE IN THE UK

Sophie Bowlby and Caroline Day

ABSTRACT

Purpose – *This chapter reflects on selected issues raised by the emotions involved in the social relations of qualitative research. We use experiences from two separate studies to explore the role of emotion and affect in the embodied, face-to-face encounter of the interview; the 'translation' of interpretations of emotional responses from one cultural context into another; the reflexivity of the researcher and the researched and the ethical implications of this form of research.*

Methodology – *The studies, one doctoral research and one funded by a Leverhulme grant, took a qualitative approach, employing individual semi-structured interviews with young people in Zambia and women in their fifties in Swindon, UK.*

Emotion and the Researcher: Sites, Subjectivities, and Relationships
Studies in Qualitative Methodology, Volume 16, 127–142
ISSN: 1042-3192/doi:10.1108/S1042-319220180000016009

Findings – The chapter argues that emotions within the interview are bound up with the potential meanings and outcomes of the interview to both the researcher and the interviewee. Emotions affect what is said and unsaid in the interview; what is communicated and hidden and how the material is interpreted.

Originality/Value – The chapter brings together experiences from conducting highly emotive research in majority and minority world contexts. It focuses on similarities in the dilemmas posed to researchers by the emotions involved in the social relations of research, regardless of location.

Keywords: Emotion; qualitative; interview; culture; majority/minority worlds; research ethics

INTRODUCTION

This chapter explores selected issues raised by the emotions involved in the social relations of research which used semi-structured interviews. We examine two very different projects: Caroline's doctoral research in Zambia with young people for which Sophie was one of the supervisors[1] (Day, 2014, 2016, 2017; Day & Evans, 2015); and a study with women in mid-life in Swindon, UK,[2] for which both of us did the interviews. Although the projects had very different cultural contexts, participant ages and research topics, we were struck by many similarities in the dilemmas posed to researchers by the emotions involved in the research process. We aim to explore these dilemmas in this chapter.

Before describing each project, we briefly discuss the significance of emotional relationships to such research. In qualitative interviews, the researcher and the participant[3] engage in a social encounter which usually asks the participant to talk about some aspect of their own lives and their reactions to their situation now, in the past or the future. Such discussions inevitably evoke emotions in both parties. Participants' accounts are often laden with emotional words, descriptions of emotional reactions and, often, implicit or explicit pleas for sympathy and understanding, and thus evoke emotions in the researcher – for example, sympathy, anger or distress. Researchers bring emotional baggage to the interview in terms of feelings about and, perhaps, commitments to particular views of the research topic and of emotions linked to fears and hopes about the research process.

There is a considerable literature on the role of emotions in social science research. This revolves, first, around the epistemological significance of the emotions of both researchers and researched (Hubbard, Backett-Milburn, & Kemmer, 2000; Mauthner & Doucet, 2008); and, second, around the harms (and occasionally the benefits) that emotions evoked during the research may bring to both parties (Hubbard et al., 2000; Widdowson, 2000).

First, commentators' views on the epistemological role of emotions in interviews are related to their understandings of the nature of emotions and their role in social behaviour. Here we start from a view of emotions as constructed in relation to other people or objects and felt as embodied, sensory experiences. We do not consider emotions to be simply biologically determined but, rather, to be shaped through culture and socialisation, which teach us to name and explain particular emotions and also to experience 'socially appropriate' emotions in specific circumstances (Hochschild, 1979; Middleton, 1989). These might be shame, pride, anger, anxiety, sexual attraction, fear or amusement. Such examples illustrate how emotional responses are often strongly linked to what participants think are the potential *meanings* and *outcomes* of a social encounter and what participants might, therefore, gain or lose from it. Consequently, emotions will be affected by the perceived status and power of those involved.

Researchers may seek to understand their participants' emotions in order to explain their behaviours and attitudes, or wish to know what emotions are felt because of particular types of event or experience – for example, death, birth, illness and unemployment. Interviewees may describe their emotions, but words rarely give a full understanding of emotion. Rather, we interpret the emotions of others through learned recognition and understandings of affect, bodily signals and social behaviours as well as words – and we are not conscious of all the ways in which we make judgements about our own or others' feelings. When researchers seek to interpret the responses of their interviewees, including their emotional responses, they inevitably rely partly on what Hubbard et al. (2000) term 'emotionally sensed knowledge' and the epistemological status of such knowledge is always complex, uncertain and provisional.

It has been argued for some time that there are significant differences in the emotional *ethos* or *style* of cultures (Lutz & White, 1986; Middleton, 1989; Solomon, 1997) as well as in notions of self and identity, and in how particular emotions 'should' be expressed and by whom. Thus, the ability to 'correctly' recognise another's emotions will be affected by the extent to which participants share cultural understandings of the meaning of bodily and verbal signals and social behaviours, and knowledge of the emotions deemed appropriate to particular social situations. Literature on cultural 'insiders' and 'outsiders' has shown both the advantages of being an 'insider' for understanding why and how people feel and act but also the disadvantages of 'taking for granted' particular ways of thinking and acting which are more visible to 'outsiders' (Mullings, 1999). It has also emphasised the multi-dimensional character of shared cultures so that it is rare to be fully an 'insider' or an 'outsider' (Chacko, 2004; see also Roberts, 2018 [this volume]).

The second area in which the role of emotions has been of concern, relates to the emotional damage a researcher may impose by raising issues that create powerful, negative emotions for the interviewee. But researchers can also suffer from the emotional impacts of interviewing. For example, observing another person's distress or their difficult living situation, without being able to alleviate their suffering, can create long-lasting pain and feelings of inadequacy. There is widespread recognition that interviews may evoke distressing, sometimes unexpected, emotional responses in participants. Attention to interviewers' ethical responsibilities in such circumstances is now widespread in the guidelines of research organisations and in student training. As Widdowfield (2000) and Hubbard et al. (2001) contend, less attention has been given to the potential distress of interviewers, although since they wrote, awareness of this has been growing as has recognition of the need for informal and formal systems of support for researchers (Evans, Ribbens McCarthy, Bowlby, Wouango, & Kébé, 2017; Watts, 2008).

THE TWO PROJECTS

Aspirations and attitudes of young carers in Zambia examined how youth experience and negotiate their socially expected transitions to adulthood in Zambia. It was a comparative study of young people with and without caregiving responsibilities for sick or disabled parents or relatives, to establish how the responsibility of caring influenced their transitions in comparison to their non-caregiving peers (Day & Evans, 2015). Interviews were conducted via an interpreter with 35 young people (aged 14–30 years),[4] comprising 15 caring for a chronically sick or disabled parent or relative (9 female, 6 male) and 20 without specific caring responsibilities for a family member (9 female, 11 male). The young people were drawn from urban and rural areas in the Central Province of Zambia. Interviews were also conducted with 12 parents or relatives of the young people, 8 of whom were being cared for by the young person, as well as with 14 strategic stakeholders.

The participants were identified through two key non-governmental organisations (NGOs) working within local communities to address and support people with various health issues, including HIV, polio, stroke and visual impairment; they were recruited using purposive sampling techniques. The young people also completed a visual timeline of their lives to map 'self-defined "fateful moments" of transition' (Worth, 2005, p. 1052) from their past and that might occur in the future (Day, 2014). They were also asked about the support they received and who this came from, and about their social relations within their communities. The interviews took place predominantly in the young people's homes, but also in the offices of a supporting NGO and a local bar/cafe.

The 'personal communities' of women in midlife in Swindon, UK, explored how women in their fifties maintained their social ties with people in their 'personal community'– that is the friends and family that were 'important' to them (Spencer & Pahl, 2006). Thirty-one women, drawn from diverse social backgrounds in Swindon, UK, were interviewed.[5] A few days before the interview, the women were asked to write down brief details of notable events in their lives and to list friends and family who were 'important' to them.

Most interviews took place in the interviewee's home. They were shown a diagram of three nested concentric circles and asked to place the people most important to them in the middle, the next most important in the second circle and the least important in the outer circle.[6] They were encouraged to discuss their relationship with each person, including how they kept in touch with them (meetings, phone calls and internet communications), what activities they shared, who amongst them they would turn to for support and the differences between family members and friends (see Bowlby, 2015).

The rest of this chapter is in three sections – the first deals with emotional exchanges of affect and emotion during the interview; the second with identifying and analysing emotions revealed through the interview data such as recordings, transcripts and artefacts and the third explores the reflexivity of the researchers and the researched during and after the interview.

EMOTIONS INSIDE THE INTERVIEW

The embodied interactions between people in interviews allow affect to be exchanged and emotions to be conveyed explicitly and implicitly. As some Swindon interviewees said about meeting face to face:

'Well, eye contact makes all the difference doesn't it you know, you can tell how some-
body's feeling about what you're saying' (Charlotte).[7]

'Obviously you have the, their expression, you see people' (Emily).

'I like to [...] actually see them and you pick up so much more' (Phoebe).

An important aspect of such emotional exchanges relates to what power
and authority over the interview exchange each party feels they have. Both
may be somewhat anxious and fearful – the interviewer about a lack of 'success' in eliciting the information they desire and the interviewee about disclosing more than they wish or simply of being in an unfamiliar social situation
where the social 'rules' are not entirely clear. Commonly used ethical protocols such as telling the interviewee they can withdraw at any time and need
not answer any question they do not wish to answer – which we adopted –
are designed to overcome some of the interviewee's anxiety. Additionally, the
interviewer is often urged to establish 'rapport' – a sense that both parties
understand each other's feelings or ideas – to encourage the interviewee to
talk more freely. Such 'rapport' is, we think, also often intended to oblige the
interviewee to give answers.

An interview's initial phases often involve emotionally significant, but
implicit, negotiations over issues of power and authority. For example, most
of the interviews with women in Swindon took place in their own homes. This
gave them an opportunity to act as a 'hostess' by offering a cup of tea or coffee, thus putting them in charge of the space and social interactions within it.
Accepting the drink with thanks, as we always did, and making small talk created the feeling of an 'ordinary' social encounter within the home and served
to allay the anxieties of both parties to the encounter. While this illusion was
then disrupted by the interviewer asking questions and 'instructing' the interviewee to carry out specific tasks, the interplay of emotionally infused social
interactions at an interview's beginning can be crucial to its progress.

This contrasted with the research in Zambia where, while many of the
interviews took place in the young people's homes, the issues of power and
authority were sometimes harder to negotiate. The young people were all living *within* the homes of older family members, rather than in their own homes,
and so the parent/relative needed to agree to the research being conducted in
the household, even where the young person was over 18. The right of the
young person to speak privately and confidentially also had to be negotiated
to ensure others did not influence their responses. Several young people chose
to be interviewed at the NGO office or at a bar/café near where they lived,
which positioned the interview in a more neutral space. However, interviewing people in the family household ensured a much better understanding of

their lives, living arrangements and the assets and resources available to them. It was harder to disentangle confused or contradictory stories from the young person or family members without such understanding.

Caroline also provided refreshments because many of the young people were living in poverty. Many had not had a meal before the interview, so this acted as a practical means of ensuring they could concentrate on the tasks in hand, while also saying 'thank you' for giving up their time. While this was the reverse of the Swindon study's process, it had a similar impact by relaxing people and making the interviews feel less formal. These initial exchanges may be seen as involving some emotional manipulation on the part of the interviewer and can raise ethical issues if this extends to lying, or suggesting implicit benefits from taking part or loss from not doing so. Even if interviewers are trying to avoid such unethical manipulation, it is nevertheless important to be aware of the emotional undercurrents of the interview relationship as it develops. Such emotional exchanges may influence what is said or not said in later parts of the interview.

Over half of the Zambian interviews were conducted through an interpreter. Introducing a third party into the conversation, while a necessity, changed the dynamics of the interview, as well as influencing the rapport that could be developed between the researcher and the participant. Relying on someone else to interpret the question and then relay back the answer meant that Caroline became both insider and outsider to the interview process, as although she was asking the questions she relied on the interpreter to feed back what was being said and was partially excluded from the conversation. This took some control away from her and made it harder to read and react to emotional signals. Choosing how to respond and what line of questioning to then pursue not only depended greatly upon the ability of the interpreter to convey the answer accurately but also emphasised the importance of seeing and hearing the emotions present in the participant's tone of voice, facial and bodily expressions.

In Swindon, many women recounted difficult aspects of their life histories such as relationship breakdowns with family members or friends; sibling suicide; domestic violence; criminal behaviour of partners or children; mental health problems and bereavement. There were also positive stories of the pleasures of kin and friend relationships such as shared activities, mutual support, grandparenting, new relationships, new activities and hopes for the future. Most women used emotive words and phrases in their accounts – for example, *supportive, tension, good laughs, hate, lonely, fondness, don't care, love him to bits, sad* – and often emotional tones of voice, facial expressions and body language. Sometimes they told their stories in a matter-of-fact tone, but more often with clear vocal indications of their emotional significance.

Similarly, in Zambia, the participants often spoke about difficult times in their lives. Stories of bereavement,[8] illness, family breakdown, poverty and abuse were common. Such experiences also came with additional challenges, such as having to 'drop out' of school, engage in risky employment, face eviction from households and early pregnancy. While some described positive relationships with family and friends, most of these encounters were reflected on in the past tense when life was perceived as having been 'good', but now the negative aspects far outweighed the positive. However, in contrast to Swindon, it was not uncommon for questions to be answered with short, monosyllabic answers, or a shrug of the shoulders, that implied they 'did nothing' or 'had nothing to say' about a topic, when Caroline knew from the project workers that the young person had been going through the exact experiences she was investigating (see also Evans et al., 2017; Hansen, 2005). This was more common amongst the young women in the study who were more socially inhibited, rather than the young men. It made it difficult for Caroline to 'read' the emotional significance of particular stories or situations.

In the interviews for both projects, it was sometimes difficult to decide during the interview on 'appropriate' reactions to stories of pain and difficulty. Interviewers are urged to be clear with themselves and with interviewees that they have neither the skills nor the right to offer advice on emotional trauma or social problems but to be prepared to provide information about appropriate services. This was the approach adopted in both the studies. In Swindon, the emotions and problems were usually not revealed to us as a means of asking for material support. What was asked of us was, most often, sympathy and understanding but also, some tacit endorsement of their feelings and responses. While this was usually easy to feel and convey, occasionally we had to suppress feelings of disapproval, lack of sympathy or simply lack of emotional understanding.

In contrast, the Zambian participants often requested advice or further support. The often-held perception that all 'white westerners' working in African contexts are doing so on behalf of large aid agencies, meant some of the participants hoped for ongoing financial support, such as school sponsorship, as a result of participating in the research. This was despite making clear that Caroline was working independently and had no means to support people after the research had ended. While most seemed to accept this explanation, Caroline often felt that they thought she was deceiving them; in their eyes she was still a wealthy, educated westerner with access to resources or agencies who could provide food, money or housing. Such encounters often left her feeling helpless and guilty in situations where it seemed no easy solution was available to support the participants or improve their lives.

The embodied expression of emotions exchanged in an interview, and the interview environment and its (dis)comfort and social meanings, affect how the interviewer feels about the experience. All this must be considered when interpreting what the interview tells the researcher about the topic of interest. It is to these issues of interpretation that we now turn.

INTERPRETING EMOTIONS

We have suggested that gaining 'emotionally sensed knowledge' during the interview itself is not straightforward. These challenges crystallise when the researcher sits down with the transcripts, recordings and other data and begins to interpret. However, having time to reflect on what was said and unsaid and to separate words and bodily signals can also suggest new understandings or questions. As we have intimated, this is particularly challenging when working within another culture, or where the participant's first language differs from that of the interviewer. We focus here on two important difficulties of interpretation. The first stems from how the emotions – fears, hopes and beliefs – of the interviewee influence their answers and the second is about the difficulties of identifying and understanding the interviewee's emotions.

A key concern in any research is understanding how the participant's emotions may influence their answers. Making emotional sense of people's stories also involves seeing the question from their perspective, including how much they want to disclose, whether they are willing to 'open themselves up' and show their vulnerabilities, and whether they are saying what they think the researcher wants to hear. People may also refrain from raising experiences they judge will be of little significance to the researcher. The young Zambians often challenged why their lives would interest someone from the UK. Some in Swindon said they were 'not worth' interviewing. In both places, we often had to assert that the 'mundane' *is* interesting and the participant's voice important and of significance to the research.

In Zambia, few of the young caregivers said they received help from family, friends or organisations with their caring responsibilities, despite visible evidence to the contrary. While this could partly have been a rapport issue, reflecting Caroline's position as a possibly untrustworthy 'outsider', it was also suggested to Caroline that this was done in the hope that she would support them and their families. While this might be thought simple 'misinformation' for personal gain, its significance is far greater. It provides a glimpse of the precarious lives these young people lead, their hopes of 'rescue' and their difficulties in negotiating the complex systems of 'development' research and aid.

The Swindon interviewees did not expect material help but did sometimes want social approval or reassurance. After reading the transcripts, looking at their personal community 'maps' and ruminating on the 'feel' of the encounter, we thought that their beliefs about how relationships with family members and friends 'ought' to be sometimes affected what they told us. This might be by exaggerating the closeness of a bond or the frequency of contact, skating over tensions in a relationship or leaving out valuable information about a relationship. Again, such 'misinformation' can provide information of another kind – here concerning beliefs about friendship and family – but we remain uncertain about how well we detected such influences. These uncertainties of interpretation relate to and question our ability to understand the emotional meaning of aspects of an interview like hesitancies, uneasiness, fervour and enthusiasm in our respondents' accounts.

The importance of not taking words at face value was frequently demonstrated in the Zambia research. As in Swindon, it mattered to pay attention to the social and cultural beliefs and practices that might be reflected in the answers people gave – sometimes reading between the lines to hear what they did not say as much as what they did. A striking example occurred when a young woman from one of the rural villages failed to mention that she had a child when asked how many people she lived with. Further analysis, discussion with the interpreter and later reflections when analysing the transcripts suggested this was probably linked to the cultural stigma surrounding young unmarried mothers. This shows the value of an interpreter born and raised in Zambia and aware of many of the cultural expectations and taboos – a cultural 'insider' (although an outsider in respect of the level of his education and his gender).

Having an interpreter was also beneficial to building rapport with the young people, helping put them at ease and open up conversation – although it complicated communication. Thus the transcriptions revealed that the interpreter did not always recount the full detail the participant gave. The interpreter also often changed the question wording or avoided certain terms due to their own, often religious, feelings and beliefs (particularly related to puberty and sexual relations). We doubt that this had a major impact on the research, but sometimes it altered the questioning, or inhibited new lines of enquiry.

A further difficulty of interpretation is understanding the interviewee's emotions – a problem exacerbated by cultural distance. We have referred to many of the young people's tendency to answer questions very briefly. It remains hard to know how far this reflected a cultural disposition to avoid acknowledging certain emotions, or the lack of the culture of self-analysis and positive valuation of emotional 'confession' common in the West, or, simply, unwillingness to trust an 'outsider' with personal vulnerabilities. The researcher also needs to be aware of emotional reactions which seem odd or inappropriate in their culture but are 'expected' in the interviewee's culture – emphasising the value of discussion with a cultural 'insider'.

It is easy to recognise the need for cultural sensitivity in situations, such as Caroline's interviews in Zambia, where there are clear cultural differences between interviewees and interviewer. However, in Swindon we became aware of subtler cultural differences linked to class, age and lifecourse experience, which hindered emotional understandings. For example, Sophie found it difficult to gauge the depth of emotion implied by the phrase 'I love him/her to bits', since this was not an expression that was common amongst her family and friends – perhaps an expression of her class background, age and place of residence, since for Caroline, who was younger and also local to the area, this expression was taken for granted.

REFLEXIVITY

Reflexivity by the researcher is generally thought to involve considering how their own positionality, experiences and theoretical views may affect interpretations of their interview material. It may also involve reflection on how their interview experiences have affected their own emotional lives, theoretical views and ontological commitments.

In both studies, we sought to retain a 'professional' distance and to remain aware of our own limitations in offering help or support. In Swindon, some of the stories of coping with abuse, hurt and loss left us feeling shaken. The material in the interviews also prompted us to re-evaluate how we practiced our own family relationships and friendships. Thus, it was impossible not to be emotionally affected by people's stories, the depth of feeling that they conveyed and, in the Zambia study particularly, the situations encountered. Caroline found that in Zambia some people assumed, because she was researching the care of people with illnesses or disabilities, that she had a medical background. This led to one of her hardest encounters. On a community visit to identify suitable participants, she was introduced to a very sick, bedridden woman, asked to decipher her medical notes and tell people what was wrong with her. This was distressing, and Caroline also had to deal with the disappointment of the project worker who had taken her there, and the woman and her family, that she could neither identify the problem nor offer a cure. In both studies, we found ourselves occasionally emotionally and professionally out of our depth and aware of our inability to help. Such encounters can have lasting impacts. Caroline still often thinks about this one, particularly as the woman died just a few weeks later.

One inappropriate response is for researchers to become habituated to the suffering of others. Feeling emotion is necessary to understanding the significance of others' emotion – but researchers must remain analytical and aim to tread the narrow line between over- and under-sensitivity to the emotions of those they are studying. We also want to acknowledge that seeing how people have coped with difficult circumstances, the joys that some have found in their lives and the warmth and care they exhibit in their relationships, can be a privilege of qualitative research. In the Swindon study, we were often left impressed and heartened by women's ways of dealing with difficult life experiences. More broadly, we believe reflecting on the experiences of qualitative research helps create greater openness to alternative theoretical interpretations, understandings of emotional responses and awareness of the fallibility of our knowledge of ourselves and others.

Our reflections on our own responses prompt us to ask honestly about the emotional impact of our research on our interviewees. What did the participants get out of the experience of being involved in the research? This was particularly pertinent in the Swindon study where on several occasions during the interviews it became apparent that the mental wellbeing of the participant was, or had been, quite fragile. A key concern was how the participants would judge themselves against each other. The women in the Swindon study, for example, listed anything between 3 and 30 family and friends in their social networks. Those with fewer contacts sometimes worried that they did not conform to social expectations. We did not want the research results, circulated to the participants as a summary, to prompt feelings of inadequacy or failure.

More positively, we often found that the participants seemed to find their participation therapeutic. Speaking to someone emotionally detached from their situation, who did not judge or try to offer advice and so remained neutral, permitted them to discuss experiences they may not have felt they could admit to family members or close friends. Several women in the Swindon study reflected on how positive the research had made them feel as it endorsed just how many friends and family they had. It emphasised to them how lucky they were – something which they had probably been aware of before but rarely took the time to appreciate. This was also highlighted in the Zambia interviews where young people talked about the value of being able to talk about their lives and feel that their voices were being heard.

However, in the Zambia study, Caroline's social position also reminded the young people of their own limited prospects. They often said they wanted to come to the UK to seek what Caroline had – education, freedom of travel, secure home and employment – and implored her to take them with her. These were things many of them will never achieve in Zambia – particularly frustrating if they had completed their education but were unemployed. However, Caroline's situation as unmarried and childless, yet in her early thirties, was a source of both confusion and amusement to many and compromised the respect that she would have received had she also achieved these life transitions.

Three years after her original study Caroline returned to share her research findings and run a workshop with the young people to develop messages for policymakers. At the workshop, the young people said how pleased they were she had returned and not 'forgotten' them. She could see that life had progressed for some, whereas many others were still dealing with the same, or additional, challenges. This made her feel both proud of the young people, and sorry for those for whom life remained very difficult. Being able to stay in touch with the projects and the young people has made the research feel more worthwhile, and raised her esteem in their community. This was highlighted when she visited Zambia last year and 'bumped into' one of the young people in the supermarket and he greeted her like an old friend. It has also affected how Caroline leads her life. She feels grateful to live in a society where she can access services, commodities and support networks that many people lack. But she recognises that in other ways this compares less well to life in Zambia that, despite its many challenges, is less tied to possessions (although many crave them) and often offers a more holistic lifestyle.

CONCLUDING THOUGHTS

While this chapter reflects on our shared experiences of two studies conducted in very different cultural contexts, it highlights similarities in the emotional and ethical dilemmas and difficulties facing researchers engaged in interview-based research. While these emotions are often rightly viewed in terms of harm to the participant, the effect on the researcher can be greatly underestimated. Writing this chapter has shown us how much we have been affected by our research. Listening to others' stories can change how you see the world and lead you to reflect critically on your own life. As researchers we seek particular answers, and as a professional you try to remain analytical but sensitive to your interviewees' feelings and social situations. This does not mean that we are emotionally unmoved.

It is important to reflect on how, as researchers, our emotions, desires and habits of thought and feeling can bound our understanding of what interviewees communicate. There is a significant tension between seeking 'rapport' and developing an intuitive understanding of how the world seems to the interviewee, whilst simultaneously maintaining sufficient emotional 'distance' to analyse and avoid taking for granted what you are being told. Awareness of cultural differences in what and how emotions can be displayed really matters here, as does the need to acknowledge the significance of both non-verbal, as well as verbal, emotional indicators and the difficulty of 'correctly' identifying emotions.

In any interview, we need to be aware of the many emotional undercur-rents at play, especially when exploring personal, and sometimes sensitive or difficult, issues. Fear, hopes for advantage and jockeying for authority can all play out, often subtly, and need to be negotiated. Here, familiar issues of researchers' power and authority over the stories of the researched should be seen through an emotional lens. In interpreting aspects of our participants' lives, we believe that we should disclose to academic and other audiences our own uncertainties of interpretation and how they entwine with the complexi-ties of 'emotionally sensed knowledge'.

NOTES

1. Dr Ruth Evans (University of Reading) was the main supervisor. The PhD was funded by a studentship provided by the University of Reading.

2. This study was funded by Leverhulme EM-2012-0061/7.

3. We recognise that some interviews may involve more than one interviewee and more than one researcher but for simplicity we focus on the situation of two people.

4. The Zambian Government defines 'youth' as young people between the ages of 18 and 35 (MSYCD, 2006). However, it also recognises the UN definition of youth as 15–25 years (UN, 2007). Pilot research revealed that few people identified themselves as 'youth' after the age of 30 as they were usually employed, married and had children. The age of 30 was therefore used as the upper age limit, while the slightly lower age

limit was used in recognition that many young people have significant responsibilities at a much younger age than age-based understandings of transitions assume.

5. Swindon is a town of about 200,000 people, situated in southern England about 80 miles from London.

6. This technique has been used in other studies of friendship such as Spencer and Pahl (2006).

7. All names are pseudonyms.

8. A total of 30 of the young people had lost at least one parent, 18 of whom had lost both parents.

ACKNOWLEDGEMENTS

We would like to thank both the University of Reading and the Leverhulme Trust for making this research possible. We would also like to thank all the women and young people in both Swindon and Zambia who participated in the research and challenged us to think about our own emotions in so many ways. Warm thanks also to Tracey and Dawn for championing the importance of attending to emotions in research. Thanks also to Peter Pearson for editorial help.

REFERENCES

Bowlby, S. R. (2015). Keeping in touch: Studying the personal communities of women in their fifties. In N. Worth & I. Hardill (Eds.), *Researching the lifecourse: Critical reflections from the social sciences* (pp. 143–160). Bristol: Policy Press.

Chacko, E. (2004). Positionality and praxis: Fieldwork experiences in rural India. *Singapore Journal of Tropical Geography, 25*(1), 51–63.

Day, C. (2014). Giving the vulnerable a voice: Research with children and young people. Experiences from fieldwork in Zambia. In J. Lunn (Ed.), *Fieldwork in the Global South: Ethical challenges and dilemmas* (pp. 192–205). Abingdon, Oxon: Routledge.

Day, C. (2016). Education and employment transitions: The experiences of young people with caring responsibilities in Zambia. In T. Abede, J. Waters, & T. Skelton (Eds.), *Labouring and learning: Geographies of children and young people* (Vol. 10, pp. 1–26). Singapore: Springer.

Day, C. (2017). Children and young people as providers of care: Perceptions of caregivers and young caregiving in Zambia. In J. Horton & M. Pyer (Eds.), *Children, young people and care* (pp. 144–157). London: Routledge.

Day, C., & Evans, R. (2015). Caring responsibilities, change and transitions in young people's family lives in Zambia. *Journal of Comparative Family Studies, 46*(1), 137–152.

Evans, R., Ribbens McCarthy, J., Bowlby, S., Wouango, J., & Kébé, F. (2017). Producing emotionally sensed knowledge? Reflexivity and emotions in researching responses to death. *International Journal of Social Research Methodology, 20*(6), 585–598.

Hansen, K. T. (2005). Getting stuck in the compound: Some odds against social adulthood in Lusaka, Zambia. *Africa Today*, *51*(4), 2–16.

Hochschild, A. (1979). Emotion work, feeling rules and social structure. *American Journal of Sociology*, *85*, 551–575.

Hubbard, G., Backett-Milburn, K., & Kemmer, D. (2001). Working with emotion: Issues for the researcher in fieldwork and teamwork. *International Journal of Social Research Methodology*, *4*(2), 119–137.

Lutz, C., & White, G. M. (1986). The anthropology of emotions. *Annual Review of Anthropology*, *15*, 405–436.

Mauthner, N., & Doucet, A. (2008). What can be known and how? Narrated subjects. *Qualitative Research*, *8*(3), 399–409.

Middleton, D.R. (1989). Emotional style: The cultural ordering of emotions. *Ethos*. *17*(2), 187–201.

Mullings, B. (1999). Insider or outsider, both or neither: Some dilemmas of interviewing in a cross-cultural setting, *Geoforum, 30*, 337–350.

Roberts, E. (2018). The 'transient insider': Identity and intimacy in home community research. In T. Loughran & D. Mannay (Eds.), *Emotion and the researcher: Sites, subjectivities and relationships* (Vol. 16). Studies in Qualitative Methodology (pp. 113 126). Bingley: Emerald.

Solomon, R. C. (1997). Beyond ontology: Ideation, phenomenology and the cross-cultural study of emotion. *Journal for the Theory of Social Behaviour*, *27*(2/3), 289–303.

Spencer, L., & Pahl, R. (2006). *Rethinking friendship: Hidden solidarities today*. Princeton, NJ: Princeton University Press.

Watts, J. (2008). Emotion, empathy and exit: Reflections on doing ethnographic qualitative research on sensitive topics. *Medical Sociology Online*, *3*(2), 3–14.

Widdowfield, R. (2000). The place of emotions in academic research. *Area*, *32*, 199–208.

Worth, N. (2009). Understanding youth transition as 'becoming': Identity, time and futurity. *Geoforum, 40*, 1050–1060.

CHAPTER 9

SHOCK AND OFFENCE ONLINE: THE ROLE OF EMOTION IN PARTICIPANT ABSENT RESEARCH

Aimee Grant

ABSTRACT

Purpose – *Drawing on a study of data extracts 'mined' from the Internet without interaction with the author, this chapter considers the emotional implications of online 'participant absent research'. The chapter argues that researchers should reflexively consider the ways in which data collection techniques framed as 'passive' actively impact on researchers' emotional lifeworlds. Consequently, it is important to ensure that researchers are adequately prepared and supported.*

Methodology/Approach – *The data introduced in this chapter were constructed around a single case study. This example documents an incident where a woman was asked to leave a sports shop in the UK because she was breastfeeding. Not allowing breastfeeding within a business is illegal in the UK, and this case resulted in a protest. The study involved an analysis of user-generated data from an online news site and Twitter.*

Findings – *Drawing on field notes and conversations with colleagues, the chapter explores the value of reflexivity for successfully managing researchers' emotional responses to disturbing data during the process of analysis.*

Emotion and the Researcher: Sites, Subjectivities, and Relationships
Studies in Qualitative Methodology, Volume 16, 143–158
ISSN: 1042-3192/doi:10.1108/S1042-319220180000016010

Originality/Value – *Whilst the role of emotion is often considered as part of ethnographic practice in studies utilising face-to-face encounters, it is underexplored in the online domain. This chapter presents, through a detailed example, a reflective account of the emotion work required in participant absent research, and offers strategies to reflexively manage emotions.*

Keywords: Reflexivity; emotion; emotion work; documents; documentary analysis; online research; Internet research

INTRODUCTION

In contemporary research, there has been a shift from qualitative approaches being largely reliant on face-to-face methods to gather data, to an expansion of methodologies that omit the participant. This includes the adoption of non-participatory visual methods (Rose, 2012), an increase in the use of documents as data (Atkinson & Coffey, 2010) and, most recently, analysis of pre-existing online content (Grant & Hoyle, 2017). Researchers investigating motherhood have adopted these non-participatory methods to contribute to a comprehensive understanding of maternal subjects. For example, participant absent research has examined how mothers organise the sharing of their excess breastmilk through (online) Facebook milk banks (Perrin, Goodell, Allen, & Fogleman, 2014). Documentary analysis principles have also been used to understand how mothers are perceived in society, drawing on data found in news articles and user-generated online dictionaries (Tyler, 2008). As such, I was interested in adopting these methods to understand public breastfeeding from the perspective of the (potential) observer, through the use of comments posted to an online news site and Twitter, a topic which has been under-researched (see Grant, 2015).

Research on the focus and content of reader-generated comments had been minimal at the time of research (2014). However, it had covered a range of topics including politics and conflict (Abdul-Mageed, 2008), immigration (Krishnamurti, 2013), murder (Hlavach and Freivogel, 2011) and domestic violence (Brossoie, Roberto, & Barrow, 2012). A significant quantity of research has since been undertaken using this method, including work exploring reader-generated comments in stigmatising pregnant women's health behaviours (Carroll & Freeman, 2016).

Attention has also been paid to the particular language used within comments. At its most basic level, a study in South Korea highlighted that the use of swearing increased approval and attention paid to comments (Kwon & Cho, 2017). Online news comments are often offensive and abusive, and arguably have the potential to cause real-world harm (Hlavach & Freivogel, 2011). For example, authors of racist comments used strategies to make their behaviour appear acceptable and in keeping with a shared moral code (Faulkner & Bliuc, 2016). Moreover, misinformation and stigmatisation, which may lead readers to undertake unhelpful behaviours, was found in online news comments regarding smoking (Carroll & Freeman, 2016; Luberto, Hyland, Streck, Temel, & Park, 2016). Accordingly, it has been reported that many online news sites in the USA had chosen to disable the comment function or retain control by strictly moderating content (Hughey & Daniels, 2013). The emotional work required for researchers analysing such comments as data has not yet been explored.

In conducting research using participant absent methods, the researcher is, by necessity, distanced from the producer of the data. Thus the emotional burden may vary compared to more traditional qualitative research techniques. For example, in their study of the Swedish judiciary, Blix and Wettergren (2015, p. 689) defined 'emotional work' as 'a necessary skill required in the building of successful rapport with the research subjects in qualitative research'. This is not required in participant absent research, where the researcher does not build a relationship with participants. Additionally, varying levels of emotion work may be related to varying levels of embodiment (Coffey, 1999). Whilst the individual is very much present in the field during traditional face-to-face data collection, this is not the case in online research, where the researcher may sit thousands of miles from those he/she is researching. However, emotion work is still required when there are no research subjects present, and attempts to understand the emotional labour involved have been reported in the literature in online research (see Eysenbach & Till, 2001; Hudson & Bruckman, 2004; McKee & Porter, 2009; Sixsmith & Murray, 2001). However, the emotional issues raised by research using user-generated comments from online news sites to understand society remain underexplored in the literature.

EMOTIONAL WORK IN PARTICIPANT-PRESENT QUALITATIVE RESEARCH

The practice of undertaking qualitative research with participants present requires researchers to familiarise themselves with the unusual, to display empathy to the circumstances of others' lives (Atkinson, Coffey, & Delamont, 2003), and to be exposed to a range of emotions from their disclosures (Denzin, 1994). In recent years, these practices, and the accompanying emotional response in the researcher, have been reported through confessional literature (Coffey, 1999). The concept of reflexivity being essential to understanding research is often related to research as an embodied, participatory experience (Coffey, 1999; Ezzy, 2010).

A wide range of 'researcher present' qualitative studies have reported how participants have articulated offensive beliefs, or had undertaken distressing crimes. Outputs from these projects provide examples of the ways in which highly emotive data is constructed and framed by participants, sometimes with the active intent of having an effect on researchers (Burr, 2003). For example, in her work on convicted sex offenders, Hudson (2013, p. 178) explored how sex offenders constructed their identities, including 'total denial' of offending behaviour, and participants making references to her own sexuality and their sexual thoughts about her during the fieldwork. Similarly, in Blee's interview study with members of the racist group Ku Klux Klan (KKK),[1] she was intimidated by participants during interviews, and reported that several years later, she still received written threats from participants (Blee, 1998). Both Hudson and Blee experienced considerable fear following their research, and Hudson (2013, p. 7) noted that 'being a researcher does not provide you with any immunity from the intensely emotional issues that arise from research of this kind'. Additionally, qualitative researchers have acknowledged that ethnographic research in dangerous or challenging contexts can result in a loss of researcher control because of the emotive nature of data collection, and this can result in researcher anxiety (Nilan, 2002).

Within qualitative research on the role of pregnancy and motherhood, the role of researcher emotion has been described in terms of embodiment and emotional labour. In her feminist research on women's experiences of in vitro fertilisation (IVF), Carroll (2012) notes that discussion of hope for children, and fears of miscarriage and divorce, were included in women's accounts as a necessary context to their IVF treatment. However, during their disclosures, she described portraying emotional responses that did not reflect her true emotional response, because of her aim to maintain a 'professional' role in the conversation. Alongside the emotion work performed in interviews, reflective field notes highlighted that participants' fertility issues affected the researcher's sense of her own biological, social and emotional identity, even though she was not currently experiencing infertility (Carroll, 2012). The effects of conducting emotion work have also been reported in research on disability and sex where the researcher self-identified as disabled (Liddiard, 2013). Thus, emotion work has been found to affect those who share characteristics with the population under study as well as those who do not.

An empirical study was undertaken with qualitative researchers to understand the emotional experience of undertaking interviews on a variety of subjects (Dickinson-Swift, James, Kippen, & Liamputtong, 2009). The study identified that researchers undertook significant emotion work in their roles, particularly if the research subject was sensitive. It was reported that when interviewees were sad, interviewers often felt sad during or after data collection, and sometimes cried during and following research interviews or following the completion of data collection. Other responses to emotionally challenging data collection reported in the research included physiological changes, including exhaustion and having a raised heart rate. Accordingly, the findings agreed with Coffey's (1999) assertion that face-to-face qualitative research is an embodied experience, and this may result in researchers considering the potential for similarities with participants' experiences in their own lives.

EMOTIONAL WORK IN DOCUMENTARY RESEARCH AND OTHER PARTICIPANT ABSENT METHODS

For Scott (1990, p. 12), 'a document in its most general sense is a written text', but the format of documents has changed over time from hieroglyphs and other markings on walls, to written words marked on parchments, to printed materials. As such, documents in contemporary society include electronic material. Compared to emotion work in participant present studies, there may be variability due to differing levels of embodiment (Coffey, 1999). However, emotion work is still required when there are no research subjects present (see also Sheppard, 2018 [this volume]).

Literature on documentary research, and analysing pre-existing online data, rarely considers the emotional implications of conducting such research, implying that using documents in research is emotionally comfortable. However, research on suicide (Fincham, Scourfield, & Langer, 2007), murder (Seal, 2012), and disability (Grant, 2011) has highlighted the emotional work of analysing reports from the coroner's court, criminal justice system and health service and the accompanying emotional responses in researchers. Fincham et al. (2007) discuss finding photographs from scenes of death in case files, and suggest that, as in face-to-face research, researchers can be unprepared for shocking insights presented to them. This burden was felt to be cumulative during periods of exposure to case files. Researchers reflected on the unbearable distress of victims and reported intrusive thoughts and a need to share the distressing details with other researchers working with the data.

These issues have also been highlighted in secondary analysis of qualitative data detailing children's experiences of abuse (Jackson, Backett-Milburn, & Newall, 2013) and adults' reports of trauma and abuse (Grant, 2011).

THE STUDY

The research aimed to gain an understanding of how public breastfeeding was understood by those viewing it. Analysis of existing research has shown that social media is able to successfully predict a range of phenomena, including voting behaviour and the spread of infectious disease (Sloan et al., 2013). Accordingly, online user-generated content can reflect real-world views (Van Dijk, 2001). Therefore, reader comments from the UK's most popular online news site, MailOnline (Media Week, 2014), in relation to one high-profile case of public breastfeeding, were used as data.

MailOnline is a subsidiary of the *Daily Mail*, a middle-market UK daily newspaper with a right of centre editorial stance. The majority of *Daily Mail* articles are repeated on MailOnline, which is accessible free of charge and funded by advertising. Jennifer Newton's online news item, published on 30 April 2014, from which the comments were taken, related to the case of a breastfeeding mother being asked to leave a UK business, and also described cases in which other breastfeeding mothers had had their rights, as outlined in the UK Equality Act 2010, breached (Newton, 2014). Data were collected from the online news site using the NCapture for NVivo tool for 24 hours following publication of the article. The rationale for this was the likely concentration of the majority of posts within the period when the article was new and highly prominent on the news site (Tsagkias, Weerkamp, & de Rijke, 2010). A total of 884 comments were posted in this time, and initial familiarisation of the data showed a high level of consistency from the majority of the posters.

Data were imported into NVivo 10 for coding. I adopted a critical discourse analysis (CDA) approach, which assumes that discourses found within text or speech are reflective of attitudes found elsewhere in society (Fairclough & Wodak, 1997; Van Dijk, 2001). Within this theoretical framework, data were subjected to discourse analysis as applied to more traditional documents (Gill, 2006). Field notes were written periodically during the analysis process, largely containing analytical memoranda and reflexive content (Sanjek, 1990). Unlike my experience of having to self-consciously write field notes during opportune moments and safe encounters in participant present research (Grant, 2013), I was free to update my notes as I collected, explored and analysed the data.

The data collected were largely focused on the (un)acceptability of the nurturing (non-sexual) female breast in public space. This discussion of female bodies was used as a vehicle to foreground acceptable female and mothering behaviours and, by association, the role of men and women as sexual beings and sexual predators (Grant, 2015, 2016). Thus, whilst the data collection did not require me (a female researcher) to be embodied, the research was very focused on bodies, sexuality, place and safety. The Cardiff University School of Medicine ethics committee stated that, as all data were already in the public domain, the research did not require ethical review.

WHOSE SIDE WAS I ON?

In undertaking this research, I reflected extensively on my own views towards infant feeding (Becker, 1966) and my belief in the superiority of breastmilk over formula-feeding. These principles were based on my understanding of the academic literature, rather than a personal experience of motherhood. They were also related to my evaluation of a breastfeeding support service (Grant, Sims, Tedstone, & Ashton, 2013), where I undertook focus groups with mothers about health information on behalf of the UK National Health Service.

Research has shown that in the UK, babies who are formula-fed are more likely to have stomach upsets, poorer cognitive development and behavioural problems; they also lack the immunity of their breastfed peers (Renfrew et al., 2012). Additionally, there are financial implications. The cost of formula feeding a baby prior to weaning at four to six months can amount to hundreds, if not thousands, of pounds (or dollars), and this money might be better used elsewhere in families who are struggling with the cost of a new child (Hamilton, 2012).

Nevertheless, I understand that breastfeeding can be physically and emotionally challenging for women who want to breastfeed; and not all mothers want to initiate or continue breastfeeding (Woods, Chesser, & Wipperman, 2013; Grant, Mannay, & Marzella, 2017). I appreciate that both breastfeeding and formula-feeding can be feminist choices, suited to women's individual circumstances (Shaw & Bartlett, 2010), and acknowledge that there is a strong pressure to breastfeed in the UK, which may result in difficult emotional responses for women who are unable or disinclined to breastfeed (Dowling & Brown, 2013). Additionally, I believe that the protection that women are awarded to breastfeed in public without harassment in the UK Equality Act 2010 is right and proper, and should be promoted and enforced. I also object to the activities of infant formula companies, in high-, mid- and low-income countries, which exploit women's fears regarding breastfeeding and regularly breach the World Health Organization's code of ethics on marketing infant formula in order to make a profit (Heinig, 2006).

More widely, I hold the feminist belief that women are not inferior to men, nor should they be treated as such. I find the scrutiny that women's bodies come under, particularly in relation to breastfeeding (Dowling & Brown, 2013), uncomfortable and unnecessary, and I believe that bodies, male or female, can be both sexual and non-sexual, although this is not currently reflected in Western culture (Grant, 2016). I am appalled by the level of normalised minor (and less minor) sexual assaults in everyday life (Phipps & Smith, 2012), and I have contributed my own experiences to the Everyday Sexism Project.[2] To conclude, my position on infant feeding is made up of conflicting and competing discourses, drawn from both the academic literature and personal experience. To more concisely answer Becker's (1966) question of taking sides, within this research, I was on the side of mothers, regardless of their infant feeding method.

SHOCK, OFFENCE AND EMOTION WORK: ANALYSING ONLINE COMMENTS

During the familiarisation process and the initial period of coding, I regularly read out extracts that I found particularly offensive to another colleague and would discuss the research with other qualitative researchers. Initially, I found the comments incredibly distasteful and shocking. When discussing the data with colleagues, family and friends I ranted; I had to share the things I had read, to somehow dilute them by having other people agree that they were both 'offensive' and not 'normal', as has occurred in other studies (Fincham et al., 2007; see also Lisiak & Krzyżowski, 2018 [this volume]).

For example, on the first day of analysis, I found the following comment particularly disagreeable. This comment was the sixth of over 800 comments collected. The poster stated that breastfeeding women are 'arrogant', public breastfeeding is 'distasteful' and that mothers should spend time expressing their milk in advance to enable bottle-feeding in public so that the poster would not have 'to see it':

> I am getting sick and tired of reading about these breast feeding mothers and wish they would just go away. I don't want to see it in public and find it very distasteful especially when they do it in a place where people eat. How arrogant of them to impose this on people. What about expressing it earlier and giving them a bottle when out and about?

A second comment from early in the analysis period suggested that women who breastfed in public were 'perform(ing)' and may be inviting an audience (of more than one) to 'watch' women feeding their infants:

'It's the most natural thing in the world'.... Then presumably you wouldn't object if we all gathered around to watch you perform this 'natural' function?

When reading and coding this comment, I was aware that my heart rate was elevated, and my face flushed. As a woman who has often received unwanted sexual attention from men, I found this statement threatening; the author appeared to be justifying aggressive behaviour with reference to the victim's behaviour, as is common in discourse on rape and other sexual assaults (Cowley, 2014). In the middle of a conversation with a colleague about this post and others sharing a similar victim-blaming discourse, we were interrupted by another colleague who commented 'You look really angry! Are you OK?'

Other comments which I found offensive claimed to be pro-breastfeeding, but provided lengthy descriptions of the type of routine breastfeeding practices they found unacceptable, largely focusing on the visibility of breasts. Alongside this, one poster suggested that the legal protection afforded to women by the UK Equality Act 2010 should be void 'IF...members of staff object' to breastfeeding on their premises:

Breast-feed all you wish in public, but you flaming well do not have the right to throw it wherever you feel to because it is in the public domain. Shop owners, vendors, managers, have policies, their policies, shaped in the way they wish to convey their businesses and business etiquette. The law should not intervene nor legislate for it on the premises IF the concerned members of staff object.

At this time, I wrote large sections with lots of exclamation marks in my field notes; my writing took on the passionate tone seen in some of the pro-breastfeeding posts woven among the many offensive anti-breastfeeding posts. For example, on day one when I was familiarising myself with the data, I wrote:

I can't believe some of these comments – v offensive!...How often do you actually get squirted with breastmilk or flashed when someone breastfeeds in public?!!! Loads of misogyny – how many women are actually flashers compared to men! Also, ideas that women are putting themselves in danger by BF because men might not be able to resist touching or staring at them! Completely absurd! (Field notes, 30/04/14)

I found it compelling to analyse the data; I took few breaks and worked late into the night. The more offensive comments, distasteful language about women's bodies, and suggestions that women who breastfed in public were inviting sexual assault, returned to my mind frequently. I found myself feeling tired and drained by the quantity of sexist and misogynistic posts, particularly in light of the presence of sexual breasts, which accompanied the news item and comments:

> Today it seems as though almost every poster wants the mums to be 'discreet' and 'cover up'. I did a search (of the data) and the word 'discreet' (or discreetly, discretion etc.) is used 51 times – the vast majority of them are negative. I can't believe they're saying these things with a strip of photos and headlines down the right hand side of the page with loads of pictures of (sometimes very) young women in bikinis and low cut tops. (Field notes, 03/05/14)

About a week later, having grown to understand the largely repetitive discourses in the data, I had undertaken about half of the initial coding. I spoke to a colleague about the potential structure for an empirical paper over lunch in a detached manner. One draft heading was 'exhibitionism and flashing' which can be illustrated by the following comment:

> I'm a mother! Notice me! Look at my breasts…(I'm pretending I'm just getting them out to breast feed but really I just want you to notice me!) Get A room idiots. Have a bit of sophistication #yuck

Another salient theme was 'breastfeeding akin to urination/defecation':

> All these people saying 'its natural' make me cross. So is defecating, but you wouldn't want to see people do that in shops would you? It is gross. Put them away love.

The third focused on 'women's behaviour', and suggested public breastfeeding had a negative impact on their children: 'Like dogs on street corners. Poor children'. These comments were not isolated cases; my coding highlighted 132 cases of 'exhibitionism', 99 cases that considered public breastfeeding as akin to another bodily function (urination, defecation, sexual intercourse, masturbation) and 56 reports of women endangering their child's well-being. Alongside this, sexist language was very common; women who breastfeed in public were referred to as: 'silly', 'disgusting' and 'the mumsnet[3] brigade'.

Calls for these women to modify their infant feeding behaviour ('Put them away love' and many others) were so common that one day, I wrote in my field notes that it felt as though every comment received this code:

> I had no idea that 'calls to action' (Gill, 2006) would be so common. Again, mostly women are asked to cover their bodies. The idea that women are consciously 'flashing' is absurd, but seems to be quite widely reported – not sure why they think women would get any (sexual) gratification… (Field notes 04/05/14)

A few days later, however, I had become immune to the negative power of these messages. I was able to report the details without feeling the original emotional connection. My colleague asked, 'Doesn't it make you angry?' At this point, I realised that I had moved beyond anger, shock and outrage to feeling fortunate for the excellent quality of my data. The repulsive statements, I knew, made my paper stronger and more likely to be published. My work has an overarching aim to contribute towards making society fairer and healthier. Therefore, this 'stronger paper', which would form part of a body of work, may in the long term help to improve breastfeeding rates. Accordingly, this positive impact would be drawn from material that, in its original form, would be likely to have a negative effect on breastfeeding intentions among anyone who read them. On my return to the office, I thought about the discussion and my feelings about the data:

> I'm shocked by how quickly I've become used to the offensive language and terminology. I still notice it, as I code, but I'm distanced from it (anaesthetised by the research?). I wonder if this is...how people coped in Jonathan (Scourfield)'s work[4] on suicide? I am still so much more angry when coding marketing materials (from infant formula companies), but I can ignore the offensive tones here. Perhaps the differential power balance – infant formula companies pose as providing health promotion advice but profit from reluctance among mothers to breastfeed publicly, but these individuals don't gain anything from this...(Field notes, 06/05/14)

Following this discussion, I began to formulate the idea for this chapter, whilst continuing to analyse the data at a more leisurely pace. I forced myself to regularly reflect on my emotional state during this process, and acknowledged that I had become distant from the negativity in the data. Dickinson-Swift et al. (2009) also discussed strategies of distancing, reporting the ways in which respondents facilitated their detachment or withdrawal from the sensitive topic by attempting to facilitate good rapport through an objective, neutral interviewer position.

However, despite my more detached emotional position, I struggled to accept some of the language and assumptions that women were inviting men to 'stand around and stare at them' whilst they breastfed on a bench in a shop. It made me concerned that women who were breastfeeding in public were vulnerable to sexual assault, as well as negative comments reported in mothers' experiences (Dowling & Brown, 2013). Moreover, in a wider sense, these posters, some of whom reported that they were women, believed that women were to blame when men attacked them. I was already aware that this view existed and was broadly accepted by sections of Western society (Cowley, 2014); but to be so closely exposed to a large volume of hateful comments

was unusual. I also found it difficult to understand why so many of the posters made negative comments about women's bodies, particularly focused on
their breasts. Alongside this, many comments suggested that the women were
lazy, scroungers, poor mothers and generally inconsiderate. I found this hard
to reconcile with my image of motherhood as one of intense activity and
unrelenting workload (Stearns, 2010).

IMPLICATIONS FOR PRACTICE AND CONCLUDING THOUGHTS

The importance of emotion work has been recognised in relation to researchers conducting participant present qualitative research (Dickinson-Swift et al.,
2009), and some forms of participant absent research (Seal, 2012). However,
the emotional lifeworlds of researchers analysing pre-existing online content
as data remain underexplored in the literature. Moreover, in my experience of
publishing from this study, reviewers have asked for this emotional content
and reflexivity to be removed. This chapter has aimed to address this lacuna
by presenting my emotional journey of anger via emotional distance to a
reflexive position of distaste.

Recording this journey in field notes was emotionally beneficial to me as
the researcher, and also in the analytical process (Sanjek, 1990); however,
the process was characterised by upsetting feelings, unwanted emotions and
physical manifestations of stress. Therefore, when undertaking documentary
analysis on emotive subjects, the emotional needs of the researcher should be
considered from the outset. Researchers should schedule regular opportunities to debrief with supervisors or colleagues. Alongside this, the use of field
notes to reflect on how the emotion work affects the analysis and potential
findings should be considered (Coffey, 2009). In reporting the findings of participant absent research on topics experienced as offensive or disturbing, it is
essential that such reflexivity is included as a valid part of analysis.

NOTES

1. The KKK is a name adopted by small unconnected right-wing white suprema-
cist 'Christian' groups in the USA since the 1940s. It had previously been used since
the 1860s in national campaigns against African Americans.

2. The Everyday Sexism Project (https://everydaysexism.com/) is an online collection of experiences of people who have experienced sexism, offensive comments and sexual assaults.

3. Mumsnet (www.mumsnet.com) was the UK's largest online website for parents at the time of the research. The website contains discussion boards for peer-to-peer parenting advice and space for members to blog their parenting experiences.

4. This reference corresponds to the citation for Fincham et al. (2007).

ACKNOWLEDGEMENTS

I would like to acknowledge the anonymous individuals from whom data was obtained, and Dr Lucy Bennett for advice on data collection issues. Thanks are also due to the editors, Dr Tracey Loughran and Dr Dawn Mannay, and to Dr Sara Delamont and the anonymous reviewers for their comments on earlier drafts of this chapter

REFERENCES

Abdul-Mageed, M. M. (2008). Online news sites and journalism 2.0: Reader comments on Al Jazeera Arabic. *Journal for a Global Sustainable Information Society, 6*(2), 59–76.

Atkinson, P., & Coffey, A. (2010). Analysing documentary realities. In D. Silverman (Ed.) *Qualitative Research* (pp. 77–92). London: SAGE.

Atkinson, P, Coffey, A., & Delamont, S. (2003). *Key themes in qualitative research.* Walnut Creek, CA: Alta Mira.

Becker, H. S. (1966). Whose side are we on. *Social Problems, 14*, 239–247.

Blee, K. M. (1998). White-knuckle research: Emotional dynamics in fieldwork with racist activists. *Qualitative Sociology, 21*(4), 381–399.

Blix, S. B., & Wettergren, A. (2015). The emotional labour of gaining and maintaining access to the field. *Qualitative Research, 15*(6), 688–704.

Brossoie, N., Roberto, K. A., & Barrow, K. M. (2012). Making sense of intimate partner violence in late life: Comments from online news readers. *The Gerontologist, 52*(6), 792–801.

Burr, V. (2003). *Social constructionism.* London: Routledge.

Carroll, K. (2012). Infertile? The emotional labour of sensitive and feminist research methodologies. *Qualitative Research, 13*(5), 546–561.

Carroll, B., & Freeman, B. (2016). Content analysis of comments posted on Australian online news sites reporting a celebrity admitting smoking while pregnant. *Public Health Research & Practice, 26*(5), e2651660.

Coffey, A. (1999). *The ethnographic self: Fieldwork and the representation of identity.* London: Sage.

Cowley, A. D. (2014). "Let's get drunk and have sex": The complex relationship of alcohol, gender, and sexual victimization. *Journal of Interpersonal Violence, 29*(7), 1258–1278.

Denzin, N. K. (1994). *On understanding emotion*. Piscataway, NJ: Transaction.

Dickinson-Swift, V. James, E. L., Kippen, S., & Liamputtong, P. (2009). Researching sensitive topics: Qualitative research as emotion work. *Qualitative Research*, *9*(1), 61–79.

Dowling, S., & Brown, A. (2013). An exploration of the experiences of mothers who breast-feed long-term: What are the issues and why does it matter? *Breastfeeding Medicine*, *8*(1), 45–52.

Eysenbach, G., & Till, J. E. (2001). Ethical issues in qualitative research on internet communities. *British Medical Journal*, *323*, 1103–1105.

Ezzy, D. (2010). Qualitative interviewing as an embodied emotional performance. *Qualitative Inquiry*, *16*(3), 163–170.

Fairclough, N., & Wodak, R. (1997). Critical discourse analysis. In T.A. van Dijik (Ed.), *Discourses as Social Interaction* (pp. 258–284). London: Sage.

Faulkner, N., & Bliuc, A.-M. (2016). 'It's okay to be racist': Moral disengagement in online discussions of racist incidents in Australia. *Ethnic and Racial Stuides*, *39*(4), 2545–2563.

Fincham, B., Scourfield, J., & Langer, S. (2007). *The emotional impact of working with disturbing secondary data*. Qualiti: Cardiff.

Gill, R. (2006). Discourse analysis. In J. Scott (Ed.), *Documentary research* (pp. 209–232). London: Sage.

Grant, A. (2011). *New Labour, welfare reform and conditionality: Pathways to work for incapacity benefit claimants*. PhD thesis, Cardiff University, Cardiff.

Grant, A. (2013). Welfare reform, increased conditionality and discretion: Jobcentre Plus advisers' experiences of targets and sanctions. *Journal of Poverty and Social Justice*, *21*(2), 165–176.

Grant, A. (2015). '#discrimination': The online response to a case of a breastfeeding mother being ejected from a UK retail premises. *Journal of Human Lactation*, *32*(1), 141–151.

Grant, A. (2016). 'I… don't want to see you flashing your bits around': Exhibitionism, othering and good motherhood in perceptions of public breastfeeding. *Geoforum*, *71*, 52–61.

Grant, A., & Hoyle, L. (2017). Print media representations of United Kingdom accident and emergency treatment targets: Winter 2014–2015. *Journal of Clinical Nursing*, *26*(23–24), 4425–4435. DOI:10.1111/jocn.13772.

Grant, A., Mannay, D., & Marzella, R. (2017). 'People try and police your behaviour': The impact of surveillance on mothers' and grandmothers' perceptions and experiences of infant feeding. *Families, Relationships and Societies*. DOI:10.1332/2046743 17X14888886530223

Grant, A., Sims, L., Tedstone, S., & Ashton, K. (2013). *A qualitative evaluation of breastfeeding support groups and peer supporters in Wales*. Cardiff: Public Health Wales.

Hamilton, K. (2012). Low-income families and coping through brands: Inclusion or stigma? *Sociology*, *46*(1), 74–90.

Heinig, M. J. (2006). The International Code of Marketing of Breastmilk Substitutes: The challenge is choice. *Journal of Human Lactation*, *22*(3), 265–266.

Hlavach, L., & Freivogel, W. H. (2011). Ethical implications of anonymous comments posted to online news stories. *Journal of Mass Media Ethics*, *26*(1), 21–37.

Hudson, K. (2013). *Offending identities*. London: Routledge.

Hudson, J. M., & Bruckman, A. (2004). "Go away": Participant objections to being studied and the ethics of chatroom research. *Information Society*, *20*(2), 127–139.

Hughey, M. W., & Daniels, J. (2013). Racist comments at online news sites: A methodological dilemma for discourse analysis. *Media, Culture and Society*, *35*(3), 332–347.

Jackson, S., Backett-Milburn, K., & Newall, E. (2013). Researching distressing topics: Emotional reflexivity and emotional labor in the secondary analysis of children and young people's narratives of abuse. *Sage Open, 3*(2), 1–12.

Krishnamurti, S. (2013). Queue-jumpers, terrorists, breeders: Representations of Tamil migrants in Canadian popular media. *South Asian Diaspora, 5*(1), 139–157.

Kwon, K. H., & Cho, D. (2017). Swearing effects on citizen-to-citizen commenting online: A large-scale exploration of political versus nonpolitical online news sites. *Social Science Computer Review, 35*(1), 84–102.

Liddiard, K. (2013). Reflections on the process of researching disabled people's sexual lives. *Sociological Research Online, 18*(3), 10.

Lisiak, A., & Krzyżowski, L. (2018). With a little help from my colleagues: Notes on emotional support in a qualitative longitudinal research project. In T. Loughran & D. Mannay (Eds.), *Emotion and the researcher: Sites, subjectivities and relationships* (Vol. 16). Studies in Qualitative Methodology (pp. 33–48). Bingley: Emerald.

Luberto, C. M., Hyland, K. A., Streck, J. M., Temel, B., & Park, E.R. (2016). Stigmatic and sympathetic attitudes toward cancer patients who smoke: A qualitative analysis of an online discussion board forum. *Nicotine & Tobacco Research, 18*(12), 2194–2201.

McKee, H. A., & Porter, J. E. (2009). Playing a good game: Ethical issues in researching MMOGs and virtual worlds. *International Journal of Internet Research Ethics, 2*(1), 5–37.

Media Week. (2014). *Newspaper ABCs: Digital statistics for January 2014.* Retrieved from http://www.mediaweek.co.uk/article/1281725/newspaper-abcs-digital-statistics-january-2014. Accessed on August 9, 2017.

Newton, J. (2014). Angry mothers stage mass breastfeeding protest at Sports Direct store that asked woman to leave because it was against 'company policy'. *Mail Online,* 30 April.

Nilan, P. (2002). 'Dangerous fieldwork' re-examined: The question of researcher subject position. *Qualitative Research, 2*(3), 363–386.

Perrin, M. T., Goodell, L. S., Allen, J. C., & Fogleman, A. (2014). A mixed-methods observational study of human milk sharing communities on Facebook. *Breastfeeding Medicine, 9,* 128–134.

Phipps, A., & Smith, G. (2012). Violence against women students in the UK: Time to take action. *Gender and Education, 24*(4), 357–373.

Renfrew, M. J., Pokhrel, S., Quigley, M., McCormick, F., Fox-Rushby, J., Dodds, R., Duffy, S., Trueman, P., & Williams, A. (2012). *Preventing disease and saving resources: The potential contribution of increasing breastfeeding rates in the UK.* London: UNICEF.

Rose, G. (2012). *Visual methodologies: An introduction to researching with visual materials.* London: Sage.

Sanjek, R. (1990). *Fieldnotes: The makings of anthropology.* Ithaca, NY: Cornell University Press.

Scott, J. (1990). *A matter of record.* Cambridge: Polity Press.

Seal, L. (2012). Emotion and allegiance in researching four mid-20th-century cases of women accused of murder. *Qualitative Research, 12*(6), 686–701.

Shaw, R., & Bartlett, A. (Eds.) (2010). *Giving breastmilk: Body ethics and contemporary breastfeeding practice.* Bradford, ON: Demeter Press.

Sheppard, L. (2018). 'Poor old mixed-up Wales': Entering the debate on bilingualism, multiculturalism and racism in Welsh literature and culture. In T. Loughran & D. Mannay (Eds.), *Emotion and the researcher: Sites, subjectivities and relationships* (Vol. 16). Studies in Qualitative Methodology (pp. 197–212). Bingley: Emerald.

Sixsmith, J., & Murray, C. D. (2001). Ethical issues in the documentary data analysis of internet posts and archives. *Qualitative Health Research, 11*(3), 423–432.

Sloan, L., Morgan, J., Housley, W., Williams, M., Edwards, A., Michael, A., Burnap, P., & Rana, O. (2013). Knowing the Tweeters: Deriving sociologically relevant demographics from Twitter. *Sociological Research Online*, *18*(3). Retrieved from http://www.socresonline.org.uk/18/3/7.html. Accessed on January 4, 2018.

Stearns, C. A. (2010). The breast pump. In R. Shaw & A. Bartlett (Eds.), *Giving breastmilk: Body ethics and contemporary breastfeeding practices,* (pp. 11–23). Bradford, ON: Demeter Press.

Tsagkias, M., Weerkamp, W., & de Rijke, M. (2010). News comments: Exploring, modeling, and online prediction. *Advances in Information Retrieval*, *5993*, 191–203.

Tyler, I. (2008). 'Chav mum chav scum': Class disgust in contemporary Britain. *Feminist Media Studies*, *8*(1), 17–34.

Van Dijk, T. A. (2001). Critical discourse analysis. In D. Schiffrin, D. Tannen, & H. E. Hamilton (Eds.), *The handbook of discourse analysis* (pp. 352–371). Oxford: Blackwell.

Woods, N. K., Chesser, A. K., & Wipperman, J. (2013). Describing adolescent breastfeeding environments through focus groups in an urban community. *Journal of Primary Care & Community Health*, *4*(4), 307–310.

CHAPTER 10

LOVE & SORROW: THE ROLE OF EMOTION IN EXHIBITION DEVELOPMENT AND VISITOR EXPERIENCE

Deborah Tout-Smith

ABSTRACT

Purpose – *The chapter explores the development and impact of the Museums Victoria's exhibition World War I: Love & Sorrow, which aimed to present an honest, graphic and challenging account of the experience and effect of World War I on Australian society. The paper describes the exhibition content and uses a range of methodological approaches to study its emotional and other impacts.*

Methodology/Approach – *A range of evaluation methodologies are used: visitor observation and summative evaluation collected in the months after the exhibition opened, and quantitative and qualitative studies produced in 2017. Comparative assessment of a large sample of visitor comments cards was also undertaken. The more recent evaluations focused particularly on emotional impacts.*

Emotion and the Researcher: Sites, Subjectivities, and Relationships
Studies in Qualitative Methodology, Volume 16, 159–176
Copyright © 2018 by Emerald Publishing Limited
All rights of reproduction in any form reserved
ISSN: 1042-3192/doi:10.1108/S1042-319220180000016011

Findings – *The research finds that emotion is central to the success of the exhibition: underpinning the exhibition concept, guiding the research process and selection of interpretative approaches, and shaping visitor response.*

Originality/Value – *The emotional aspects of museum work have received relatively little attention, and few studies focused on the evaluation of visitor emotions have been published. The chapter uses a case study to highlight the role of emotions in museum exhibitions and historical interpretation, argues for more central place for emotions in historical enquiry, and addresses concerns about subjectivity, authenticity and evidence.*

Keywords: Museums; emotions; visitors; evaluation; authenticity

INTRODUCTION

Museums Victoria's exhibition *World War I: Love & Sorrow* opened at Melbourne Museum in 2014, marking 100 years since the outbreak of war. The exhibition aimed to present an honest, graphic and challenging account of the experience and effect of World War I on Australian society, and to shift understandings of the war towards its costs and consequences. The exhibition follows eight personal stories through the chronology of the war and post-war years, ending with films of descendants reflecting on the experience of their loved ones and the impact of the war on their families. Research for the exhibition actively sought to interrogate the emotional landscapes of the war: how it felt to live in those times, endure those experiences, survive through the post-war years and try to make sense of it all as the past receded from living memory. Our team actively sought interpretative approaches which maximised access to these emotional landscapes.

THE MUSEUM CONTEXT

Before the centenary of World War I, the representation of the war in cultural institutions paid little attention to emotional engagement or to the graphic nature of war, as recent commentators have noted (McKernan, 2015; Witcomb, 2016, p. 206). The Australian War Memorial, for example, stepped tentatively through the minefield of representation, the dead depicted largely whole, rarely in photographs; the wounded with faces and minds largely intact; families in mourning but not collapsing in distress. A reverence sometimes bordering on religiosity, a sense of the heroic, pervaded the loss of life and provided a suite of words to soften the blow, as Paul Fussell noted so long ago (1975): *sacrifice, the fallen, the brave.*[1]

In recent years, though, museums have increasingly mounted exhibitions which build emotional connections, offer alternative ways of seeing and support social change. Examples at Museums Victoria include *Identity: Yours, Mine, Ours* (opened 2011, Immigration Museum) and *First Peoples* (opened 2013, Bunjilaka Aboriginal Cultural Centre), both developed with close community contact, rich with personal voices and including challenging and sometimes disturbing content. Each includes consciously affective elements and deep emotional content, strengthening the impact of the story on visitors and bringing the narrative into the present. *First Peoples,* for example, presents the devastating impact of smallpox on Aboriginal communities through a contemporary art installation by Koori artist Maree Clarke, showing images of mourners wearing *kopi* caps coupled with a haunting soundscape.

Importantly, these types of exhibition acknowledge the past that cannot be presented as objectifiable, capable of being teased away from the complex internal emotional lives of its players and their communities, or from the internal worlds of the curators who represent them. These exhibitions present a case for the incorporation of emotions in both research and interpretation, and argue that the emotional responses of visitors should be encouraged, supported and shaped to develop deeper understandings of the past. Some scholars have identified market drivers for this increased focus on emotions: Del Chiappa, Andreu, and Gallarza (2014, p. 421) note that 'museums, to maintain their competitiveness, are changing the way they approach their target, becoming more able to deliver experiences and to inspire emotions than effectively present "objectives"'.

In this environment, the centenary of World War I offered an opportunity to mount an exhibition built on personal feelings, with primary sources laid open to view, inviting deep personal engagement by visitors. Marina Larsson's recently published *Shattered Anzacs: Living with the Scars of War*, with its notions of suffering, of war's toll realised through slow, bitter wounds, helped to shape my ideas for the exhibition.

FRAMING THE PROJECT

Exhibitions, like other research projects, are a complex interplay between research and outcome. We start with a broad concept, then begin to imagine how to interpret the concept so it becomes accessible to our audience and generates meaningful engagement. We then use this concept as a frame onto which our research is built. In the case of *Love & Sorrow*, our approach was driven by what several scholars have called the 'experiential paradigm', which considers visitor behaviour subjective, emotional and symbolic (in contrast to objective and rational behaviours), with authenticity and uniqueness as important underpinnings (Del Chiappa et al., p. 422, cite Hirschman and Holbrook, 1982, amongst others). This approach was appropriate to our key messages, our content and our desire to create an exhibition that could change visitors' minds. As Mazda (2015), Hayes (2016) and many others have noted, visitors are more receptive to new feelings, ideas and ways of seeing when in an emotional state, in part because their own memories are being triggered and accessed. And there is arguably an even greater benefit: an authentic and emotions-based approach could allow us to come closer to representing lived experience.

Our approach required two things: research that interrogated emotional experiences, and an exhibition environment that supported the communication of those experiences and encouraged emotional engagement. Inclusion of primary sources would also be critical. The scholars who formed the academic advisory committee for *Love & Sorrow* were selected for their particular engagement with emotional histories, and their brave approach to tackling challenging content such as deep mourning, wounding, mental illness and suicide: Marina Larsson, Joy Damousi, Alistair Thomson, Peter Stanley, Bart Ziino and Kerry Neale. Significantly, the exhibition drew on their many years of research, including personal stories of veterans and their families, underlining the length of time it takes to develop the deep connections needed to produce emotional histories.

It was also important, at this early stage of interpretative and research planning, to acknowledge the particular qualities that war as a topic brings. At its most basic level, war is an act of violence. The moment we try to get close to the experience of soldiers, or those in intimate relationships with soldiers such as family members, we expose ourselves to extremes of behaviour and experience. Pain, anguish, terror and desperation are the currencies of war. To fully interrogate war, and to represent it accurately in a museum, it is necessary to relinquish our desire to uplift visitors, and to include content that can be emotionally uncomfortable, disturbing and distressing. We need to accept that sometimes the past 'enters the present as an intruder, not a welcome guest' (*Traumascapes*, 2005, p. 12, quoted in Byrne, 2013, p. 607).

The interpretative approaches we selected drew on techniques honed by the film industry: building engagement and empathy through interconnecting narrative, imagery, sound, personal connection, character development, one or more climaxes and an ending that leaves a lasting impact. And we could offer more: artefacts of the physical world, in front of visitors, right at the moment where they have the most intense meaning.

We selected a chronological structure within which personal stories could gradually unfold, in contrast to the more typical museum presentation of personal stories in single cases or contexts. This would allow visitors to follow a person not knowing the outcome, more closely mirroring lived experience, and evoking emotions such as fear and worry of the unknown. As Willis has noted, when a life is re-enacted its loss is more keenly felt (2014, cited in Hayes, 2016, p. 58). I was particularly inspired by Peter Englund's then-recently published book *The Beauty and the Sorrow: An Intimate History of the First World War*, which follows 20 real-life characters through the chronology of the war, building in power as each faces the vagaries of their fate. I wanted to extend this framework into the present too: how had the war affected, in the long-term, the families and loved ones of those who lived through it? I wanted to create an emotional history, 'mapped across the canvas' of individual lives, as Byrne says, even smaller and closer in scale than community (2013, p. 597).

Our main 'characters' were selected for the power and poignancy of their narratives, each with mementoes and personal diaries or letters to support their story and a family member who could reflect on its meaning today. The characters also needed to work effectively as a group, reflecting diversity of experience and context, underlining how much and how little was shared by those who lived through the times. In the end, we chose a teenage telegraph messenger, an orchardist, a butcher with a young family, a coach-builder, a mother, a nurse, two Aboriginal brothers and two Jewish brothers who fought for Germany.

Amongst the characters who had already risen to the attention of several scholars was the orchardist Frank Roberts.[2] Frank married his sweetheart Ruby before he embarked overseas with the 21st Battalion in 1917, aged 27. Their daughter Nancy was born later that year. Ruby sent Frank a parcel containing one of a pair of booties worn by Nancy (see Fig. 1), with a note purporting to be from her: 'Daddy dear this is my shoe / can you put it on dear daddy I wonder?...Mummy tells me its 16 months since she saw you.

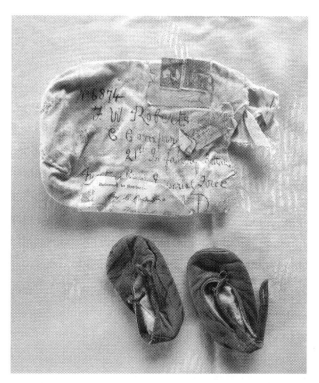

Fig. 1.   Baby Booties and Parcel Sent by Ruby to Frank Roberts, Marked 'Undeliverable', 1918. *Source*: Museums Victoria/Photographer: Deborah Tout-Smith (2013).

Come home soon…Good luck to you daddy / Mummy and I want you home so badly / lots of love from your little daughter Nance'.

Frank never received the parcel: he was killed at Mont St Quentin in September 1918. The unopened parcel was sent back to Ruby. She saved it all her life and passed it onto Nancy, whose daughter Jilba lent the booties and parcel to Museums Victoria for *Love & Sorrow*. Jilba is shown on film at the end of the exhibition, deeply moved as she remembers that her grandmother would still cry when remembering Frank many decades later. The moment allows visitors to both witness and share something of her grief, in the 'enchanted landscape of love where objects and places have a peculiar vibrancy' (Byrne 2013, p. 599).

THE EXHIBITION

Much of the material culture in the exhibition focuses on the personal and poignant: letters from a worried mother to her son; a runner's arm band worn by a teenage telegraph messenger as he fled through the trenches, soon to be buried alive; a simple message posted in a German newspaper, 'in deepest sorrow', for the death of a beloved son. Young Ethel Kemp struggles to write to her father serving far away, her words fading off the postcard as she says 'dear daddy I am waiting and watching day by day for you' (see *Fig. 2*). These objects were chosen for their ability to carry emotional power – they are sticky objects, to use the term coined by Sara Ahmed and extended by scholars such as Andrea Witcomb (2016, p. 214). They lie in 'quiet ambush' for the visitor (Byrne, 2013, p. 604).

The display cases are laid out casually, with bits of fabric and other props, to create a sense of a personal, intimate space, breaking from the regimented lines of typical museum displays that hint at the impersonal and objective. The cases instead become mini-vignettes, fragments of the everyday, the lived-in 'object world' (Byrne, 2013, p. 600). Between the cases are enlarged photographs, focusing on people. Some are very disturbing: wounded soldiers receiving triage, devastating facial wounds, a burial in the mud marked with a cross and dead bodies at Guillemont Farm, northern France, where the curatorial voice explains how people actually die in war:

> Soldiers were said to 'fall' in battle or 'make the ultimate sacrifice'. These words softened the blow of what really happened: they were blown apart, shot, gassed, stabbed, buried alive, crushed or drowned. Large numbers also died of disease or infections from the putrid battlefields.

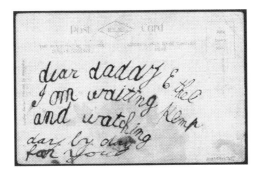

Fig. 2.   Ethel Kemp's Postcard to Her Father Albert, circa 1917. *Source*: Museum Victoria/Copyright Estate of Ethel Kemp.

In the longer panels each text is written in narrative form, mirroring the narrative approach in the exhibition as a whole. Adjectives and descriptions of personal feelings are used, breaking the mould of the deliberately impersonal (or impartial) museum voice. Different perspectives are included, such as women who spoke against the war and men interned because they (or their ancestors) had emigrated from 'enemy' nations.

In the Glencorse Wood interactive (see *Fig. 3*), words work in a different way. As visitors look across photographs of the terrible war landscapes east of Ypres between 1915 and 1917, and watch their shadows projected dynamically as the scene changes from the battlefield into the green forest of today, behind them are the names of the 1,771 men of the Australian, British and German armies killed in the vicinity in little over a week. The names are organised alphabetically, no matter for whom they fought, in the same way that the remains of so many of them now lie together in the forest, indistinguishable. The Glencorse Wood interactive has thus become more than 'an emblem of the lives that were lost there' (Waterton & Watson, 2015, p. 99) – in naming those people it has reclaimed them, bringing them from the symbolic underworld into the world of the lived. The unspeakable personal impact of those deaths is underlined with a quote from a single family:

Fig. 3.   The Glencorse Wood Interactive, Love & Sorrow Exhibition, 2015.
Source: Museums Victoria/Photographer: Benjamin Healley.

Tread softly by
Our hearts are here
With our beloved Jack[3]

We also worked carefully with sound in this space to boost the emotional response and further construct a sense of place: the birds of Glencorse Wood today can be heard, giving way to faint gunfire. These sounds interplay with patriotic music drifting through from the exhibition entrance, becoming increasingly ironic as pain, pathos and suffering build.

The other key immersive space focuses on the Queen's Hospital in Sidcup, Kent, where facial wounds were treated. The graphic display includes an operating table and surgical tools, shown against a large image of a Sidcup theatre, and prostheses used to cover and complete appallingly damaged faces. Four personal stories are presented, including photographs, paintings and plaster casts, illustrating the progression from wounding, through repeated operations, to some semblance of recovery.

The visitor's journey ends with short films of descendants, reflecting on the continuing relevance and emotional impact of the stories. Each descendant holds an object from their story as they talk, such as the baby's bootie or a letter, the same objects displayed in the exhibition, giving a physicality to their connection. Each also reads original words from their relative for the audio 'Storyteller' device,[4] so that they became, in a sense, the mouthpiece for their relative, channelling their words into the present time. It becomes, briefly, their own story, an artefact of both memory and imagination.

EVALUATION

The emotional aspects of museum work have received relatively little attention, as Munro notes (2014, p. 46); specific investigation of emotions as a measure for understanding of visitor satisfaction has been similarly neglected (Del Chiappa et al., 2014; Hayes, 2016, p. 8). Yet emotions are a useful determinant of the museum experience. Del Chiappa et al. suggest that the higher the level of emotional affect, the more the museum is considered a 'fascinating and authentic place' (2014, p. 421 & 426), and it has already been argued that people are more receptive to new ideas when emotionally engaged.

Museums Victoria's Audience Insights team has evaluated the *Love & Sorrow* exhibition several times, exploring visitor emotions as well as other responses. The team conducted visitor observations in the exhibition in

October 2014, two months after it opened, tracking approximately 70 visitors, then interviewing them briefly after they had left the exhibition. Online summative evaluation was conducted after visits between October 2014 and January 2015, with a sample of 191 people. Most recently, in March 2017, the team conducted in-depth qualitative interviews with 19 visitors and quantitative questioning of 56 visitors at the exit of the exhibition. The focus of this evaluation was the emotional impact of the exhibition.[5] In addition, I undertook an assessment of 3,360 visitor comments cards in mid-2015 to explore their key meanings. The following discussion considers the evaluations collectively, focusing on visitor behaviour in the exhibition, the types of emotions reported and the impacts of these emotions on engagement and learning.

During the October 2014 tracking, most visitors were seen to move chronologically through the exhibition (as intended), and they paused an average of 22 times. Visitors aged over 50 stopped one-third more often than visitors under 50 – an average of 27 times. This is a relatively high pause rate for a small exhibition, indicating a high level of engagement with the exhibition content. The proportionately large number of visitors who choose to fill comments cards at the end of the exhibition is also significant. Museums Victoria has found that exhibitions that emotionally engage visitors attract increased visitor comments.[6] The only exhibition at Melbourne Museum that has previously come close to this level of comments was the emotionally powerful *Inside: Life in Children's Homes and Institutions* (2013–2014).

Love & Sorrow was found to be moving and thought-provoking by 75% of visitors (up to 85% in the 55+ age group) in the online summative evaluation. Of the quantitative group, 64% of visitors said they had felt more emotional than in other exhibitions, while 30% said they had felt about the same. More than half of the summative group (56%) found the content distressing, but felt it was important to hear; 40% were fascinated; 30% were tearful and 9% were surprised. Above all, the quantitative group reported feeling sadness and sorrow (40%); a smaller number used the words 'sympathy' and 'empathy' (12%); almost the same number felt shock, grief and anger. Visitors were then given a list of emotions and asked *which* they had felt. They indicated strong empathy (75%), sadness (73%) and reflectiveness (59%). The 18 qualitative interviews indicated that the experience of the exhibition was usually associated with feelings of being both 'confronted' and 'enlightened'.

Emotional responses seem focused on two aspects of the exhibition: personal stories and medical content. Broadly, stories (and the objects that carry them) were considered the most memorable part of the exhibition for visitors.

Tracking observations found that visitors paused longest at the first cluster of soldiers' stories and again in the stories of life at home, and finally the post-war stories (where they stopped for longest of all, with one visitor pausing for 29 minutes) – in other words, they focused on the more personal accounts, where they could have a deeper engagement with the content. Qualitative interviews also indicated that personal stories were clearly effective in building empathy.

Interestingly, the descendants' films received relatively low levels of emotional response from the qualitative group: most of the 19 respondents said they were 'worn out' by the end of the exhibition. However, two respondents chose the films as the most powerful part of the exhibition, and visitors who did access the films reported high levels of emotional engagement. (Unfortunately access to the films was hampered by maintenance issues, with activation buttons and instructional signage becoming difficult to see, which may have affected the sample). It is tempting to wonder if the lack of response to the final films relates to the low interest in *the act* of following a single person's story through multiple stages – only 2% of the quantitative group felt that that this act generated 'the most powerful' emotional impact. Perhaps we succeeded too well in presenting each personal story case as both self-explanatory and as part of a larger narrative, even though the larger narrative offers a much deeper reading.

Perhaps, too, it is particular objects that have the greatest impact. Certainly, visitors had a strongly positive response to the objects in the exhibition, with 95% of the quantitative group agreeing or strongly agreeing that the show-cases and the layout of the objects in them made the space feel personal and intimate. A significant number mentioned the power of objects such as the baby's booties, letters and stories – those objects with 'peculiar vibrancy'. Some of the quantitative group also emphasised the impact of personal objects, such as, '... the few mementoes that were returned to people when they found out their loves ones were dead. That was kind of hard, but also illuminating'. (Female, 28)

Responses to other content are also helpful in understanding the power of the exhibition. When asked more broadly about what had made an impact on them, 90% of the quantitative group selected disturbing content such as the dead on the battlefield, triage and facial wounds. Importantly, 42% of this group then reported that the most powerful *emotional* impacts also came from the disturbing content – the Sidcup immersive space, images of wounds and images of damaged veterans such as Geoffrey Carter, shown in underwear so the stumps of his missing legs are graphically visible. For this survey group, personal stories had the next most powerful impact. Interviews at the end of tracking found a similar pattern: although visitors paused for longest in the personal story clusters, as noted above, they reported that wounding and hospital stories were the highest points of interest for them, with personal stories a close second.

Text (and labels) were also important to visitors. As many as 97% of the quantitative group noticed that the text was 'written as a story and described how people were feeling'. Many self-reported the importance of text that was narrative in style but not too long, and carrying information effectively. Text was identified as the exhibition element that had the greatest contribution to their learning (19%), followed by objects (18%) and images (15%).

Another key factor in visitor experience was photographic imagery. Nearly three-quarters of the quantitative group reported that large images had an emotional impact on them. One visitor in the qualitative group described the photographs as 'really touching but also very informational' (Female, 83); another felt photographs are 'a very good way to tell the story because they're real' (Male, 60s). Two-thirds of visitors felt they were 'really in' Glencorse Wood and the hospital at Sidcup.

Response to the soundscape of the exhibition – the patriotic period music from the entry film, and the sounds of the forest and occasional weapons fire in Glencorse Wood – is harder to assess. Visitors in the qualitative group found it difficult to recall the soundscape, with one speaking for many when she said '[It was] really more background for me' (Female, 28). The summative group were asked specifically about their satisfaction with sound in the exhibition – which might have also included ambient visitor noise – which they felt (on average) rated 7.8 out of 10 on a satisfaction scale. The challenge in understanding the effectiveness of the sound was that it was intended to be largely subliminal in the exhibition space, and the lack of conscious awareness of the sound cannot be used to measure its effectiveness.

With an understanding of the experiential impacts of *Love & Sorrow*, learning outcomes can now be considered. These are closely linked to the reasons that people visited the museum. Of the quantitative group, almost one-third hoped to reinforce and expand their 'intellectual understanding'; almost the same number hoped to enjoy themselves in a 'casual atmosphere in a cultural location', and 20% wanted to 'share and experience world and natural history with others'. Being informed and enriched, expanding their understanding and connecting emotionally were the leading descriptors of what they wanted to experience and feel from a museum visit. Interestingly, 84% had a family member who had served in a war. Perhaps visitors with their own stories might be more receptive to the personal stories of others, and might want to make sense of what they already know.

Online summative evaluation showed that learning outcomes were extremely successful: 97% said it made them think of the impact of World War I on Australian society; 89% learned new things and around 72% said it had given them new perspectives. About the same number again said they would share what they had learned with others. In the qualitative group, 87% of visitors indicated they had learned something new or different in visiting the exhibition. The learnings focused around medical experiences of the war (31%) – for example '...we had no idea the injuries people had and what they lived through' (Female, 53). Personal impacts (27%) and the nature and extent of Australia's involvement (14%) were also key learnings. Asked to indicate what contributed to their learning, the majority mentioned personal stories, pictures, objects and letters, with several referring to graphic plaster casts of facial wounds.

Most importantly, 84% of respondents thought that feeling emotional made them more able to learn new things. The 18 qualitative interviews provided further insight into this finding, with Sidcup 'constantly mentioned' as a section associated with new understanding.[7] Arguably, visitors learned most when they knew least: this explains responses to content dealing with the nature and treatment of facial wounds, and the long personal impacts of war. Their deepest emotional connections came from the combination of graphic content and personal stories – Sidcup (28%) and images of wounds (14%).

And what else did our visitors learn? Online summative evaluation found that the messages they received were (from most to least significant) that war causes pain, suffering, hardship and loss of lives; it comes at a high human cost, and impacts on individuals and families; war is a terrible thing that affects everyone; wars should be avoided; and there are no winners. One visitor in the qualitative group spoke for many when she said, 'What strikes me the most is the fact that we still haven't learned. We're still at war' (Female, 33). An older visitor reflected the 4% of visitor comments cards which expressed anti-war sentiment: 'That just makes me more a pacifist than I was before' (Female, 83), while a Canadian visitor appreciated 'a different country's perspective on the allied front' (Male, 35). These messages were exactly what we hoped that visitors would receive. We also wanted to encourage thinking and reflection, and succeeded in this respect too. Compared to other recent exhibitions at Melbourne Museum, *Love & Sorrow* scored most highly in the category of '[I was] was made to think of...'[8]

A small number of visitors in the summative evaluation group felt that our message was about bravery and heroism, although remarks about bravery were only made on 1.5% of comments cards. In fact the largest group of visitor comments cards were those which expressed gratitude or thanks to soldiers (43%); 34% wrote 'Lest we forget'. Virtually none used words like 'sacrifice' or made comments obviously reflecting religious views. Other comments about war generally made up just under 4% of the cards surveyed, most anti-war or pro-peace; a further 2.3% wrote 'rest in peace'.

As these words are deliberately not included in the exhibition, what did our visitors mean? Arguably these expressions are not a retreat into unthought or un-weighed words; rather, they are part of a shared language where deep emotions can be expressed in a kind of shorthand. They highlight the importance of the existing framework within which war is articulated, and which can be repurposed with new meanings and ideas. We see this in some of the comments which say 'lest we forget' but also elaborate, such as 'There is no good in any war – lest we forget'. Of all the visitor comments, the repercussions of the war emerge as a leading theme – a 'continuation of the sorrow'.

REFLECTIONS

When all of the visitor evaluation is considered together, it highlights the success of the exhibition's methodology. *Love & Sorrow* has a high level of impact, strongly linked to visitors' emotional responses to the exhibition content. Evaluation has shown that visitors feel more able to learn new things when they feel emotionally engaged, particularly when the content is new to them. They become engaged through personal stories that gradually unfold, objects which are imbued with deep meaning, imagery that confronts, and texts that are written in simple narrative form, often including original voices.

Should we be concerned that this focus on emotions could affect our ability to create histories that are objective and trustworthy? After all, the perceived impartiality of museums is a large part of why museums remain the most trusted source of information about the past and our world (see, e.g., Hamilton & Ashton, 2003, p. 27; Silberglied, 2017). There are several counters to this concern.

The first argument relates to authenticity. The reason museums are trusted is that they hold and display primary evidence about the past in a range of different media, including highly compelling material culture. As Kavanagh notes, there is 'no real parallel with the museum and the way it works with such a complete spectrum of evidence' (2000, p. 173). The content of *Love & Sorrow* deliberately included as many primary sources as possible, and in some areas, laid our process of historical enquiry bare, such as the interactive that allows visitors to see what was happening in every house in the street where butcher Albert Kemp lived. Visitors are able to see digitally the documents including rate books, newspapers and war records that were used to build the story of each house, and each source is specified. This authenticity applies to all of Museums Victoria's exhibitions: they must have a high level of accuracy, and be shaped and approved by content experts who include both scholars and the community members whose stories are represented.

The second argument relates to the notion that visitors' emotional (feeling) responses are unpredictable and therefore somehow less valid than their cognitive (thinking/rational) responses. Visitors' responses are conditioned by variable factors including memory, historical knowledge, nationality and personal experience, as Sheila Watson and many others have noted (2015, p. 296; Kavanagh, 2000, p. 4; Waterton & Watson, 2015, p. 92). These variables impact on *both* cognitive and emotional responses, which are inextricably entwined, suggesting that cognitive responses are no more valid. And museums do hold considerable control over emotional responses: evaluation of visitor types in *Love & Sorrow* has shown a notable consistency in the type and depth of emotional responses. The line between encouraging and proscribing emotional responses is very fine, as Crang and Tolia-Kelly note (2010, cited in Munro, 2014, p. 52).

Yet emotional responses *are* much more subliminal, complex, hard to define and harder to work with. Munro (2014, p. 45) notes that some museums are now actively embracing the idea of uncertainty, the idea that responses and outcomes are not always controllable, nor should they be. With this comes a relaxing of authority, a trend closely allied to the incorporation of differing voices, collaboration with diverse communities and the embracing of new and challenging modes of representation. The most important thing is that we act ethically when we create emotional experiences, and continue to encourage critical thinking (Watson, 2015, p. 296).

The third argument focuses on the status of emotions and subjectivity. While the incorporation of subjectivity broadly, and emotion specifically, seems to find currency in a 'post-truth' world (Silberglied, 2017), this is arguably a misreading. The exploration and acknowledgement of the beliefs and feelings of both the subject and the researcher or commentator lays the groundwork for *greater* accuracy and deeper interpretation. For example, the poignant collection of 27 scrapbooks put together by bereaved father Garry Roberts in the years after his son Frank's death at war can only be understood in the framework of his emotional response to the tragedy. The scrapbooks were more than a distraction during years of mourning: they provided a way of holding onto Frank's existence, gradually becoming a physical entity in the space that Frank could never fill. As Denis Byrne reflects, although death is final, experientially it is not. The loved one lives on in the marks they have left in the world, the memories, the dreams and even in the creations made during memorialisation (2013, p. 606). Garry's scrapbook creates a place where connection and reconnection is possible, and even though actual connection is a fantasy, it likely provided respite and comfort for Garry, and today offers both an insight into his thinking and his times, and a point of connection for the viewer. The scrapbooks serve as an expression of deep grief in the way that few objects or words can.

In the end, the *Love & Sorrow* exhibition makes a case for a more nuanced understanding of the role of emotions in the historian's craft, and in the museum. Emotions make us human and are critical to understanding how other humans have behaved. We can see ever more clearly the constraints that striving for objectivity has placed on our practice.

NOTES

1. It is encouraging that the Australian War Memorial has somewhat moved its position during the centenary, including a story about facial wounding and a section at the end of its new World War I gallery which movingly presents the longer-term impacts of loss and mourning.

2. Frank Roberts' story is discussed by Stanley (2009), Damousi (1999) and Luckins (2004).

3. Grave inscription for Jack Edwards by his parents, quoted by Ziino, 2007, p. 143.

4. The 'Storyteller' device provides additional content on each character such as readings of letters, photographs and moving footage. Unfortunately, technical issues have hampered its use, particularly in relation to beacons that should progressively release content.

5. Marsh and Meehan (2015), Borisova and Meehan (2015) and Nabila and Meehan (2017) and Meehan (2017). All of these evaluations assessed the *Love & Sorrow* exhibition specifically.

6. Carolyn Meehan, Manager, Audience Insights, Communication & Partnerships, Museums Victoria (personal communication, 2015).

7. Unfortunately, the other immersive space, Glencorse Wood, had technical problems at the time of the qualitative interviews so cannot be included in this discussion.

8. Compared to *The Melbourne Story, Afghanistan, Bond 007, Aztecs and Mind* exhibitions (Borisova and Meehan 2015).

REFERENCES

Borisova, A. & Meehan, C. (2015). *WWI: Love & Sorrow summative evaluation report.* Audience Insights (Unpublished report), February. Melbourne, VIC: Museums Victoria.

Byrne, D. (2012). Love & loss in the 1960s. *International Journal of Heritage Studies, 19*(6), 596–609.

Damousi, J. (1999). *The labour of loss: Mourning, memory and wartime bereavement in Australia.* Cambridge: Cambridge University Press.

Del Chiappa, G., Andreu, L, & Gallarza, M. G. (2014). Emotions and visitors' satisfaction at a museum. *International Journal of Culture, Tourism and Hospitality Research, 8*(4), 420–431.

Englund, P. (2011). *The beauty and the sorrow: An intimate history of the First World War.* London: Profile Books.

Fussell, P. (1975). *The Great War and modern memory.* Oxford: Oxford University Press.

Hamilton, P., & Ashton, P. (2003). At home with the past: Initial findings from the survey. *Australian Cultural History, 23*, 5–30.

Hayes, J. (2016). *Creating discomfort: Exploring the use of emotional immersive experiences to address social issues in Museums.* Unpublished Dissertation. University of Washington Museology Program.

Hirschman, E.C. and Holbrook, M.B. (1982). Hedonic consumption: Emerging concepts, methods, and propositions, *Journal of Marketing, 46*(3), 92–101.

Kavanagh, G. (2000). *Dream spaces: Memory and the museum.* London: Leicester University Press.

Larsson, M. (2009). *Shattered Anzacs: Living with the scars of war.* Sydney, NSW: UNSW Press.

Luckins, T. (2004). *The gates of memory: Australian people's experiences and memories of loss and the Great War.* Fremantle, WA: Curtin University Books.

Marsh, R., & Meehan, C. (2015, February). *WWI: Love & Sorrow exhibition observation study.* Audience Insights. Unpublished report, Museums Victoria, Melbourne, VIC.

Mazda, X. (2015). Exhibitions and the power of narrative. Museums Australia Conference, 23 May, Sydney.

McKernan, M. (2015). WWI: Love & Sorrow, *Recollections, 10*(1), April. Retrieved from http://recollections.nma.gov.au/issues/volume_10_number_1/exhibition_reviews/wwi_love_and_sorrow. Accessed on March 21, 2017.

Meehan, C. (2017). *Love & Sorrow exhibition: Power of emotion.* Audience Insights (Unpublished report) No. 1045, 15–26 March, Museums Victoria, Melbourne, VIC.

Munro, E. (2014), Doing emotion work in museums: Reconceptualising the role of community engagement practitioners. *Museum & Society, 12*(1), March, 44–60.

Nabila, A. & Meehan, C. (2017). *Analysis summary. Love & Sorrow exhibition.* Audience Insights (Unpublished report), Museums Victoria, Melbourne, VIC.

Silberglied, G. R. (2017, 17 January). *Be a truthteller. Advocate for museums.* Centre for the Future of Museums, American Alliance of Museums. Retrieved from http://futureofmuseums.blogspot.com.au/2017/01/be-truthteller-advocate-for-museums.html. Accessed on March 21, 2017.

Stanley, P. (2009). *Men of Mont St Quentin: Between victory and death.* Carlton North, VIC: Scribe Publications.

Waterton, E., & Watson, S. (2015). A war long forgotten. *Angelaki, Journal of Theoretical Humanities, 20*(3), 89–103.

Watson, S. (2015). Emotions in the history museum. In A. Witcomb & K. Message (Eds.), *International handbooks of museum studies: Museum theory* (pp. 283–301). Chichester: John Wiley & Sons.

Witcomb, A. (2016). Beyond sentimentality and glorification. In D. Drozdzewski, S. de Nardi, & E. Watson (Eds.), *Memory, place and identity: Commemoration and remembrance of war and conflict* (pp. 205–220). London: Routledge.

Ziino, B. (2007). *A distant grief: Australian war graves and the Great War*. Crawley, WA: University of Western Australia Press.

PART III
SUBJECTIVITIES AND SUBJECT POSITIONS

CHAPTER 11

THE EXPECTATION OF EMPATHY: UNPACKING OUR EPISTEMOLOGICAL BAGS WHILE RESEARCHING EMPATHY, LITERATURE AND NEUROSCIENCE

Lauren Fowler and Sally Bishop Shigley

ABSTRACT

Purpose – *This chapter details the collaborative investigation of a neuroscientist and a literature scholar into whether reading literature increases empathy in health professionals, pre-health professionals and students outside of health care. It also reflects on the role of different epistemologies that inform researchers' approaches, and muses on how ethnicity, sexual orientation and class inform research and teaching.*

Methodology/Approach – *Students watched or read Margaret Edson's play* W;t *and were asked if the medical drama increased their sense of appropriate empathy in medical encounters. The original research*

Emotion and the Researcher: Sites, Subjectivities, and Relationships
Studies in Qualitative Methodology, Volume 16, 179–195
Copyright © 2018 by Emerald Publishing Limited
All rights of reproduction in any form reserved
ISSN: 1042-3192/doi:10.1108/S1042-319220180000016012

employed the Jefferson Scale of Physician Empathy, electromyography and galvanic skin response to measure physiological markers of empathy. These results were then compared to the self-reflection of participants to determine whether or not the physiological responses mirrored the self-report. The reflections on how emotion impacted the research were primarily narrative essay-based accompanied by feminist other literary theories.

Findings – *All participants in the original study reported an increase in empathy after reading or viewing the play. This affect was even stronger when they viewed a live performance. The researchers determined that the role that their ethnicity, age, sexual orientation and class needed further study, perhaps with different pieces of literature.*

Originality/Value – *This chapter reflects the interdisciplinary and epistemological challenges of two researchers from very different backgrounds and training and investigates the relationship between reading, physiological empathy and perceptions of empathy. It considers the difficult and controversial challenges to quantifying emotions and the role emotions play in academic collaboration.*

Keywords: Empathy; neuroscience; literature; pedagogy; epistemology; medicine

INTRODUCTION

We are currently participating in an experiment to find out whether it is possible to use literature to teach empathy. In this chapter, we explore our individual epistemologies and our emotional responses to them: what things informed the ethos of our training and what has changed throughout our careers. We discuss how our research and teaching has evolved and changed based on our experiences working with each other.

Sally's Story

When I was an undergraduate, I changed my mind weekly: should I major in biology or English? I was good at both. Cell biology and xylem and phloem tugged at me with the same insistence as James Joyce's 'Araby' and the poetry of Elizabeth Bishop. The decision made itself eventually, as the demands of calculus overcame my math-phobic brain: no calculus, no biology. Even though I still love natural science and have eagerly taught courses on literature, medicine and science, I was not in the biological sciences long enough to have developed a scientist's habits of mind: objectivity, developing a workable hypothesis, manipulating quantitative data and reporting on research in the passive voice. Instead, I developed the habits of mind of the humanities, with their emphasis on diversity, communication, ethics, culture and cooperation. The humanities also lean in the direction of social justice because literature is often about people in peril of one kind or another, about social responsibility and what it means to be human. The humanities do not maintain ownership of these qualities at the expense of other disciplines, but I cut my scholarly and pedagogical teeth on these ideas.

I trained as a PhD student just as literary theories (feminist, Marxist, structuralist and post-structuralist, reader-response and psychoanalytical) trickled into lesser schools from the high-powered universities on either coast. I was aware of theory as a graduate student, but I never had a class devoted to it. I was mostly trained as a New Critic. The early twentieth-century New Critics were possessed of science envy (Middleton, 2015), but their attempt to apply the scientific method to literature was a little misguided. New Critics believed in the text and nothing but the text. Context, authorial intention and the reader's emotions took second place to close reading of the mechanics of poetic literature. Students trained by the New Critics can sniff out a synecdoche in the darkest corners of a poem, but they do not focus on situating literature in the emotions and politics and furore of the world.

I spent my early years as a scholar camped out in the brain of twentieth-century American poet Elizabeth Bishop. Bishop's poetry was perfect for my analytically trained mind: she was allusive, indirect and closed off from many of her own emotions. I wrote a book about her, which was good for my tenure chances, but I felt trapped. I knew how to do traditional literary scholarship, and it bored me, but it felt like cheating to do 'frivolous' research about topics just because I found them interesting, especially before I received tenure. In my academic life, what I thought would be compelling and fun was irrelevant.

Looking at things through a feminist lens helped, as feminist scholarship in the 1990s reclaimed 'the feminine' and the personal as legitimate objects of study. My scholarship became a mite more diverse. I wrote a book chapter here and an article there on a wide range of subjects. I was not ready to write confessional essays, but for the first time in my career, I let what I wanted to write about overpower the scholarly manacles that I had willingly accepted in graduate school. Other women, especially feminists, had started writing about their personal experiences in a scholarly way (Heilbrun, 1996; Nelson, 1995; Tompkins, 1996). It seemed like they were getting away with something, a kind of academic naughtiness. Like all other forms of naughtiness, this was exciting in all the connotations of that word: scary, stimulating and thrilling in the small way that academic discourse is thrilling.

I began looking for conferences that combined literature with the love of science that had started my university journey. In 2010, I went to a conference at Duke University called 'Poetry and Medicine'. Physicians, nurses, ethicists and literary scholars spent three days together watching the interdisciplinary field of medical humanities take shape. I came home in that obnoxious state of scholarly intoxication where you trap people in hallways to try out your ideas and make lots of lists and buy lots of books. I taught classes on medicine and literature for different programmes, including one with a colleague from nursing. It was exhilarating. I went to other conferences on science and the humanities. Many of the participants taught at medical schools. They argued about whether literature could help teach empathy to physicians-in-training (Shapiro & Rucker, 2003; Wear & Zarconi, 2007), whether empathy is a desirable quality (Garden, 2007), and why the humanities should provide concrete evidence that teaching literature has a measurable effect on physician empathy. The medical schools wanted evidence (Strauss & McAlister, 2000). The humanities people resented their work being quantified by a science rubric (Macnaughton, 2011). I thought that there ought to be a middle ground. So I set up a meeting with Lauren. My goal: to find out if there was a way to get quantitative and qualitative data to suggest that reading literature had an impact on perceptions of empathy. I bounced it off a medical humanities colleague. She warned me that it would be poorly received. I did it anyway.

Lauren's Story

I knew that I wanted to be a neuroscientist from the age of nine. I used to spend summers with my grandparents on a farm in Texas, and when I grew bored with what the farm had to offer, I explored my grandfather's books. In the summer of 1979, a book on the brain captured my attention. I got my grandmother to purchase note cards so that I could type up interesting things I found in the book and keep the cards with me throughout the year. One of the scientists in the book was a behavioural neurobiologist, which is someone who studies the biological basis of behaviour, and I remember typing that onto a card and thinking, 'One day I will be a behavioural neurobiologist!'

While the path was not a direct one, in 1999, I eventually received my PhD in Neuropsychology and Behavioral Neuroscience.

When I was in college, I loved all things science, and loved the idea of going to medical school. I was sure that I was destined to be a neurosurgeon (as well as a concert pianist on the side). However, after taking several courses in the traditional sciences, I discovered that while I loved the information I was learning in those classes, I didn't really know what to do with it. The college I attended had an extensive shadow programme that encouraged all students to become involved with members of the profession they hoped to enter. During my sophomore and junior years I shadowed physicians, most of them female. Every single female physician I shadowed told me that if they had the chance to do it over, they would choose *not* to go to medical school. They were either unhappy in their jobs, or found it too difficult to juggle their family lives, jobs and the way they felt they needed to act as physicians. I asked one of the physicians, a paediatric oncologist, how she dealt with seeing children in pain on a daily basis. She told me point blank that she had to separate out those feelings and assume her role as a doctor and a scientist. I didn't like the idea that I couldn't be a scientist *and* have feelings.

At the same time, my psychology courses really spoke to me. I was able to learn about physiology and apply it to behaviour and cognition. For example, I studied how sleep loss not only makes us feel tired and grumpy but also what happens neurologically to produce the grumpiness. While I performed really well in those psychology courses, I was only slightly above average in some of my science courses (curse you, Organic Chemistry!). So I chose to major in psychology, but I still completed my pre-med courses in case I decided to go to medical school. I liked the idea of being a doctor, but didn't think that it was really in the cards for me. That way of applying science did not fit.

During my senior year in college, I decided to pursue my education certificate. I knew that I could use this to get a job at any time, especially because I liked science and math (the toughest teaching jobs to fill in many areas). At the same time, I managed to get some lab experience with a neurobiologist at Emory University, and to see firsthand what it was like to be a straight-out researcher at a research-intensive institution. This neurobiologist's life was spent in the lab. His goals were always to publish, get more grants and spend more time in the lab. I liked his freedom in the lab, but it seemed that the outcome of the research drove the science, rather than the science driving the outcome. If his results were not significant, he wouldn't get published or get a grant, even if the results were interesting or important in other ways. Because I wanted to apply the information I was learning, I felt that to be happy, I needed more than just doing science for its own sake. This lab experience was invaluable partly because at the same time I was learning how to apply my knowledge in the real world through teaching. This experience showed me that I liked research but loved teaching. While I was teaching I got to explore concepts and think about things from different perspectives, and this drove more exploration, regardless of the outcome. Thus, when I graduated from college, I decided to teach middle-school science so that I could incorporate science and teaching.

After a year of teaching middle school, I knew I had found what I wanted to do for the rest of my life. I *loved* teaching, especially the fact that I learned as I taught. I went to class prepared to share information with students, but when I incorporated their experiences and thoughts, I ended up learning as much as they did. But I did not like teaching in a public school system that suppressed free thought. In the state of Georgia during this time, you were not legally allowed to say the word 'evolution' when teaching. I tried substituting the word 'adaptation' and talking about the *theory* of evolution, but I still got into trouble with the administration and some of the parents for allowing the students to consider ideas that were not ideologically compatible with the dominant religion in the area.

At the same time, I experienced two things in my classes that pushed me to go further with my education. First, I loved teaching science, but my curriculum was fairly set and not open to much interpretation. Second, things I noticed in class made me curious. I taught the same material four times a day, but the classes were very different in their dynamics at different times of day. Teaching students about cell structure at 10 a.m. was elegant and orderly. By 2 p.m., the science classroom sounded like a zoo, and cell biology was the least of my worries. I decided to explore this concept and discovered a fascinating area of research on circadian rhythms, which demonstrated that people are physiologically different at different times of day, meaning that their cognition and behaviour are different, too.

These combined factors drove me to apply to graduate school. Georgia State University had a programme in neuroscience that combined psychology and biology, as well as researchers studying biological rhythms, so it seemed like the perfect opportunity. The year I applied, they had created a new interdisciplinary programme and were seeking people with backgrounds in both psychology and biology, as well as looking for people with teaching experience. The planets aligned for me, and I was admitted to the first class of the Neuropsychology and Behavioral Neuroscience PhD programme at Georgia State.

During graduate school, I explored both my interest in biological rhythms and my desire to teach. I worked with chimpanzees to study the effects of rhythms on cognition, and I found that dealing with them was very similar to teaching 13-year-olds. I also conducted some research in a lab setting, which was valuable to my training, but reinforced my unwillingness to play the big science game and work exclusively in a lab. I finished graduate school knowing I wanted to teach for a living, conduct research and apply my knowledge in a real-world situation.

I was hired by Weber State University to teach in the Psychology Department right after I completed my PhD. I thrived in the classroom, because I suddenly got to teach what I wanted, how I wanted. I got to explore more information to share with my students and to learn from them at an even higher level than before. Students from all over the campus took my class, so students from genetics or nutrition came along and then applied what they had learned in those other classes to the material I was teaching. This allowed me to integrate many different areas of study into my teaching, and the diverse interests of my students made me a much better teacher and learner. While I enjoyed teaching and learning in the classroom, I also explored science through research. I applied for and received two National Science Foundation grants for research with undergraduates to conduct biological rhythms research in our community. Over a 10-year period, I worked with students to help solve problems related to circadian desynchronisation. In real terms, we studied ways to help medical, military and law enforcement personnel adapt to the demands of a 24/7 job, usually by helping develop effective shift-work schedules and/or working to develop fatigue countermeasures that were specific to each setting. This work helped reinforce my belief in the power of making a difference with knowledge. I was able to apply basic research for a positive influence in our community.

In 2013, Sally approached me about studying empathy. I did not know much about empathy, but Sally was known on campus as an outstanding teacher and a force for interdisciplinarity, so I was keen to discuss ideas with her. That meeting was one of the best experiences I have had at Weber State. We were both enthusiastic about studying empathy, but we came at it from completely different perspectives. Most gratifying, though, was how neither of us was threatened by the other's ideas and ways of thinking. We both saw that by working together, we could come up with a much more complete picture of empathy than if we worked alone. Sally's goal of studying whether literature could affect empathy inspired me, because I wanted to know if we could teach it and change people physiologically, as well as perceptually. That meeting has spurred four years of research that has no end in sight. The more we explore, the more we discover we have to learn. The success of our research and our subsequent class has raised an interesting question.

Was our research and teaching improved because we liked each other, had young daughters and neuroses in common and could flow seamlessly from discussing research variables to Girl Scout camp? We do not know how to quantify that, but it certainly did not hurt.

OUR RESEARCH

There is an enormous need to study empathy in the healthcare system. Much is unknown about both the perceived and physiological effects of empathy on healthcare workers and patients. Many studies have shown that professional empathy improves medical practices and lowers the incidence of malpractice lawsuits (Moore, Adler, & Robertson, 2000). Studies have also shown that for physicians, empathy can decrease burnout, increase longevity and decrease errors (Crane, 1998; Krasner et al., 2009). But physician empathy can also benefit the patient. With increased physician empathy, there is a resulting decrease in patient stress, levels of pain relievers used and the duration of hospital stays, as well as an increase in patient satisfaction (Hojat, 2009; Kim, Kaplowitz, & Johnston, 2004; Zachariae et al., 2003). However, other research suggests that sometimes empathy by healthcare professionals (HP) can be a bad thing. Trifiletti Di Bernardo, Falvo, and Capozza (2014) found that stress-related symptoms among nurses rose the more they empathised with their patients. Empathy can be good for both the HP and the patient, but there is also evidence that it might have some adverse effects.

Getting Started (Sally)

Before the first meeting about the empathy research, Lauren and I did not know each other well. Our daughters were in the same Girl Scout troop, and we had served on committees together, but we were not exactly friends. I was tentative about that first meeting. Despite my professional persona, I am instinctively an introvert and need some sense of personal connection for scholarly collaboration not to be completely exhausting. Plus, Lauren is a titan on our campus, beloved of students and colleagues alike and affectionately known as Dr Brain. Lauren and I approached each other with more care than was productive. We were self-deprecating to a fault, by turns cheering each other on and humbly downplaying our expertise. We apologised a lot. We eventually got over that initial hesitation through discussions outside our research interests. Talking of kids, colleagues and favourite foods, and reassuring one another about everything from body image to thyroid health, created a safe space for us to talk honestly about our scholarly strengths and weaknesses. It was very different from meetings or conferences I had attended in which territory had to be marked and professional dialogue was more of a series of self-aggrandising monologues. Lauren and I listened to each other. We were not competing and pontificating. Dare I say that our empathy made our research relationship more productive?

The Research (Lauren)

We wanted to study how to measure empathy in general, as well as determining if you could teach empathy through literature. For the past four years, then, we have studied physiological and perceived levels of empathy in college students, pre-healthcare professionals (PHPs) and HPs including physicians, nurses and physician assistants. Our research asked:

- Are empathy levels different in students, PHPs and HPs?
- How do students, PHPs and HPs compare on physiological and perceived empathy?
- Does literature affect empathy?
- Does the form of literature have an effect on empathy?
- Can you use different forms of literature to create lasting changes in empathy?

Our first study looked at how people perceive their own empathy levels, how this perception relates to physiological measures of empathy, and if reading literature affects either or both types of empathy. We were also interested in assessing whether PHP students were different to non-PHP students. Research suggests that the empathy of medical students drops in their third year of medical school (Chen, Lew, Hershman, & Orlander, 2007; Neumann et al., 2011). We wanted to see if differences in empathy existed even earlier, when the students were undergraduates. To assess this, we measured perceived empathy and physiological empathy: perceived empathy primarily through self-report and button-pressing, although we eventually used the Jefferson Scale[1] too; and physiological empathy through facial electromyography (EMG) and galvanic skin response (GSR) before, during and after PHPs and non-PHPs read the play *W;t*. *W;t* tells the story of Vivian Bearing and her sometimes callous treatment at the hands of her

cancer doctors. We chose *W;t* because it was short, easily understood and
had many concrete scenarios demonstrating characters' empathy or its lack.
We found that each person had a slightly different definition of empathy,
but all indicated that their perception of empathy had changed as a result
of reading *W;t*. The non-PHPs had a significantly bigger change than the
PHPs ($p < 0.05$) in perceived empathy after *W;t*, but both groups showed
increases when compared to pre-testing. In fact, the PHPs' post-assessment
of empathy was virtually identical to the non-PHPs' pre-assessment of perceived empathy, which indicates that just by reading *W;t*, the PHPs 'normalised' their empathy levels (see *Fig. 1*).

Participants were given a button to press when they experienced empathy while reading the play. Interestingly, the PHPs pressed the button *more*
than the non-PHPs did. This is notable because the PHPs self-reported
lower empathy when asked directly, but when presented with a patient scenario in *W;t*, they self-reported higher levels of empathy than the non-PHPs.
Physiological empathy had drastically different effects in PHPs compared
to non-PHPs. Students bound for the health professions showed very little
activation of facial EMG muscles, while non-PHP students had activation
that corresponded to their perceptions of their own empathy. In other words,
non-PHP students showed a stronger physiological empathetic response to

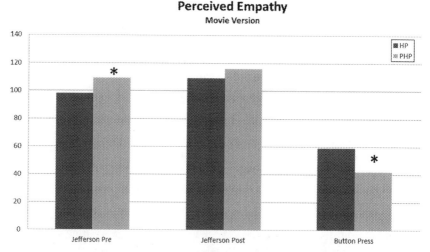

Fig. 1. Perceived Empathy in PHPs Versus HPs Who Watched the Movie *W;t*.
The '*' indicates a significant ($p < 0.05$) difference between the two groups.
Source: Courtesy of Lauren Fowler.

reading *W;t* than pre-healthcare students, and this physiological response resembled the perceived responses of the non-PHPs.

We found the combined results of the button-pressing and physiological data most interesting. The perceived and physiological empathy of non-PHPs were clearly related: they *perceived* higher levels of empathy when they *showed* physiological measures that reflected empathy. However, the PHPs button-pressed at points in the play that were socially acceptable times to feel empathy, but their levels of physiological empathy did not reflect those changes: they pressed the button because they thought they *should* feel empathy, even though they did not. Our qualitative data reflected this, when a physician in a later study said, 'I pressed the button because I thought I should be feeling empathy, so I pressed it'.

We also had two pre-medical students assisting us with the research, and their input was especially interesting. They felt that reading the play had an enormous effect on their empathy levels and were fascinated by the discrepancies between the PHPs and non-PHPs. One of these students told us that reading *W;t* and participating in this study taught him not to treat patients as if they were research subjects. Seeing things from the perspective of a researcher looking at empathy changed his outlook on life. So the take-home message from our first study was a resounding yes: literature (in particular *W;t*) had an effect on empathy, and it was something that we *could* measure, both physiologically and perceptually. We also learned that maybe HPs were different even before they went to medical school.

Our next step was to assess the effects of watching the movie *W;t*. We believed that viewing a movie would create a stronger physiological empathetic response than simply reading the play. Dimberg, Andréasson and Thunberg (2011) demonstrated that brain activity is significantly different when people are viewing video rather than reading text. Videos are processed up to 60,000 times faster than written text. In addition, viewing action increases bilateral mirror neuron brain activation, whereas reading texts usually increases mirror neuron brain activation primarily in the left hemisphere (Carr, Iacoboni, Dubeau, Mazziotta, & Lenzi, 2009). Based on current physiological empathy research, we expected the movie to produce at least as strong an empathetic response as reading the play, if not stronger.

The results of watching the movie and reading the play version of *W;t* were similar to each other. We tested PHPs to non-PHPs, but we also compared PHPs to practising HPs. Results indicated that regardless of its form, literature increased the perceived empathy of non-PHPs, PHPs and HPs.

Prior to the study, the Jefferson Empathy Scores were significantly lower for the HPs ($p < 0.05$) than the PHPs – this supports research indicating that the longer someone is in the field of healthcare, the lower their empathy scores. But after viewing the movie, while there was still a difference in perceived empathy, PHPs and HPs were much closer in their empathy scores. Most interestingly, the Jefferson post-score for HPs was the same as the pre-score for PHPs. One way to interpret this is to infer that watching *W;t* reminded HPs about empathy, and transformed their state of empathy to its PHP level.

The Live Play (Sally)

Bolstered by the success of the research so far, we approached a colleague in the theatre department about directing a live performance of the play on campus. We were curious about whether the increase in perceived and self-reported empathy found in students viewing the movie version of the play would hold when participants were watching a live performance. The three of us wrote and won a collaboration grant and the director slotted the play into her schedule. Lauren and I had very little to do with the production until it was in the final stages of rehearsals, and we had to negotiate where we would put research participants during the performance. The director was very concerned that people hooked up to the EMG, GSR and laptops recording data would interfere with the verisimilitude of the play. Lauren was frustrated because her research students would be relegated to a dark corner of the theatre. I was worried because everyone was agitated, and it seemed like our whole reason for getting the grant money and finding more participants was unravelling before my eyes. Nobody behaved badly, but the disciplinary boundaries that had seemed flexible when melding literature and neuroscience seemed very solid as the necessities of the quantitative research bumped up against the complexity of putting on a live show. The director had the cast, the crew and the audience to think about: live bodies that might be distracted by the apparatus of the research. We despaired because the whole reason for putting on the play was to get more data.

Looking back, it was an ironic mirroring of the play. Jason and Kelekian (Vivian's primary physicians) want data and treat Vivian like a research project (that will, to be fair, produce results that will help save people in the future). The play hates them for it, preferring the human and healing touch of the primary nurse Susie. It was strange for me to be on the side of the data. We had worked so hard to get to the live performance that the erection of disciplinary boundaries felt personal. I felt thwarted, and like a jerk for feeling thwarted. Attendance was good for all the performances, but Lauren and I felt buffeted by the conflicts. Our passion for the project narrowed our objectivity. Mistakes on flyers, legal wrangling and the director's impatience felt personal. We were empathy researchers, but we did not feel much empathy for the people getting in our way.

But once the play started its run, things changed. The play was an enormous success, to the point where some people returned to see it multiple times. We were able to fill our research spaces with participants, and all of the participants, regardless of health profession status (PHP or HP), were moved by the play. Everyone involved had an emotional response to the play itself, although the responses were very different depending upon the individual. For example, a paediatrician was very upset after the play because she had never seen another physician behave so carelessly and thought that the playwright misrepresented medicine. However, a neurosurgeon felt like this was a fairly accurate portrayal of the doctor/patient relationship. He identified with Jason and did not feel that Jason's treatment of Vivian was at all unusual.

When we analysed the data, we saw a similar effect to past results. For the physiological data (GSR and EMG), the results looked very much like the physiological data when people read the book and watched the movie. HPs had a lower physiological response than PHPs, but they had more button presses. However, overall responses were higher than with either the book or the movie. Seeing the play evoked a stronger physiological response in all of those who participated than watching either the movie or reading the play. In addition, all of those involved pressed the button more during the play than during the movie, indicating that they all had a stronger perceived empathetic response to watching the play. *Fig. 2* shows that perceived empathy increased after the play and movie, and it also demonstrates that viewing the play had a stronger effect on perceived empathy. These results were not statistically significant, but we had a small sample size of healthcare professionals ($N = 22$); the small sample size makes it more challenging to find a significant effect without increasing the probability of error. In addition, every participant tested during the play (as well as the movie and the book) indicated that they felt their levels of empathy had changed as a result of reading and/or seeing the play.

So what have we learned from over three years of data collection, working with non-HPs, PHPs and HPs working in the field? We have learned that literature has an effect on perceived and physiological empathy. This effect was found using the written version of the play *W;t*, the movie version of the same play, and the live stage performance of the play. The written version of the play had the weakest effect, but results were still statistically and

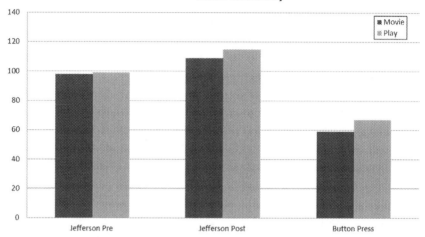

Perceived Empathy in Physicians
Movie versus Play

Fig. 2.   Perceived Empathy in HPs, Comparing the Movie to the Play *W;t.*
Source: Courtesy of Lauren Fowler.

clinically significant. This means that regardless of the form that we used, 100% of the participants felt that empathy was enhanced by exposure to *W;t.* Physiologically, there were some differences in individuals, but the differences were not always reflected in the perceived empathy (especially in HPs).

These results indicate that literature can be used to help teach empathy. Research on the decline in empathy in HPs during training and clinical experience has led to increased interest in teaching empathy in medical and nursing schools. Brunero, Lamont, and Coates's (2010) examination of effectiveness of empathy training in nurses found that the majority of training programmes significantly improved empathy scores. So empathy can be taught, and it can make a noticeable difference in those in the health professions. The results of our study support the findings of Shapiro, Morrison, and Boker (2004) and Ubukawa and Miyazaki (2014) that literature can be used to teach empathy to PHPs and HPs.

WHERE DO WE GO FROM HERE?

As we review our respective histories, our success as academics, our research collaboration and our teaching, two issues repeat themselves.

First, the balance between desire and safety. We both felt conflict between what we wanted to do and what we should do. Was our desire for teaching or poetry or biology as important as what we felt like we should be doing? Would we risk working together even if we didn't know precisely how, or stay in our disciplinary boxes and do what was expected? Letting go of personal, pedagogical and scholarly safety nets has produced dividends for us. It has made us better at our jobs, and it has made us happy, a word that does not get much play in academic environments. Second, our affection and admiration for each other translates into our teaching, scholarly presentations and scholarship and makes them better. Because we are enjoying ourselves our audiences and students feel relaxed and enjoy themselves as well. Certainly, our research would not work if we were friends and did not put in the time to do good research. Friendship alone does not make us successful. But in our interdisciplinary work, interpersonal trust and a willingness to be vulnerable opens us up to see and imagine things that we would not have access to if we restricted ourselves to our disciplinary world view.

In the next step of our collaboration, we will turn our research lens towards empathy and poverty. Do the clothing, speech, hygiene and socio-economic status of characters in fiction change readers' empathy towards them? Once again, we two straight, white, upper-middle class, overly educated mothers will have to honestly examine our emotional baggage so that we can look directly at our subject without our personal and epistemological assumptions getting in the way.

NOTE

1. The Jefferson Scale of Physician Empathy is a 7-point Likert scale which attempts to quantify empathy using a self-report measure. On the validity of the scale, see Hojat, 2003; Glaser, Markham, Adler, McManus, and Hojat (2007).

REFERENCES

Brunero, S., Lamont, S., & Coates, M. (2010). A review of empathy education in nursing. *Nursing Inquiry, 17*(1), 65–74.

Carr, L., Iacoboni, M., Dubeau, M. C., Mazziotta, J. C., & Lenzi, G. L. (2003). Neural mechanisms of empathy in humans: A relay from neural systems for imitation to limbic areas. *Proceedings of the National Academy of Sciences, 100*(9), 5497–5502.

Chen, D., Lew, R., Hershman, W., & Orlander, J. (2007). A cross-sectional measurement of medical student empathy. *Journal of General Internal Medicine, 22*(10), 1434–1438.

Crane, M. (1998). Why burned-out doctors get sued more often. *Medical Economics, 75*(10), 210–212, 215–218.

Dimberg, U., Andréasson, P., & Thunberg, M. (2011). Emotional empathy and facial reactions to facial expressions. *Journal of Psychophysiology, 25*, 26–31.

Edson, M. (1999). *W;t*. London: Faber and Faber.

Garden, R. (2007). The problem of empathy: Medicine and the humanities. *New Literary History, 38*(3), 551–567.

Glaser, K. M., Markham, F. W., Adler, H. M., McManus, P. R., & Hojat, M. (2007). Relationships between scores on the Jefferson Scale of physician empathy, patient perceptions of physician empathy, and humanistic approaches to patient care: A validity study. *Medical Science Monitor, 13*(7), CR291–CR294.

Heilbrun, C. (2008). *Writing a woman's life*. New York, NY: W.W. Norton.

Hojat, M. (2009). Ten approaches for enhancing empathy in health and human services cultures. *Journal of Health and Human Services Administration, 34*, 412–450.

Kim S. S., Kaplowitz, S., & Johnston, M. V. (2004). The effect of physician empathy on patient satisfaction and compliance. *Evaluation & the Health Professions, 27*, 237–251.

Krasner, M. S., Epstein, R. M., Beckman, H., Suchman, A. L., Chapman, B., Mooney, C. J., & Quill, T. E. (2009). Association of an educational program in mindful communication with burnout, empathy, and attitudes among primary care physicians. *JAMA, 302*(12), 1284–1293.

Macnaughton, J. (2011). Medical humanities' challenge to medicine. *Journal of Evaluation in Clinical Practice, 17*(5), 927–932.

Middleton, P. (2015). *Physics envy: American poetry and science in the cold war and after*. Chicago, IL: University of Chicago Press.

Moore, P. J., Adler, N. E., & Robertson, P.A. (2000). Medical malpractice: The effect of doctor–patient relations on medical patient perceptions and malpractice intentions. *Western Journal of Medicine, 173*, 244–250.

Nelson, N. O. (1995). *Private voices, public lives: Women speak on the literary life*. Denton, TX: University of North Texas Press.

Neumann, M., Edelhäuser, F., Tauschel, D., Fischer, M. R., Wirtz, M., Woopen, C., & Scheffer, C. (2011). Empathy decline and its reasons: A systematic review of studies with medical students and residents. *Academic Medicine, 86*(8), 996–1009.

Shapiro, J., Morrison, E. H., & Boker, J. R. (2004). Teaching empathy to first year medical students: Evaluation of an elective literature and medicine course. *Education for Health, 17*(1), 73–84.

Shapiro, J., & Rucker, L. (2003). Can poetry make better doctors? Teaching humanities and arts to medical students and residents at the University of California, Irvine, College of Medicine. *Academic Medicine, 78*(10), 953–957.

Strauss, S.E., and McAlister, F.A. (2000). Evidence based medicine: A commentary on common criticisms, *CMAJ, 16*(3), 837–841.

Tompkins, J. (1996). *A life in school: What the teacher learned*. New York, NY: Perseus Books.

Trifiletti, E., Di Bernardo, G. A., Falvo, R., & Capozza, D. (2014). Patients are not fully human: A nurse's coping response to stress. *Journal of Applied Social Psychology, 44*(12), 768–777.

Ubukawa, E., & Miyazaki, Y. (2014). Using Tuesdays with Morrie for in-training future healthcare professionals: A pilot study. *Annual Report of JACET-SIG on ESP, 16*, 8–24.

Wear, D., & Zarconi, J. (2007). Can compassion be taught? Let's ask our students. *Journal of General Internal Medicine, 23*(7), 948–953.

Zachariae, R., Pedersen, C. G., Jensen, A. B., Ehrnrooth, E., Rossen, P. B., & von der Maase, H. (2003). Association of perceived physician communication style with patient satisfaction, distress, cancer related self efficacy, and perceived control over the disease. *British Journal of Cancer, 88,* 658–665.

CHAPTER 12

'POOR OLD MIXED-UP WALES': ENTERING THE DEBATE ABOUT BILINGUALISM, MULTICULTURALISM AND RACISM IN WELSH LITERATURE AND CULTURE

Lisa Sheppard

ABSTRACT

Purpose – *This chapter reflects upon my experiences as a PhD researcher examining the portrayal of multiculturalism in contemporary Welsh- and English-language fiction about Wales. It discusses my emotions regarding my identities as a second-language Welsh speaker and as an early career researcher, and how they affected my participation in this field.*

Methodology/Approach – *The chapter draws on my PhD research, which examined how different cultural groups were portrayed in fiction as 'others' due to Wales's complex linguistic and cultural position. This involved analysing contextual research about multiculturalism in Wales to explore*

Emotion and the Researcher: Sites, Subjectivities, and Relationships
Studies in Qualitative Methodology, Volume 16, 197–212
Copyright © 2018 by Emerald Publishing Limited
All rights of reproduction in any form reserved
ISSN: 1042-3192/doi:10.1108/S1042-319220180000016013

discourses of belonging and alienation. This chapter reflects upon my emotional responses to the field as a Welsh speaker and new academic, and how this in turn affected my research.

Findings – *Embracing my changing relationship with my Welsh-speaking identity, I reflect on how my research touched upon contradictory feelings I had about the Welsh language and Welshness. I discuss the effects my changing feelings over time about linguistic hybridity, and my growing confidence as a young academic, had on my engagement with different texts and writers. This is discussed in light of the relationships I was able to form with some creative authors and academics in Wales's close-knit literary and scholarly society.*

Originality/Value – *This chapter argues that confronting their own emotional engagements with their research topics enables researchers to better understand why certain subjects are so contested. It can also prepare researchers to communicate their ideas effectively in the difficult debates that arise around such subjects.*

Keywords: Welsh language; identity; multiculturalism; literary criticism; hybrid identities; literary culture; early career research

INTRODUCTION

In her autofictional novel *Sugar and Slate* (2002), Welsh author and sociologist Charlotte Williams explores her identity as a mixed-race woman and expresses her sympathy for 'poor old mixed-up Wales, somehow as mixed up as I was' (Williams, 2002, p. 169). Although I am not mixed race and have therefore not suffered the same racial inequalities as Williams, her vision of 'mixed-up Wales' and a mixed-up self resonate with me both personally and professionally. I am a literary critic, interested in how the complicated politics of Welsh-English bilingualism affects Wales's literature and literary culture. My doctoral research, completed in 2015, examined how bilingualism affects contemporary fiction's portrayal of multiculturalism in Wales. I am also one of the 19% of Welsh inhabitants who speak Welsh (Office for National Statistics, 2012) – it is my second language, although, by now, I use it just as much as English. I am, therefore, often emotionally affected by linguistic debates in Wales. This chapter explores how my emotional investment in bilingualism affected my doctoral research. It demonstrates how my complicated personal feelings about language at times restricted my academic work, but ultimately helped me to forge my own space in a contentious field. These interactions are set against my identity as an early career researcher, and how wanting to feel accepted as both an academic and a Welsh speaker was an important emotional drive as I conducted my research.

MY JOURNEY AS A WELSH SPEAKER

Describing my life as a Welsh speaker as a 'journey' is appropriate as my fluency, use of Welsh and positive attitude towards Welsh culture and society has changed over time. Welsh is my second language. I was raised in an English-speaking home in the Afan Valley, and educated at Welsh-medium primary and secondary schools in Aberafan and the Swansea Valley. Many pupils of such schools in south Wales, including some of my own first cousins and most of my primary school classmates, have a similar linguistic background. In line with the findings of research regarding the attitudes of Welsh-medium educated children towards the Welsh language (Geraint, 2016, pp. 57–61), my own feelings towards the language have always been overwhelmingly positive, and I perceive my peers' feelings to be similar. As a literary critic who takes a postcolonial approach to Welsh literature and culture (Aaron & Williams, 2005; Bohata, 2004), I am, by now, comfortable in my linguistic 'hybridity' (Bhabha, 1994). Indeed, this hybridity, in part at least, drives my research. Yet despite this positivity towards Welsh and my current contentment, at certain times, I have felt insecure about my validity as a Welsh speaker.

It is not entirely clear to me why this might be. My journey as a Welsh speaker began in the Welsh-medium classroom, in much the same way as many other people's. Furthermore, my use of the language and relationship with it in childhood and adolescence reflects the findings of academic research conducted with other Welsh-medium educated children in the area of Wales in which I was raised (Gruffudd, 1997). Children's use of Welsh tends to reflect their family's view of the language and linguistic background (Geraint, 2016, pp. 44 and 61), and children are most likely to use the language usually spoken at home (Gruffudd, 1997, pp. 201–205). Despite our family's positive attitude towards the language, my Welsh-medium educated cousins and I always spoke English with each other, and still do, despite us all using Welsh professionally. Although we feel somewhat guilty, I also worry about excluding the rest of our English-speaking family through speaking Welsh.

Conforming to the linguistic majority is a factor in the linguistic choices of Welsh-medium educated children at school, too (Geraint, 2016, p. 55). The catchment areas of my primary and secondary schools, both situated in Neath Port Talbot County Borough Council, is majority English-speaking (although certain areas, such as the Tawe Valley and the eastern Amman Valley, have a significant Welsh-speaking population), so English is the majority language of the community too. English was perhaps considered a more 'fashionable' language (Gruffudd, 1997, p. 213), although for me it was not such a conscious choice. My best friends at secondary school all came from homes where at least one parent spoke Welsh, and our friendships were maintained despite the differences in our linguistic backgrounds. My integration into Welsh-language culture has also been aided by my high level of fluency in Welsh – my mother recounts that at every parents' evening, my teachers were always amazed when her own preference for English (she lacks the confidence to use Welsh) reminded them that I was not from a Welsh-speaking home.

My happy hybridity, and my feelings of being a bona fide Welsh speaker, developed most fully when I went to university to study Welsh and English Literature. Here, Welsh truly became a language for socialising. My best friends at university were all Welsh speakers who were studying Welsh. As a group, our relationship with, and fluency in, Welsh varied, from first-language speakers from the Welsh-speaking heartlands to second-language speakers who had been taught Welsh at English-medium schools. Despite these differences, we spoke Welsh with each other inside and outside the classroom, and still do so now. When I continued to my masters and doctoral-level studies, and then employment as an academic in a Welsh department, Welsh became the language of work too. My colleagues, like my university friends, have diverse linguistic backgrounds as Welsh speakers. Therefore, although Welsh is technically my second language, it is now the main language of my work and leisure time. I am now equally confident and fluent in Welsh or English, and have been for a long time. In my experience, Welsh is a language spoken by a variety of people of differing circumstances and for different purposes too.

My relationship with the literatures and languages of Wales as objects of academic study, then, illustrates Amanda Coffey's (1999, p. 22) argument that 'who is a stranger or a member, an outsider or an insider, a knower or an ignoramus is all relative and much more blurred than conventional accounts might have us believe'. Although I have been a Welsh speaker from an early age, it was not inevitable that I would maintain this identity in later life. In addition, my relation to the English-speaking Welsh communities in which I was raised and have always lived is complicated by the fact that, unlike most other members, I speak Welsh. Whilst I do not feel excluded from either language group, I am neither wholly inside or wholly outside one or the other (see also Roberts, 2018 [this volume]). This sense of 'otherness' or 'duality' is perhaps amplified by my own academic interests in hybrid identities, multilingualism and multiculturalism.

I think such 'otherness' and 'duality' is also a preoccupation in Wales, though, brought about by certain cultural divides. Literary critic Katie Gramich has noted that 'the cultural situation of Wales does seem ineluctably divided: north versus south, Welsh versus English, town versus country, industry versus agriculture, chapel versus pub and so on. Such dualism seems to pervade Welsh culture: is it apparent or real?' (Gramich, 1997, p. 101). As bilingual playwright Alun Saunders recently put it, 'people like to put things in boxes' (Sheppard, 2017).[1] Whilst it is true to say that nobody's identity fits neatly into preordained categories, my hybrid linguistic identity means that clumsy or inflammatory statements on linguistic division (e.g., Tickle & Morris, 2017) frustrate and even anger me: such attacks feel personal. Binary categories are untenable in my experience of contemporary Wales.

I have not always revelled in the ambivalence and ambiguity of my position as a Welsh-speaker from an English-speaking background. Charlotte Williams, has commented upon the imagined link between the ability to speak Welsh and a stronger claim to Welsh identity: she claims that the Welsh language's 'place in the national imagining as the most authentic marker of Welsh identity is unchallenged. In turn this produces the "not-identities" of Wales as inevitably the lack of language skills is felt to compromise some people's claim to Welshness' (Williams, 2005, p. 223). Although no one ever levelled such accusations at me when I was at school, at the back of my mind I did worry that my linguistic background made me less 'Welsh' than others. Non Geraint's study of Welsh- and English-medium educated children in northern Powys demonstrates that some believed that 'speaking Welsh may result in a deeper level of national identity' (Geraint, 2016, p. 54). It is possible that similar ideas unconsciously influenced my feelings as a young person.

RESPONDING TO ACADEMIC DEBATES ABOUT BILINGUALISM, MULTICULTURALISM AND RACISM IN WALES AS AN EARLY CAREER RESEARCHER

On a personal and emotional level, then, I understand that some Welsh people might see a grain of truth in Charlotte Williams's perception of a link between linguistic ability and Welsh identity. I feel strongly, however, that this should not be the case. Despite my sympathies with those who feel excluded from 'Welshness' because they do not speak Welsh, I also find presentations of Welsh-speaking society as particularly exclusive or homogeneous deeply problematic. They are simply unrepresentative of the literature and society upon which my research concentrates and are often based on unintentionally misleading interpretations of data and sources. But as a new doctoral researcher, I found it difficult to discuss these opinions because Williams is undoubtedly the most important voice in debates on multiculturalism in Wales. She co-edited the pioneering volume, *A Tolerant Nation? Exploring Ethnic Diversity in Wales* (Williams, O'Leary, & Evans, 2003) which sought to dispel the powerful myth of Welsh tolerance of ethnic diversity. Williams's own writings argue that Welsh speakers' campaigns for linguistic recognition hinder the realisation of a truly multicultural Wales (Williams, 2003a, p. 220). Her work has also advanced the idea that Welsh-language culture is 'monocultural' (Williams, 2003b, p. 23). More than anything, her work demonstrates how the emotive subject of language is crucial in debates about Welsh multiculturalism. Multiculturalism is often an emotive topic in itself, as it inevitably invokes ideas of belonging, national sovereignty, and both positive and negative manifestations of nationalism (Sheppard, 2018). In addition, some language campaigners have been accused of racism, and, as will be seen, this was particularly relevant to my own research on Welsh multiculturalism.

To fully understand my emotional response to Charlotte Williams's claims about Welsh-language culture, it is necessary to realise her importance as a creative writer. *Sugar and Slate* won the English-language Wales Book of the Year Award in 2003, and was praised by prominent literary critics for its portrayal of multicultural Wales. Jane Aaron has called it the 'fullest literary exploration to date of such hybrid ethnic identities in Wales' (Aaron, 2016, p. 34), and Katie Gramich, one of my own doctoral supervisors, has applauded its 'unique and powerful, and specifically Welsh' exploration of belonging and alienation (2007, pp. 191–192). Despite my reservations about Williams's academic claims, I not only agree that *Sugar and Slate* is the most important Anglophone text about multicultural Wales, but find Williams's persona in this autofictional novel sincere and likeable.

As I began my doctoral studies, I felt that I was responding to two different Charlottes. One was the creative writer whose work I admired. The other was the sociologist with whom I disagreed. My other doctoral supervisor, the literary and cultural critic, and Welsh language campaigner, Simon Brooks, had also published research that challenged Williams's claims about the monocultural nature of Welsh-speaking communities (Brooks, 2006, 2009). Although my supervisors both actively encouraged me to challenge their (sometimes divergent) readings of texts and contexts, I found this prospect daunting. As experienced academics, they inevitably held institutional and experiential power (Wisker, 2012, p. 54). I also found it near-impossible to balance the positive responses to Williams's creative work and the more controversial debate surrounding her academic work. For example, I felt that her suggestion that Welsh-language culture 'strives increasingly towards mono-culturalism' (Williams, 2005, p. 224) ignores the multifarious ways speakers of the language have engaged with other cultures, as strongly evidenced by the Welsh-language fiction I was researching (Sheppard, 2018). As other commentators have noted, charges of monoculturalism, exclusivity, and even racism, have plagued Welsh-speaking society since the turn of the twenty-first century (Brooks, 2006). I found that such charges were obstacles to my goal of discussing multiculturalism in an academic setting. As Brooks argues in relation to this matter, 'to be branded a racist is to have one's discourse delegitimised' (2006, p. 160). As a new researcher trying to contribute for the first time to academic discussions of topics such as multiculturalism, who wanted to seem progressive and open-minded, I was extremely apprehensive about the possibility that my own research would be described in this way.

I was also becoming increasingly aware of how rare black and minority ethnic (BAME) voices, literary or academic, were in the field of Welsh multiculturalism. Williams's prominence added such a voice to the debates. In addition to this, whilst my own experiences led me to disagree with Williams's assessment of Welsh-language culture, I do not possess the same knowledge of Wales's BAME communities. I felt I could not challenge findings based on Williams's own personal and professional involvement with those communities. One of the aims of my research was to explore the literary voices of marginalised groups, and so I felt a weight of responsibility to ensure that diverse voices were heard. In my mind, however, Welsh speakers were marginalised too, and their voices were not being adequately heard in this debate.

Some of Williams's most damning evidence supporting her arguments about Welsh cultural exclusivity was based on the mistranslated statements of Welsh language campaigners. Williams's argument draws upon concerns expressed by Welsh language activists about the effect of migration, specifically migration from England, in decreasing the proportion of Welsh speakers in the Welsh-speaking heartlands known as '*Y Fro Gymraeg*' (Williams, 2003a, 2003b, 2005). These concerns had been mistranslated and misrepresented by various media outlets (Brooks, 2006). Both this misrepresentation, and Williams's neglect of the original sources, seemed to show the disregard afforded to the Welsh language and those who write in it. This frustrated me and I wanted to advocate for language rights, for my own sake as a Welsh speaker as well as that of those who had been directly misrepresented.

As my research progressed, I found that focusing on fictional portrayals of otherness, alienations and marginalisation was a way to include Welsh, English and other multicultural voices in my analysis. At the beginning, however, I felt restricted by competing and sometimes divisive understandings of multiculturalism in Wales. I worried that whatever research choices I made, I would ultimately isolate myself from one group or another, and forego any opportunities (including for future employment or publication) that may have been available had I taken a different line in the debate.

WELSH LITERARY AND SCHOLARLY COMMUNITIES

For new researchers in the field of Welsh literature, opportunities to engage directly with authors and critics are readily available. As a doctoral student, I had personal and professional relationships with people whose work informed my research, and whose work I might have to challenge. This familiarity is common in Welsh literary and critical circles, and is particularly true of Welsh-speaking literary culture, where events like local and national *Eisteddfodau* (literary festivals) are especially important. Although literary events in Wales are usually informal and friendly arenas, they are also often implicitly or explicitly politically symbolic. Wales's literary sphere is politically self-aware, particularly in terms of the politics of language and culture. For instance, Jane Aaron's analysis of 'Bardic anti-colonialism' (2005) shows how, since the thirteenth century, Welsh-language poets, and, more recently Welsh poets writing in English, have creatively expressed resistance to English cultural and political dominance. For Welsh-speaking society, literary prosperity is linked to language survival (Price, 2002, p. 16), and to a certain extent this affects how literature in created, critiqued, and consumed by this community (Marks, 2013, p. 26). Whilst contributing directly to the literary and critical scene is fruitful, or even necessary, for Welsh-language literary critics, it can also be emotionally tricky to navigate relationships between authors, critics and lay readers, as my own experiences of participating in Welsh-language literary culture reveals.

I believe literature (and all art) has a dialectical relationship with society and culture – simply put, literature is influenced by the world in which it is created, and, in turn, it influences the world in which it is consumed. If this is true, then a diversity of authors and literary voices will help create a more inclusive society (Sheppard, 2018). In this respect, the apparent conservatism of much Welsh-language literary criticism, right up until the recent past, frustrates me. Williams and Roberts (1982, pp. 10–11) have remarked that in such a small community of authors and critics, there is less chance of finding opposing opinions about texts, and so ultimately it becomes easier to rely on traditional voices, myths and forms, at the expense of creating a truly representative literary sphere. Since the 1980s Welsh literature and criticism have deconstructed what could be deemed a restrictive literary culture (Hallam, 2007; Marks, 2013; Price, 2002; Williams & Roberts, 1982). In addition, from the early 1990s student-run magazines such as *tu chwith* (1993–2015) and *Y Stamp* (2016–ongoing) have provided an important space for new literary and critical voices. While the Welsh literary scene might seem static, and although some influential figures can be seen as gatekeepers of tradition and culture, I have always felt that everyone is very welcoming, and that there are many people who share my feelings about Welsh literature. On many occasions, discussing certain points of frustration with like-minded colleagues has been liberating, and their support has been uplifting.

More challenging, in my experience, is the relationship between the critic and the author who is the object of that critic's work (Hallam, 2002; Marks, 2013). In my doctoral thesis, I analysed the work of 15 authors, and during the research and in the time since completing my PhD I have met six of them. Of this six, I have worked on projects, interviewed, connected on social media, personally corresponded or socialised with at least four of them, and these relationships have developed over an extended period. I have also forged relationships with other writers whose work I study or teach, which falls short of friendship but goes beyond mere acquaintance. They are certainly more than simply authors whose work I study. When one of the four authors recently died, I felt very sad and shaken for many days afterwards, and found it difficult to engage with his work for a project I needed to finish at that time. The types of relationships that one can forge with authors in this kind of literary culture has implications for how criticism is produced. Critics may not only be thinking of editors and presses as they write but also the authors with whom they have personal relationships. I know that honest criticism is essential to the continual development of a robust and inclusive literary and critical culture in Wales, but I have had to grapple hard with the thought of responding negatively to the work of authors I know.

These feelings were most pronounced in my engagement with one of my favourite authors, Llwyd Owen. As a doctoral student and academic I have interviewed Llwyd, been interviewed with him, invited him to speak at events I have organised and attended his book launches, so our relationship has developed over a period of around six years. I refer to him here as Llwyd because it feels unnatural to refer to him as just 'Owen'. I feel indebted to Llwyd for more than this personal support though – his novels are the reason I do what I do. Had I not been introduced as an undergraduate student to his graphic, funny and challenging novels, my serious interest in contemporary Welsh-language literature might not have developed. His first novel, *Ffawd, Cywilydd a Chelwyddau* (Fate, Shame, & Lies, 2006) became infamous not only for its dark portrayal of Cardiff's media industry, but because its early manuscript version lost out on the Daniel Owen Memorial Prize in the 2005 National Eisteddfod – the judges believed that its language, a mix of code-switched Welsh and English, and purposely mistranslated and grammatically incorrect Welsh, made it unworthy of the prize (Orwig, 2015; Pritchard, Mair, & Davies, 2005). Although Llwyd was raised in a Welsh-speaking home, as a new undergraduate student and a second-language speaker, I think I was drawn to the rebellion against standards and traditions that his 'incorrect' Welsh symbolised, as well as to his daring subjects, which were a world away from the old-fashioned Welsh novels I had studied at school. His second novel, *Ffydd Gobaith Cariad* (Faith Hope Love, 2006) was equally popular, with me, and readers more generally, and it won the Welsh-language Wales Book of the Year in 2007.

As an academic whose work analyses ethnic, racial and linguistic communities, and how they are portrayed, I find the reliance on linguistic stereotypes in Llwyd's second novel problematic. I have written and published on this novel, and noted my objections to this stereotyping that polarises Wales's two main linguistic communities (Sheppard, 2015; Sheppard, 2018). In writing about the novel, I felt that my identity as a critic and scholarly standards required me to point out this unfortunate dichotomy, but my personal relationship with Llwyd made me feel awkward about doing so. I do not know whether he is aware of my criticism, but the familiar nature of Welsh literary society, which also includes a great number of well-read and proactive lay readers, means that if he has not heard about it already, it is very possible that he will in the future. Criticising his work, then, felt like betraying an author to whom I feel I owe a lot. I felt guilty about criticising his novel (albeit in one sentence in a 10,000-word article, and another in an 80,000-word thesis/monograph) when I had always been enthusiastic about his work in his presence. I was also aware of the criticism Llwyd's previous work had received from Eisteddfod judges and felt uncomfortable with the potential power my negative words, as a critic, could hold over the work of someone I knew and would undoubtedly meet again.

MY DISTAL RELATIONSHIP WITH CHARLOTTE WILLIAMS

While the closeness of the Welsh-language literary scene means that I have forged personal relationships with several authors during my research, I am always aware of those authors whom I have not met, and that my relationship with the different authors I research is unequal. I am further troubled by the different reasons for my apprehension about criticising the work of different authors. In commenting on the work of Llwyd Owen, for example, I was mostly worried about how Llwyd would feel, and how this might affect any future engagement between us. I also study Charlotte Williams's creative work in my doctoral thesis, but have never met her. When it came to challenging her academic findings, I was more worried about how I would be perceived by others – would I seem progressive, or racist? This has led me to consider how the personal relationships Welsh literary researchers forge within the field might affect their work. Additionally, my awareness of the access and influence I have within different academic circles of interest has been heightened. As a doctoral researcher and early career academic, meeting Welsh authors and critics, and discussing work with them, has not been difficult. Creating networks in the broader field of multiculturalism, however, has been more challenging. As my research developed, Williams's work and her role as an influential figure in the academic study of multiculturalism complicated my engagement with the field. My feelings about this might be best explored in relation to a six-month period towards the end of my time as a doctoral student, where I came into more direct, albeit still distal, contact with her.

Williams is professor of Social Work at Royal Melbourne Institute of Technology (RMIT) University in Australia. She was undoubtedly the creative author I was least likely to meet of all those whose work my research considers. Whilst attending a public lecture, my supervisor Katie Gramich had spoken to Neil Evans, one of Williams's co-editors on *A Tolerant Nation?*. Evans had suggested that I contact him about the new edition of *A Tolerant Nation?* which was in preparation, and even sent me the revamped introductory chapter. A few days later, he emailed again to say that he had told Williams and O'Leary about my research, and they were happy to let me see the new, unpublished edition in its entirety. I was extremely grateful for the opportunity to enhance my own research – after all, the content of this new edition might have impacted upon my own work, and the future possibilities for publishing or using the research after I received my doctorate. Mentioning Charlotte and Paul by their first names, he explained that all three editors understood my dilemma, and did not wish me to have to delay completing my thesis until the volume was published. The use of first names and the expression of sympathy added a personal feeling that made me feel valued as a fellow researcher in the field, and instantly more familiar with them. I felt excited that I was in contact with important figures in my field.

Upon reading the new edition, however, I found that despite other substantial changes, the same core ideas regarding the exclusivity of Welsh language speakers and communities, with which I disagree, remained an important factor in the text. I was partly relieved that the points to which my own research responded had remained, as at least that meant my thesis had something different to contribute. My feelings about challenging Williams's work, however, now became more complicated. I had previously felt concerned about silencing diverse voices, and about becoming embroiled in the discourse of racism that had developed in discussions of migration, multiculturalism and the Welsh language. But I now also felt indebted to Williams and her co-editors for their support. I also did not want to alienate people who I perceived as powerful influences in the field of multiculturalism, who might be able to help me with future research and work. Additionally, now that I knew Williams was aware of my work, I imagined she would be more likely to read it, and was apprehensive about her response. I therefore declined the opportunity to directly cite the new edition in my thesis, to avoid feeling even more awkward and ungrateful for disputing its claims (although I do now dispute them in my forthcoming monograph).

This was not the end of my interaction with Charlotte Williams. Coincidentally, at that time I was due to attend some academic conferences to present papers on her creative work. My supervisor Simon Brooks had left Cardiff University, and thus, I had a new supervisor. Although Brooks had not attempted to influence my view of Williams's work, despite some of his own research publications challenging it, the fact that I began to engage more with Williams's work might suggest that, subconsciously, I felt less inhibited in his absence. The first of these conferences was the Contemporary Women's Writing Association's biennial conference, which in 2014 was held in Melbourne, Australia. RMIT University was one of the conference's host institutions. My experience of familiar literary circles in Wales, where colleagues and I have often discussed an author's own work with them, or even presented conference papers on their work in their presence, led me to wonder whether Williams would attend the conference, even though it was outside her academic discipline. I agonised over the phrasing of my paper, avoided including any readings that challenged Williams's academic work and concentrated instead on discussing how her academic scholarship could illuminate her creative work and vice versa. When I entered the room where I was to give my paper, I scanned the audience and was both relieved and a little disappointed to find that Williams was not present. Although I now knew conclusively that I did not have to worry about her response to my work, at least at that moment, part of me imagined a scenario where she really enjoyed my paper, and we had a chat about it afterwards.

Ironically, after the conference I received some confirmation of Williams's awareness that I was interested in her work. Around two weeks after returning from Melbourne, I attended the 'What Happens Now: 21st Century Writing in English Conference', hosted by the University of Lincoln, to present the same paper I had given in Australia. An academic from Keele University chaired my panel, and one of his Keele colleagues was in the audience. Charlotte Williams has previously worked at Keele University. In conversations before the session began, they both told me that they knew Williams, and that they were looking forward to my paper. The audience member also mentioned that she was still in regular contact with Williams, and had emailed her the night before to tell her about my paper. Their obvious fondness for Williams confirmed my own positive impressions of her as a person, gleaned from my indirect interactions with her. The paper went well, and I was pleased to hear that Williams's former colleagues had enjoyed it. Afterwards I had an email from the academic social network, Academia.edu, notifying me that someone had searched for my name on Google and viewed my profile. Although the viewer remains anonymous, Academia.edu allows users to see the viewer's location. I felt a flicker of excitement as I saw that the viewer was in Melbourne, and was taken aback to think that Williams might have actively tried to find out more about me. I still do not know whether the viewer in Melbourne was Williams or not, but the possibility of her interest was heartening. Even if she entirely disagreed with what I had to say, it would at least mean that she felt I was worthy of further investigation as an academic.

CONCLUSION

This incident made me feel validated at a pivotal moment in my academic career. I was about to finish my thesis, experience my doctoral viva and begin my first academic post, and this momentary incident made me feel like a 'real' academic. Reflecting upon it reveals how emotion can play a significant role in research, how our emotions towards our work change over time, and the impact they can have on our research. Confronting my own emotions as a second-language speaker in the debate about multiculturalism in Wales, and recognising my sympathies for speakers of both languages, was essential to the path my doctoral research eventually took. My thesis ultimately engaged with the idea that all cultural groups in Wales – including native Welsh and English speakers – could feel excluded on the grounds of their ethnic, racial or linguistic background, and proposed how to develop a more inclusive society all round. Indeed, the process of writing a paper for the Emotions and the Researcher conference held in Cardiff in early 2014, from which this chapter has developed, was an important first step in understanding what I wanted to argue in my thesis as I began to bring disparate chapters together into a whole.

As well as recognising the role emotion can play in shaping research topics and outcomes, my emotional engagement with the Welsh literary scene reflects many of my hopes and apprehensions as an early career researcher. Recognising the emotions involved in my participation in Welsh literary culture has contributed to my development as a researcher in this field. The act of criticising or challenging the literary or academic work of people I know, like and respect has not only strengthened my resolve to be as honest as possible in my criticism but has also helped me to criticise in a constructive and thoughtful manner. As an early career researcher, I have been the (by now) grateful recipient of such beneficial comments, and hope my experiences help me in the next step in my career: co-supervising my first doctoral student. She is one of my university friends – but that is another chapter yet to be written.

NOTE

1. This translation of a Welsh-language source has been undertaken by the chapter's author.

REFERENCES

Aaron, J. (2005). Bardic anti-colonialism. In J. Aaron & C. Williams (Eds.), *Postcolonial Wales* (pp. 137–158). Cardiff: University of Wales Press.

Aaron, J. (2016). Devolved voices: Welsh Women's writing post 1999. In D. Mannay (Ed.), *Our changing land: Revisiting gender, class and identity in contemporary Wales* (pp. 22–41). Cardiff: University of Wales Press.

Aaron, J., & Williams, C. (Eds.) (2005). *Postcolonial Wales*. Cardiff: University of Wales Press.

Bhabha, H. K. (1994). *The location of culture*. London: Routledge.

Bohata, K. (2004). *Postcolonialism revisited*. Cardiff: University of Wales Press.

Brooks, S. (2006). The idioms of race: The 'racist nationalist' in Wales as bogeyman. In T. R. Chapman (Ed.), *The idiom of dissent: Protest and propaganda in Wales* (pp. 139–165). Llandysul: Gomer Press.

Brooks, S. (2009). Tiger Bay a'r diwylliant Cymraeg. *Trafodion anrhydeddus Gymdeithas y Cymmrodorion, 15*, 198–216.

Coffey, A. (1999). *The ethnographic self: Fieldwork and the representation of identity*. London: SAGE.

Geraint, N. (2016). Only inside the classroom? Young people's use of the Welsh language in the school, community and peer group. In D. Mannay (Ed.), *Our changing land: Revisiting gender, class and identity in contemporary Wales* (pp. 43–63). Cardiff: University of Wales Press.

Gramich, K. (1997). Cymru or Wales? Explorations in a divided sensibility. In S. Bassnett (Ed.), *Studying British cultures* (pp. 97–112). London: Routledge.

Gramich, K. (2007). *Twentieth-century women's writing in Wales: Land, gender, belonging*. Cardiff: University of Wales Press.

Gruffudd, H. (1997). Young people's use of Welsh: The influence of home and community. *Contemporary Wales, 10*, 200–218.

Hallam, T. (2002). Eilunyddiaeth. *Tu Chwith, 17*, 31–36.

Hallam, T. (2007). *Canon ein llên: Saunders Lewis, R. M. Jones ac Alan Llwyd*. Cardiff: University of Wales Press.

Marks, R. (2013). *'Pe gallwn, mi luniwn lythyr': Golwg ar waith Menna Elfyn*. Cardiff: University of Wales Press.

Office for National Statistics. (2012). 2011 Census: Key statistics for Wales, March 2011. Retrieved from https://www.ons.gov.uk/peoplepopulationandcommunity/population-andmigration/populationestimates/bulletins/2011censuskeystatisticsforwales/2012-12-11#proficiency-in-welsh. Accessed on August 3, 2017.

Orwig, S. (2015). *Cyfnewid cod mewn llenyddiaeth: Nofelau Cymraeg a Ffrangeg Canadaidd: Datblygu methodoleg newydd*. Unpublished M.Phil. dissertation, Cardiff University, Cardiff.

Owen, L. (2006). *Ffawd, cywilydd a chelwyddau* (2nd ed.). Talybont: Y Lolfa.

Owen, L. (2007). *Ffydd, gobaith, cariad* (2nd ed.). Talybont: Y Lolfa.

Price, A. (2002). *Rhwng gwyn a du: Agweddau ar ryddiaith Gymraeg y 1990au*. Cardiff: University of Wales Press.

Pritchard, E., Mair, B., & Puw Davies, C. (2005). Beirniadaeth Gwobr Goffa Daniel Owen. In J. E. Hughes (Ed.), *Cyfansoddiadau a beirniadaethau Eisteddfod Genedlaethol Cymru, Eryri a'r Cyffiniau 2005* (pp. 92–100). Llandysul: Llys yr Eisteddfod.

Roberts, E. (2018). The 'transient insider': Identity and intimacy in home community research. In T. Loughran & D. Mannay (Eds.), *Emotion and the researcher: Sites, subjectivities and relationships* (Vol. 16). Studies in Qualitative Methodology (pp. 113–126). Bingley: Emerald.

Sheppard, L. (2015). Pulling pints, not punches: Linguistic tensions in the literary pubs of Wales. *International Journal of Welsh Writing in English, 3*, 75–101.

Sheppard, L. (2017). Trafodaeth Ford Gron – Dwyieithrwydd a chreadigrwydd [video resource]. In *Eitha' different yndyn nhw…but it works*, Llyfrgell y Coleg Cymraeg Cenedlaethol. Retrieved from https://llyfrgell.porth.ac.uk/View.aspx?id=2981∼4u∼vy7Iupmy. Accessed on August 3, 2017.

Sheppard, L. (2018). *O'r Gymru 'ddu' i'r ddalen 'wen': Aralledd ac amlddiwylliannedd mewn ffuglen Gymreig, er 1990*. Cardiff: University of Wales Press.

Tickle, L., & Morris, S. (2017, 20 June). 'We're told we're anti-Welsh bigots and fascists': The
     storm over Welsh-first schooling. *The Guardian* [Online]. Retrieved from https://www.
     theguardian.com/education/2017/jun/20/storm-welsh-only-schools-minority-language.
     Accessed on August 3, 2017.
Williams, C. (2002). *Sugar and slate*. Aberystwyth: Planet.
Williams, C. (2003a). Claiming the national: Nation, national identity and ethnic minorities. In
     C. Williams, P. O'Leary, & N. Evans (Eds.), *A tolerant nation?: Exploring ethnic diversity
     in Wales* (pp. 220–234). Cardiff: University of Wales Press.
Williams, C. (2003b). Strange encounters. *Planet, 158*, 19–24.
Williams, C. (2005). Can we live together? Wales and the multicultural question. *Transactions of
     the Honourable Society of Cymmrodorion, 11*, 216–230.
Williams, C., O'Leary, P., & Evans, N. (Eds.) (2003). *A tolerant nation?: Exploring ethnic diversity
     in Wales*. Cardiff: University of Wales Press.
Williams, I. L., & Roberts, W. O. (1982). Myth y traddodiad dethol. *Llais Llyfrau*, Autumn,
     10–11.
Wisker, G. (2012). *The good supervisor: Supervising postgraduate and undergraduate research for
     doctoral theses and dissertations* (2nd ed.). Basingstoke: Palgrave Macmillan.

CHAPTER 13

THE EMOTION OF 'DOING ETHICS' IN HEALTHCARE RESEARCH: A RESEARCHER'S REFLEXIVE ACCOUNT

Geraldine Latchem-Hastings

ABSTRACT

Purpose – *This chapter reflects on the importance of being reflexive as a socio-legal researcher whilst seeking to address the practicalities, challenges and methods of being reflexive during the research process. The chapter demonstrates 'doing it' by reporting on the use of an internal dialogue of the researcher's feelings and choices during research encounters to reflect on the status of insider knowledge in the interview process. It also charts the unexpected emotional reactions of participants, and in doing so, highlights the challenges of reflection in and on everyday practice as a physiotherapist.*

Methodology/Approach – *The research reported here was an empirical ethics study using in-depth interviews and the voice-centred relational method as practical means of doing and being reflexive.*

Emotion and the Researcher: Sites, Subjectivities, and Relationships
Studies in Qualitative Methodology, Volume 16, 213–228
ISSN: 1042-3192/doi:10.1108/S1042-319220180000016014

Findings – *The chapter sheds light on the role of emotion in the research process, the author's emotional position as researcher and the unexpected emotional reactions of participants.*

Originality/Value – *The chapter presents a practical method of reflexivity in qualitative research and considers the personal and ethical issues that arise during the research process from the competing perspectives of both insider and researcher. The key lesson learnt is the importance of reflecting on ethically important, and at times uncomfortable, moments in the research process so that other researchers can learn about the 'how to' of reflexivity and reflexive writing.*

Keywords: Reflexivity; emotion; ethics in healthcare research; insider research; role duality; voice-centred relational method

BACKGROUND

This chapter draws on the empirical ethics study undertaken for my PhD, which explored the values of paediatric physiotherapists working in the community (Hastings, 2013). Paediatric physiotherapy is a specialist area of physiotherapy 'concerned with the assessment, treatment and management of babies, children and young people with physical problems' (Association of Paediatric Chartered Physiotherapists, 2009, p. 7). My interest in the research topic originated from past clinical experience as a paediatric physiotherapist. Whilst working in the acute hospital environment, I encountered many patient and family scenarios that gave rise to an array of complex legal and ethical dilemmas for physiotherapists and other healthcare professionals. Such was the complexity of these interactions that I began studying, researching and ultimately teaching healthcare law and bioethics.

Why might physiotherapists experience complex legal and ethical dilemmas in their practice? The very nature of the physiotherapist's work entails close and prolonged physical and emotional contact with patients. The touching practices of this profession, which was developed initially to legitimise and de-sexualise massage (Barclay, 1994), give rise to complex legal and ethical questions in practice. Physiotherapists are required to make autonomous clinical and ethical decisions based on connections and relationships with patients, families, other health professionals, health institutions and changing health policies. Both touching practices and autonomous decision making carry responsibilities in respect of scope of practice, requiring knowledge and observance of professional standards. Moreover, physiotherapists' clinical practice raises issues of fundamental ethical importance because it deals with the nature of life from its very beginning until its end.

Despite the ethics embedded within physiotherapeutic practice, when I began my PhD, there was both a dearth of studies exploring ethical dilemmas in physiotherapy practice generally, but particularly within paediatrics, and a lack of empirical methodological work focused on the *doing* of ethics-based research. As the literature provided little guidance or consensus on methods I developed my own approach. I conducted what Kon (2009, p. 60) refers to as a 'Lay of the Land' study where I defined and described values, beliefs and practices of a group of paediatric physiotherapists. I took this approach to describe the *what* and *how* of bioethical reasoning and decision making as experienced by these physiotherapists in various contexts (Ives & Draper, 2009).

THE ETHICS OF 'DOING ETHICS' RESEARCH IN HEALTH CARE

As a qualitative researcher conducting an empirical ethics study, being reflexive about my research practice was crucial. Reflexivity requires the qualitative inquirer to be attentive to and conscious of one's own voice and perspective, as well as to the perspectives and voices of interviewees and those to whom one reports (Patton, 2002, p. 63). I, like Guillemin and Gillam (2004), view reflexivity as closely connected with the ethical practice of research. I experienced a very rigorous research ethics review prior to conducting my study. Some concerns raised by the ethics committee were role duality as a researcher and a physiotherapist, and the potential for psychological harm to the participants, unethical conduct that might warrant reporting to professional regulatory bodies.

I, as a former paediatric physiotherapist, came to the research study as someone with insider knowledge of physiotherapy practice. I was mindful that being an insider could be a benefit because it might bring me closer to the participants and assist in gaining richer data (see Mannay & Creaghan, 2016; Roberts, 2018 [this volume]). However, it could also be disadvantageous, as participants may have been concerned that I would judge their practice through my interpreting and reporting on their accounts (see also van den Scott, 2018 [this volume]). In addition, as a lecturer in physiotherapy, it was important to be conscious of how participants might view me. Therefore, I was careful to focus upon my role as a researcher rather than a physiotherapist or a teacher.

In reality, this was more challenging when caught up in the kaleidoscope of feelings experienced during a given interview. Overall, my research practice necessitated what Etherington (2007, p. 600) refers to as 'ethical mindfulness' contributing to 'an ethic of trust' in the relationships formed with the participants during the research journey – a journey that was constantly challenged by issues of transparency, equality and power.

Emotional Risks for Participants

Guillemin and Gillam (2004, p. 272) suggest that the potential harms to participants in qualitative research are often 'quite subtle and stem from the nature of the interaction between researcher and participant'. I was aware that asking participants to reflect on practice might involve emotive thinking as sensitive and potentially upsetting experiences were recalled. The notion of harm or distress to participants was one of the main ethical issues raised during ethics review prior to conducting the research. However, knowing theoretically what might happen and dealing with the emotional responses of the participants turned out to be more challenging than anticipated. As a novice researcher, I did not anticipate that the first interview would become as emotionally intense as it did, at least for some of the participants, who found the retrospective journey of describing and discussing their careers at times upsetting. Being interviewed was an unusual experience for most of the participant physiotherapists – a role reversal if you like – as they were usually the listeners (Legard, Keegan, & Ward, 2003). None of them had previously had the opportunity to discuss their experiences, so, unintentionally, each interview became a cathartic experience. These issues undoubtedly influenced the way I approached the study, as is evident in my reflexive account below.

THE EMPIRICAL ETHICS STUDY: APPROACH AND METHOD

My theoretical and ontological position as a researcher was influenced by my own values of care, compassion, empathy and placing the child at the centre of the therapeutic relationship. I was drawn to theoretical ideas/concepts that supported these values. Eventually, my perspective as researcher became influenced by the work of the feminist theorists Carol Gilligan and Joan Tronto on the ethic of care and the concept of relational ontology. Relational ontology posits the notion of the human being as embedded in a complex web of intimate and larger social relations where people are viewed as interdependent rather than independent (Gilligan, 1992; Tronto, 1993). Taking this ontological position into my research practice, I undertook in-depth biographical interviews, which focused on the clinical practice experiences of participants, and adopted Brown and Gilligan's (1992) voice-centred relational method.

I chose in-depth interviews to gain a rich understanding of each individual practitioner's values, and how these influenced their approach to ethics in practice (Johnson, 2002; Seidman, 2006). A researcher who uses such a method commonly seeks information concerning personal matters such as an individual's self, lived experience, values and decisions, occupational ideology and perspective (Seidman, 2006). Kvale (1996, p. 109) describes interviewing as a 'moral enterprise', one in which forming relationships with participants seems rather inevitable. But in-depth interviews differ from conversation with friends because the interviewer seeks to use the information obtained in the interaction for some other purpose (Johnson, 2002): in this instance, to uncover the values of paediatric physiotherapists working in the community.

I interviewed participants three times. In interview one, I gathered information (including demographic characteristics) about the participants' personal and professional experiences over the course of their careers. Each participant revealed fascinating stories about their experiences of working with children and their families in the community. In the second interview, the questions elicited each participant's attitudes, beliefs, opinions, reasoning and decisions in relation to two fictional vignettes. The aim was to explore each participant's perspective on several topics: the influence of evidence-based practice on physiotherapy practice; understandings of morality and ethics as general issues; personal values, beliefs, ethical frameworks and moral codes. The final interview explored the status of children during physiotherapy intervention. I asked each participant to describe and discuss experiences related to the topics of informed consent, the assessment of capacity in relation to child patients and their families, and the usage and significance of ethical codes and professional guidance in the clinical setting. Discussions around the ethical dimensions of practice seemed to emerge naturally, although in colloquial physiotherapy language rather than the language of bioethics. These discussions were a critical part of the way in which therapists expressed and showed their professional values.

Brown and Gilligan's (1992) voice-centred relational method offered me a continuous process of critical scrutiny and interpretation, not just in relation to the research methods and the data but also to the researcher, participants and the research context. Their method involves a set of four transcript readings, where the original audio files are listened to and four different 'readings'

applied, each with a different emphasis. I used the process to illuminate relationship development with the person speaking in the text and to be reflexive
about the impact of my own values, assumptions and prejudices.

What follows is my narrative account of how, through reflexivity during
the research process, I recognised the emotional impact of the research on the
researched and, in turn, the emotion I experience as the researcher. I focus on
extracts from the transcript of one participant, 'Connie', for several reasons:
she was one of the first physiotherapists I interviewed so I was particularly
attentive to data analysis and reflexivity; her narrative told a story about a
forgotten area of physiotherapy history; and these interviews provide a good
example of emotional tension.

MY REFLEXIVE ACCOUNT: USING THE
VOICE-CENTRED RELATIONAL METHOD

All three interviews took place in Connie's home as it was most convenient
to her but, in doing so, Connie allowed me to come into a private part of her
life. The interviews were preceded by general conversation and cups of tea. In
this way, a relaxed atmosphere was created and rapport established between
us. I was conscious of making sure that I developed a strong well-founded
relationship with her to access her personal and professional story. However,
I either did not think about, or was naive about, the implications of building
this kind of relationship and the consequences of doing that over time.

From the start, I made it clear that at any time, if Connie wished, the
recording would be stopped. This occurred on two occasions and a conversation ensued that was not considered part of the research project. The
interviews continued at her request. In this way, I tried to establish my own
integrity and ensure that, if required, Connie could assume a measure of
control over the process. Gaining trust is enhanced by the researcher showing
genuine feelings and responding honestly to comments and questions posed
by the participants; it is an integral element of qualitative research (Brown
and Gilligan, 1992).

Reading 1: Reading for the Storyline and for My Responses to the Narrative

The first reading comprises of two elements: the text is first read for the overall
story that is being told by the participant, and then for the 'reader response',

where the researcher reads for herself in the text (Brown & Gilligan, 1992). On the first reading of Connie's interview transcripts I read for the overall story told by Connie – the main happenings, characters and subplots. Connie's transcript (italicised) is followed by my reflexive narrative (non-italicised) which are presented in different ways to distinguish the transcript from my 'reader response' reflections.

The first interview revolved around the open question, 'Tell me about yourself and your career'. Connie began by telling me why she had chosen to train as a remedial gymnast[1] rather than as a physiotherapist.

Now then, going back to the reason why I trained (laughs), when I was in school, having decided I was going to be a physio, and then changed to a remedial gymnast, and having done A-Levels, I decided to drop an A-Level because it was too hard. So I had too much spare time according to my sixth form tutor. So he said, 'Well that's fine, you can drop your A-Level, but find if there's anything you can do that is relevant to what you want to do in the future, go off and see if you can arrange it'. I actually worked, I went every Wednesday afternoon to [a] Special School.

[…]

I worked with a class – the physio didn't want to know me, so that was the beginning of me knowing that there were tensions, the physio didn't want to know. I ended up spending that Wednesday afternoon with a class teacher whose class was having PE that afternoon. I had an absolute ball with all these kids with spina bifida having a PE lesson, it was great. So that was every Wednesday afternoon while I was a sixth former. And I knew I wanted to work with kids. I was a gymnast and then a gymnastics coach, and a gymnastics judge, so I had always worked with children, you know, as a 16-year-old taking the little ones…

There were multiple reasons for her choice to work with children as a physiotherapist – she loved working with children and wanted to work with them long-term. Connie describes working with disabled children in a special school which fitted with her current role as paediatric physiotherapist, she was a gymnast and gymnastics coach and judge and the remedial gymnast training appeared to be less academically challenging. However, a subplot is already evident – the tension between physiotherapists and remedial gymnasts. In the second half of the extract Connie talks about this tension, the impact and the emotional toll that the merger of the Remedial Gymnasts Association with the Chartered Society had on her personally.

You know, so there was always the physio stuff, RG stuff, in the background – but at that time the physio/RG stuff in the background was very unsettling.

[…]

…and by this time, [two children later], I definitely wasn't going to go back to work ever (laughs), just totally lost everything mentally then. But by now they were training up all the ex RGs in the electrotherapy skills…and everything else they perceived that we'd missed in our training.

I extensively reviewed the historical accounts of physiotherapy as part of my thesis so was fascinated by Connie's story as I knew from a research perspective that this part of the history of the physiotherapy profession has been overlooked. Physiotherapy had become an organised and self-regulated profession formed originally to legitimise and regulate therapeutic touch and, in doing so, to take possession of healthcare terrain that had existed for many years before: massage, remedial exercise and electrotherapy (Wickstead, 1948; Barclay, 1994). Such a move secured physiotherapy's place as the first and largest profession allied to medicine and the formalisation of physical rehabilitation as a professional discipline.

During this first reading, I felt enormously privileged to listen to Connie's story and realise that I was really drawn in by the storytelling. There is also a sense of the 'tin-opener effect' (Etherington, 1996), that is, encouraging Connie to talk about an aspect of her life that she had never discussed in this way before. I recognise that my interest in the historical aspects of Connie's story has lead me to influence the direction of the interview by continuing to pursue the discussion of this challenging time in Connie's life and career. In the following extract, I reflect with Connie on how she was made to feel all those years ago and how I am making her feel in the interview.

Geraldine: *You're surviving a lot of things here when put to the test, lots of little challenges for you I think?*

Connie: *Big ones yeah. I think that's why I can probably hold my own now. You know, I don't know what this tells you, but you just think, 'Oh', and then you just think, 'hang on, I'm here, you know, now'. if I could hang on to all those years of feeling abandoned, feeling as though I was never going to get any training from anywhere, feeling as though I'd never be accepted, you know, I can – I can (do what I do now).*

Geraldine: *So yeah it's very interesting what you've been saying.*

Connie: *Yeah.*

Geraldine: *And in some ways possibly you're the first person who is actually talking about emotions here.*

Connie: *Really?*

Geraldine: *Because you're sharing…like this was traumatic…*

Connie: *Oh, it was terrible yeah.*

Geraldine: *But it's also stuck with you so it was that terrible.*

Connie: *Well I'm not in tears, that's a good thing. I mean it took me years not to think about that exam part…*

Geraldine: *…and I've brought you back there.*

Connie: *Anyway I'm through it.*

My emotional reaction to the realisation of how I had shaped this interview is drawn out in the discussion that follows of the reader-response.

In the 'reader-response' element of the first reading, the researcher reads for herself in the text. I positioned myself, with my background, history and experience, in relation to Connie. I wrote out what I was hearing and how I responded emotionally and intellectually to Connie's experience. This allowed me to consider how my thoughts and some of my own assumptions and views might affect my interpretation of Connie's words and, importantly, how I would write about her (Brown & Gilligan, 1992, p. 27).

Being reflexive about my data analysis process also involved locating myself socially in relation to Connie, attending to my emotional responses to her, examining how we make theoretical interpretations of the participant's narrative, and documenting these processes for myself and others. My first reading of the interview one text thus represented my attempt to come to know my response to Connie and her story. The underlying assumption here is that by trying to label how I am located to her, I retain some grasp over the blurred boundary between the narrative and my interpretation of the narrative:

> Whilst listening to Connie, I began to recognise what a traumatic event this professional upheaval had been for her and others like her who had chosen this different but complementary career pathway to physiotherapy. Connie was obliged to undergo further study and take exams to ensure she could return to work but as a physiotherapist rather than a remedial gymnast. I suddenly feel a sense of guilt about taking her back to this obviously terrible time but this feeling is counter balanced by an understanding that my role as researcher is to facilitate disclosure. In this instance, my role duality has enabled me to establish a good rapport with Connie which in turn has influenced how much of her life story she has disclosed to me. I also begin to recognise that she is sharing a great level of emotion about how she was made to feel by others and a sense of not fitting in. These events had stayed with her for over 20 years.
>
> My guilt increases when I arrive two months later for the second interview. As became customary I was invited to have a cup of tea and a chat. Connie reflected on events post the first interview, explaining that she had not slept for three nights afterwards tossing and turning things over in her head. She was surprised that revisiting the past had affected her in this way. As I listened, I realise that internally I was horrified and felt obliged, indeed had an ethical responsibility, to talk over these feelings and events.

My response is in keeping with research that shows researchers can experience a mixture of feelings including guilt, anger and frustration in response to participants' stories or when they feel they may be exposing their participants to emotional distress (Bourne, 1998; Hubbard, Backett-Millburn, & Kemmer, 2001). The emotionality of this interview influenced how I managed emotion in the next consecutive interviews, as this interview situation evoked such a powerful emotional response from me.

Reading 2: Reading for the Voice of the 'I'

The second reading represents the first step of a phased process of listening to participants as they speak about themselves, their lived experiences and the broader social contexts within which they live. This reading is important for a method that is not only interested in the processes of reflection and decision making of the person but also in illuminating their values and value systems. Brown and Gilligan (1992, p. 27) describe this process:

> We listen for 'self' for the voice of the 'I' speaking in this relationship. Listening for the voice of the other is crucial to bring us into relationship with that person, in part by ensuring that the sound of her voice enters our awareness and in part by discovering how she speaks of herself before we speak of her.

Attempting to get some sense of participants' voices through the empirical data I used a highlighter pen to physically trace words in their transcripts – specifically where they used personal pronouns such as 'I', 'we' or 'you' in talking about themselves. This process was a valuable empirical technique as it helped centre my attention on the active 'I' telling the story to discover 'how she speaks of herself before we speak of her' (Brown & Gilligan, 1992, pp. 27–28).

During Connie's first interview, there were recurring phrases like, 'I'm struggling, 'I couldn't', and 'I'm going to burst into tears in a minute'. Tracing the 'I' in Connie's interview transcript (indicated by underlining in the extract below), and how she spoke about herself in this period of her life, brought me to a different interpretation of her account. I feel I would have missed this interpretation had I not paid close attention to the way she spoke about herself. It brought to life the emotions of this traumatic time and the impact it had not only on her clinical career but also on her personal life, where she was raising her young family with no intention of returning to work.

> *I was offered a place in the summer of '86 I think, but I couldn't, couldn't even think of it, so I deferred that place then till the summer of '87. I did the complementary skills course knowing that it was funded by somebody else, didn't have to pay, knowing that my mum could do my childcare while I did it, knowing that this was the last opportunity ever. So, I had [various physiotherapy managers] ringing me up saying, 'I hear you're on the complementary skills course, does that mean you're interested in work?'*
>
> *It was wow. So my answer to that was, 'I'm struggling to learn about electrotherapy, I've never done physics in my life, and I've got exams to do, and I've got a young family'. The exam was in December of 1987, and all being well I would have been ready to accept employment in the January of the following year,'88. However, I missed the date of the*

exam by having the wrong date on my calendar, and I failed one of the parts – I can't remember which part I failed, but there was a bit I had to re-sit. Oh it was dreadful. I'm going to burst into tears in a minute, I tell you, it was awful (laughs nervously) and for what? They don't use it now.

Reading 3: Reading for Relationships

In the third reading, I listened for how participants spoke about their interpersonal relationships with family, work colleagues and patients. Consciously, reading for relationships was particularly valuable in revealing the challenges each participant faced in their everyday lives, both private and public, and in revealing the values and beliefs of each participant. Separating relationships from cultural context and social structure was challenging as the relationships in Connie's interviews were influenced by both cultural and organisational contexts, which is illustrated further below.

Reading 4: Placing People within Cultural Contexts and Social Structures

In the fourth reading, I placed the participants' accounts within broader social, political, cultural, religious and organisational contexts. Here I looked, for example, on the moral context of physiotherapy practice. I looked for the use of moral terms such as 'should', 'ought', 'right', 'wrong', 'good' and 'bad' to indicate places in the narrative where the participants spoke in terms of cultural norms and personal and professional values. There was often tension in these 'moral voices'. Another important setting was the organisational context, which had a major impact on how Connie spoke about some of her more challenging relationships in the day-to-day practice setting. One aim of my research was to provide descriptions of the process of clinical practice and the reasoning behind actions. Much of interview three was spent asking each participant to describe processes and actions, recognising that this was a necessary but very complex and challenging request. Extracts from readings three and four of Connie's third interview are presented jointly as there is much overlap between interpersonal relationships and organisational contexts.

For a reason (not apparent that day), we seemed to get off on the wrong foot despite the usual 'chat over tea' ritual. During interview two, there had been a few times when Connie had become silent, looking at me in bewilderment, and we seemed to be in that place again. Despite my explanation to the contrary, she clearly felt that she was being tested, a phenomenon

Silverman (2005, p. 31) refers to as 'a professional self-consciousness' (perhaps a flashback to the horrible exam experience Connie describes in the extract above). As the following extract evidences, Connie was confused about what I was asking her to discuss, and we evidently had different understandings of choices associated with treatment decisions.

> Geraldine: *So what I'm trying to find out is about whether you involve your patients in assessment and treatment decisions. Do you give them choices, do you feel you can give them choices, are there decisions that you would allow them to make, but feel that a lot of the time there are some decisions that maybe they can't make? That kind of thing is what I've got in mind.*

> Connie: *Yes okay, well I like choices so, you know, that's a good start.*

> Geraldine: *So I'll leave it up to you (laughs) [She's going to be silent again].*

> Connie: *What, you want me to talk about choices?*

> Geraldine: *I do.*

> Connie: *Oh right.*

> Geraldine: *What choices do you give?*

> Connie: *What choices do I give? Well (laughs) usually it's to obtain cooperation really, the choice that I generally start with is, 'Are we going to do this on the floor or on the plinth?' And I'm hoping to goodness they choose on the plinth, because that's where I'd like them to be because it's easier for me.*

> Geraldine: *Hmm, hmm.*

> Connie: *So I give them that choice, but if they stay on the floor, fine, we'll do the assessment on the floor, we'll do the exercises on the floor, and I might then move them to a place where I want them to be at a later point saying, 'Well yes, great, you've done that there, we're going to do them somewhere else', they don't have a choice then.*

> Geraldine: *So taking you back before that then, so when they show up with mum, dad or whoever…*

> Connie: *Oh yeah.*

> Geraldine: *What choices do they have at that point? Because are you giving them a choice of, 'You can be here if you want to, but if you don't want to you can go'. Do you go there?*

> Connie: *No.*

> Geraldine: *So how do you approach that?*

> Connie: *I usually say, 'Thank you for coming. I'm Connie, your physiotherapist. Shall we go up to the physiotherapy room, where we'll have a look at your child?' I don't really include the child in that.*

It was only after completion of the 'reader response' part of the process that I became fully aware of my part in setting the tone of the interview. My strong opinions in favour of children's participation in decision making were clearly influencing the atmosphere in the room through my body language and tone of voice. Connie was focusing on her relationship with the accompanying adult rather than the child. I recalled that I was inwardly irritated by this description and struggled to uphold any neutrality. It was also apparent that the conversation had different meanings or perspectives, and that I, as the researcher, had the power to structure the interview. This prompted me to reflect on whether there could be genuine dialogue in such situations (Brown & Gilligan, 1992, p. 23).

I could also see how Connie might feel she was being tested as I asked many challenging questions such as 'what choices do you give?' and 'how do you approach that?' The answers required lots of description. However, there was obviously something else troubling Connie, which unfolded as the interview proceeded:

Connie: *...in the light of having a horrible complaint letter recently, I'll see anybody who wants to stay on my caseload, you know. Yeah, yeah I'm very reluctant to persuade anyone that their child doesn't need physiotherapy any more. It wasn't a very nice letter...*

I think I – I usually feel that I've done a jolly good job at sowing the seeds into how they access different things that will be of benefit to them, you know, like community-based leisure activities, plus a home exercise programme, plus maybe, you know, things like referral to podiatry.

Geraldine: *Hmm, hmm*

Connie: *But then you still get people who insist that there's more to be done and, you know, school staff are still saying that she's the least co-ordinated in a PE lesson. So, you know, I'm a bit nervous about getting rid of them at the moment.*

I now recognised that there was a sub-plot regarding the workplace that is clearly troubling. Connie describes how her professional judgement and reasoning have been challenged by a complaint based on the parents' desire to continue with physiotherapy even though she considered it beneficial and timely for the family to access readily available community-based resources. Connie describes organisational constraints and a loss of professional autonomy that now deterred her from discharging patients from her caseload, even if this seemed warranted in her professional opinion. This event had happened very recently so Connie had lost confidence in her decision-making abilities. So it was no wonder she found the interview very perplexing, if not threatening (Sinding & Aronson, 2003). However, that day I was exhausted from facilitating the interview, so I did not feel able to pursue the issue. I had a sense that Connie was exhausted too and wanted to get the interview over with rather than stop.

Consequently, a while later I had a post-interview debrief. Connie told me that at different times through the research process there were quite a few personal/professional situations that made her question her career. She said that the experience of being interviewed, and having time to digest our discussions, had made her realise her value and worth as a physiotherapist, so she viewed participation as a positive experience despite the emotional toll it had taken on her (and me).

Reflecting on My Data Analysis

This detailed and time-consuming work was valuable for understanding the depth and complexity of individual experiences, as well as the significant differences between the participants' narratives. Overall, performing four readings of the interview transcript emphasises the multilayered nature of narratives and helps to trace voices across and within a given transcript. Tracing voices through individual interview transcripts, as opposed to linking themes across interviews, helped me create a narrative portrait for each participant which was especially important in a study about values. This process made me acutely aware of my own role and power in choosing the specific issues I emphasised and the ones I glossed over or ignored. My detailed and lengthy focus on the individual interviews also represented respect for each participant within the research context and therefore supported my relational approach. This approach also respected my own role as researcher and the need for my own perspective to receive full consideration in the process.

CONCLUSION

This chapter has discussed the practicalities, challenges and methods of being reflexive as a socio-legal researcher when undertaking a qualitative empirical ethics study. For the duration of my doctoral research, I chose a voice-centred relational framework within which I located myself and through which I heard and analysed my participants' lives. This position and frame influenced my data analysis, how and what I attended to, and, equally, what I left out. Critically, through reflexive research practice, I attended to my influence on data collection, the influences upon my own position, and the interactions between me, my participants and the data produced. Reflexivity also helped me to discuss my emotional position as researcher and the role of emotion in the research process. It is only with the course of time that I have come to appreciate fully the meaning of reflexivity in the context of my own research. The key lesson learnt was the importance of reflecting on ethically important, and at times uncomfortable, moments in the research process, so that other researchers can learn about reflexivity and the 'how to' of reflexive writing.

NOTE

1. The Association of Remedial Gymnasts and Recreational Therapists merged with the Chartered Society of Physiotherapy in 1988. Remedial gymnasts (RGs) brought group instruction and a focus on exercise to the physiotherapy profession. From the 1960s there had been a lot of animosity and professional jealousy between RGs and physiotherapists. However, the work of the two groups overlapped so significantly that by the 1980s both parties had decided that the only sensible way forward was to join forces. The merger clearly had a less positive effect for some RGs.

REFERENCES

Association of Paediatric Chartered Physiotherapists. (2007). *Information to guide good practice for physiotherapists working with children*. London: CSP.

Barclay, J. (1994). *In good hands: The history of the Chartered Society of Physiotherapy, 1894–1994*. Oxford: Butterworth-Heinemann.

Brown, L. M., & Gilligan, C. (1992) *Meeting at the crossroads: Women's psychology and girls' development*. Cambridge, MA: Harvard University Press.

Etherington, K. (1996). The counsellor as researcher: Boundary issues and critical dilemmas. *British Journal of Guidance & Counselling, 24*, 339–346.

Etherington, K. (2007). Ethical research in reflexive relationships. *Qualitative Inquiry, 13*, 599–616.

Gilligan, C. (1992). *In a different voice: Psychological theory and women's development*. Cambridge, MA: Harvard University Press.

Guillemin, M. & Gillam, L. (2004). Ethics, reflexivity and 'ethically important moments' in research. *Qualitative Inquiry, 10*(2), 261–280.

Hastings, G. M. (2013). *Researching the values of paediatric physiotherapists working in the community*. Ph.D. thesis, University of Bristol, Bristol.

Hubbard, G., Backett-Millburn, K., & Kemmer, D. (2001). Working with emotion: Issues for the researcher in fieldwork and teamwork. *International Journal of Social Research Methodology, 4*(2), 119–137.

Ives, J., & Draper, H. (2009). Appropriate methodologies for empirical bioethics: It's all relative. *Bioethics, 23*(4), 249–258.

Johnson, J. M. (2002). In-depth interviewing. In J. F. Gubrium & J. Holstein (Eds.), *Handbook of interview research: Context and methods* (pp. 103–120). Thousand Oaks, CA: SAGE.

Kon, A. A. (2009). The role of empirical research in bioethics. *American Journal of Bioethics*, 6–7, 59–65.

Kvale, S. (1996). *InterViews: An introduction to qualitative research interviewing*. Thousand Oaks, CA: SAGE.

Legard, R., Keegan, J., & Ward, K. (2003). In-depth interviews. In J. Ritchie & J. Lewis (Eds.), *Qualitative research practice: A guide for social science students and researchers* (pp. 138–69). London: Sage.

Mannay, D., & Creaghan, J. (2016). Similarity and familiarity: Reflections on indigenous ethnography with mothers, daughters and school teachers on the margins of contemporary Wales. In M. Ward (Ed.), *Gender identity and research relationships* (Vol. 14). Studies in Qualitative Methodology (pp. 85–103). Bingley: Emerald.

Patton, M. Q. (2002). *Qualitative research & evaluation methods* (3rd ed.). Thousand Oaks, CA: SAGE.

Roberts, E. (2018). The 'transient insider': Identity and intimacy in home community research. In T. Loughran & D. Mannay (Eds.), *Emotion and the researcher: Sites, subjectivities and relationships* (Vol. 16). Studies in Qualitative Methodology (pp. 113–126). Bingley: Emerald.

Seidman, I. (2006). *Interviewing as qualitative research: A guide for researchers in education and the social sciences* (3rd ed.). New York, NY: Teachers' College Press.

Silverman, D. (2005). *Doing qualitative research* (2nd ed.). London: SAGE.

Sinding, C., & Aronson J. (2003). Exposing failures, unsettling accommodations: Tensions in interview practice. *Qualitative Research*, *3*(1), 95–117.

Tronto, J. C. (1993). *Moral boundaries: A political argument for an ethic of care*. New York, NY: Routledge.

van den Scott, L. K. (2018). Role transitions in the field and reflexivity: From friend to researcher. In T. Loughran & D. Mannay (Eds.), *Emotion and the researcher: Sites, subjectivities and relationships* (Vol. 16). Studies in Qualitative Methodology (pp. 19–32). Bingley: Emerald.

Wickstead, J. H. (1948). *The growth of a profession*. London: Edward Arnold.

CHAPTER 14

BEING BOTH RESEARCHER AND SUBJECT: ATTENDING TO EMOTION WITHIN COLLABORATIVE INQUIRY

Mary Morris and Andrea Davies

ABSTRACT

Purpose – *This chapter represents a dynamic cycle in a collaborative inquiry conceived some six years ago. The aim of this study is to share some of our reflections, tensions, questions and uncertainties in positioning our own emotional responses as legitimate research data.*

Methodology/Approach – *We adopted a collaborative second-person methodology within an action research framework in the process of inquiring into our own practice as systemic psychotherapists and women.*

Findings – *We offer reflections on the positioning of emotion as researchers, tutors and psychotherapists. We discuss three themes from the emotional landscape of the inquiry, research process, research product and gendered voices, in anticipation that they will connect with and be useful to other researchers.*

Emotion and the Researcher: Sites, Subjectivities, and Relationships
Studies in Qualitative Methodology, Volume 16, 229–244
Copyright © 2018 by Emerald Publishing Limited
All rights of reproduction in any form reserved
ISSN: 1042-3192/doi:10.1108/S1042-319220180000016015

Originality/Value – The chapter introduces our sense-making framework for reflexively exploring the salience of emotion in research. It argues that attenuating, listening and responding to the emotions we feel as researchers both serves as a guide to inquiring into critical social constructs and engenders opportunities to promote social change.

Keywords: Collaborative inquiry; gender; emotion; researcher

AN INQUIRY INTO GENDER

The mainstream dictum tells us that in Western society, women's right to vote, receive education, have sexual freedom and control their own finances and their increased presence in paid employment stand as testimony to the success of gender-aware policies of feminism (Kelan, 2009b). Whilst post-feminist agendas such as 'girl-power' and 'ranch-culture' offer evidence that feminism has grown increasingly redundant (McRobbie, 2004), there is still an argument that the nature of 'gendering' in relationships has not changed significantly and a feminist sensibility is as relevant now as in the early 1970s (Kelan, 2009a, 2009b).

The field of systemic psychotherapy mirrors some of these tensions. There is a sense that gender has been sufficiently 'taken into account' as we are all trained in and expected to be aware of issues around gender and power. Implicit in this position is an idea that we no longer need to engage critically with our prejudices as they have been openly declared and worked on. Yet, as women, we believe we have different experiences because we identify as women, and not as men, and so we position ourselves within the discourse that claims gender to be a socially constructed concept. When we, in this article, talk of gender, we are not claiming an essentialist view of gender; we understand that the categories of 'man' and 'woman' are still powerful descriptors of human relationships, influencing our communication and positions in hierarchical ways (Kemp & Squires, 2009a).

We are both employed in sectors (education and health care) which would identify themselves with some principles of feminism, although they would not identify themselves as feminist institutions. Both sectors have a wide range of policies that speak to equality and anti-discriminatory practices, whilst at the same time being critiqued for the unsuccessful implementation of these practices (Higher Education Authority, 2016). In 2010, we were both working as members of family therapy teams.

For Andrea, as a clinical psychologist and systemic psychotherapist, this involved clinical work with adults in secondary mental health services and a regional medium-secure unit, supervision of trainee clinical psychologists and consultation to colleagues and teams within the mental health directorate. Alongside psychotherapy and consultative work, Mary was a senior lecturer in systemic psychotherapy in a university, training and supervising counselling and systemic psychotherapy trainees. We have known each other since 2007 when Andrea was a systemic psychotherapy trainee and Mary was a clinical tutor on the programme. Our project grew out of a connection between us based on the fact that at that time we were both working in family therapy teams where we were the only woman. Our initial conversations posed a number of questions for us including:

- What interests us in terms of gender?
- What do we each *mean* by 'gender'?
- *Should* either of us be raising the topic, or is it unnecessary in this era of post-feminism where gender roles are not considered so binding?
- What are the potential implications of holding the responsibility to be the one who raises issues of gender?
- How might we invite our male colleagues into a position of collaborators?
- How do we talk about an issue from 'the inside'?
- How do we each value our own experience without reducing it to anecdotes and generalisations?
- What pressures do we experience to *not* talk about gender?

METHODOLOGY

There is a long-standing debate within the field of psychotherapy, including systemic psychotherapy, on the most appropriate research methodologies for our discipline. Tensions exist between those that voice the need to conduct large-scale effectiveness and outcome studies to confirm the place of psychological therapies in wider medical and accountability contexts, and those that privilege process studies as more useful in furthering our understanding of the complexity of the human endeavour of therapy. Put simplistically, the former tend to rely more on quantitative, positivistic, and empirical methodologies, whilst qualitative methodologies tend to offer opportunities to study therapeutic activity through a more intimate lens, engaging with constructionist epistemologies.

Our curiosity to turn an inquiring lens on our relationship with gender within our working practices fitted with our understanding of ourselves as self-reflexive practitioners; a concept embedded within the practice of reflection-in-action (Schön, 1991) and the ability to adapt and respond within the real-time unfolding of the therapeutic relationship to feedback. Additionally, we wished to collaborate together in our endeavour to research into our own experience so that we could learn from each other and pay attention to the quality and integrity of our inquiring process (Marshall, 1999, 2016).

Action research (Reason & Bradbury, 2008) is widely described as research *with,* not *on* people, and subsequently there is no separation of researcher from participant. The word 'action' in the name privileges the idea that the very act of researching in and of itself can initiate change. This sits neatly alongside a 'post-modern systemic epistemology' (McNamee, 1998), positioning the researcher participation *within* the system of inquiry, and engaging with the process of research as an intervention into that system. This 'second-order' description of the researcher/researched system, which notes the impossibility of separating the researcher from the researched subject, is isomorphic with the therapist/family system, where the therapist cannot impose change on a family from an objective stance, but is embroiled in the change with the family. Attending to the *self* of both therapist and researcher becomes necessary.

Within action research, there are different 'territories of action': first-, second-, and third-person inquiries (Marshall, 2016, p. 7). There is some resonance of a first-person inquiry in all therapeutic practices that involve taking a self-reflexive position and including reflections both in-action and on-action (Schön, 1991), albeit with a relatively narrow focus. The research frame could be said to bring some formality and a different quality to that process. Marshall advocates a position of 'living life as inquiry' (1999), which would extend the focus of the inquiry to all aspects of lived experiences. Accordingly, the researcher, the professional (lecturer, psychotherapist and psychologist), and the personal (woman, mother, partner, sibling and daughter) are all intertwined.

The territory of 'second-person inquiry' best fitted our process of inquiry. We were both separately engaged in inquiring into our relationship and experience of gender as a defining theme in our lives and practices, and were doing so collaboratively to understand and effect change to the ways we worked with gender as a theme in our working practices, as well as our professional and personal lives. We acknowledged and welcomed the influence we were having on each other and were open to the structural differences inherent in our early relationship.

Whilst the subject of mutual concern was 'gender', we found that this was inseparable from 'emotion'. Our own identity as gendered people, with experiences of being treated in particular ways as a consequence of our gender, and our knowledge of feminist theories that had (or had not) made a difference to our lives or the field of systemic psychotherapy, both evoked emotions in us and the friends, colleagues and clients we talked with. We experienced emotions such as indignation, anger and frustration, alongside hope, laughter and a sense of fellowship. Maturana (1988) views emotions as 'dispositions for actions', and the emotions we noted led us to action and a conclusion that the theme of 'emotion and the researcher' was integral to us as research practitioners.

Action research methodologies often involve spirals of inquiry cycles, moving the researcher through a process of formulating questions, eliciting feedback, formulating new questions and considering further directions of inquiry. Space prevents a detailed sharing of the ideas that were pertinent to our thinking as we embarked on a number of cycles of inquiry, the questions we were asking ourselves, points of action and the meaning made. However, we offer the readers some headings as a rough map of the journey:

- *Cycle 1*: What does 'gender' mean to each of us?
- *Cycle 2*: Consultation with colleagues.
- *Cycle 3*. Writing to each other.
- *Cycle 4*: Consultation with a 'critical friend'.
- *Cycle 5*: An unsuccessful attempt to construct a 'traditional, academic' written account of the research process.
- *Cycle 6*: Presentation at 'Emotion and the Researcher Symposium', Cardiff University (Morris & Davies, 2014).
- *Cycle 7*: Preparing for and constructing this chapter.

THE EMOTIONAL LANDSCAPE OF INQUIRY

As we proceeded, we were aware of 'moments'. These were ideas, events and moments of realisation, connection and activity that struck us as significant, and formed the data for our research. Reviewing this data through the lens of emotion provided an opportunity to re-engage with moments that connected with the emotional landscape of the inquiry. We have grouped these moments under three themes: research as process, research as product and gendered voices.

Research as Process

An action research frame welcomes complexity, challenges notions of clarity and aims to foster uncertainty as a process of learning. The frame is isomorphic with a systemic approach to psychotherapy, 'perturbing' systems to create new configurations or meanings. In our experience, most research involves moments of uncertainty and questions of confidence. As Coleman (2001) reflected on her research journey, 'I have had a strong sense of attempting to pin down a moving process, which is as yet offering me no conclusion, no end, although many 'findings', and much movement, journeying on my part'. It is our contention that the potential for becoming stuck in the mire of confusion and befuddlement is greater in a methodological frame that looks to engage with 'chaos'.

Since the emphasis is on research *with* rather than research *on,* there is not the separation of researcher from subject that can sometimes protect the researcher from strong emotions instigated by the research topic. Researchers are not automatons, and other chapters in this book describe processes by which researchers are affected by their work (e.g.,Grant, 2018; Roberts, 2018 [this volume]). However, for us there is a subtle but significant difference in the demands for self-reflection and self-reflexivity of a first- or second-person inquirer, which requires that the whole person of the researcher is present, taking part in what is essentially a dialogical process.

When we first met, the definition of relationship between us was student and tutor/supervisor. We had to negotiate a shift away from this hierarchical relationship to one framed by collegiality and equality. This was crucial as otherwise we might slip into privileging the lived experience of one over the other, and assuming propositional knowledge without attending to the varieties of contextual influences on both of us that were informing our interpretations of our experiences. Most of this negotiation was unspoken between us. However, an extract from Mary's journal acknowledges our changing roles:

> I am also aware of the re-negotiation of our relationship that has been happening. Moving on from tutor-tutee. But not consultant-consultee. Peer endeavour. But how can I acknowledge my ignorance on issues? (December 2010)

It was helpful to us that the course on which we both met promotes a collaborative style of teaching and close connection between students and tutors, albeit not an equal one. However, as the quotation above demonstrates, this did not mean that we were without anxieties about how each would be perceived by the other. We both sat with different versions of what might be called 'imposter syndrome' (Jarrett, 2010). Nonetheless, the developing collaborative relationship between us has been empowering, allowing us both to acknowledge a variety of feelings and not to feel so organised by them.

The prevailing question of what constitutes legitimate research activity, and a convincing methodology, is, we realise, ingrained within us, even though we aspire to advocate for qualitative action inquiry as part of a mixed economy of research methodologies. The positivist traditions in which we were both schooled early on still appear to be a dominating influence on our relationship with research activities, as became evident to us when we considered our anxieties about validity. Looking at our endeavours from the perspective of our different experiences of engaging in research, and sitting within organisations that in their different ways extolled other research practices, we were continually plagued by feelings of self-doubt and worries about being overly self-indulgent. Marshall (2011) makes reference to this as a common concern and proposes that the question 'to what purpose?' is key to demonstrating quality. We were then steadied by the claim that a 'mark of quality in an action research project is that people will get energised and empowered by being involved, through which they may develop newly useful, reflexive insights as a result of a growing critical consciousness' (Bradbury & Reason, 2006, p. 344).

Research as Product

A pressing, and possibly over-organising question for us became 'what product should we achieve?'

> Good to meet Andrea today, feel re-energised and re-invigorated about the project which I was feeling a bit despondent about. I was worrying we hadn't been doing enough action but…meeting is action…reading and writing is action…that's the problem with all my 'research' endeavours I think they have to be big projects. (Mary, Journal Entry, June 2012)

Many voices enter into this question: how legitimate was it to be a practitioner researcher? Could we only legitimise this enterprise if we 'disseminated' our results? What would dissemination entail in our various contexts? How would seeking a product, or end goal, influence the process of inquiry? Were we in danger of privileging propositional knowing over other forms of knowing (Heron & Reason, 2008)? Marshall (2016) writes of the paradox of product versus process within this kind of inquiry, where the seeking of a goal overshadows or perverts the emergent research findings. Whilst we were instinctively aware of the benefit to our practices of engaging in this project, we were not so confident in how we might convey this to others.

Looking back, we can see how we were sitting with opposing tensions which intensified our anxieties about the legitimation of our inquiry. On the one hand, we queried whether we were being self-indulgent and not doing 'proper' research. On the other hand, we were aware of the trap of thinking it was our problem (not a systemic one) and we knew of the well-documented value of first- and second-person action inquiry in generating changes. We became for a while focused on achieving a 'goal', on producing something, as a way of justifying the project to ourselves.

We settled on the idea of trying to write up our experiences for publication, and this became the cycle of inquiry headed, 'An unsuccessful attempt to construct a "traditional, academic" written account of the research process'. This generated paroxysms of self-doubt, connecting with Etherington's (2001) struggles to finding voice as a woman, and we became aware that our emotional responses, anxieties and lack of confidence in the prospect of seeking publication were the very subject matter of our research. Etherington (2001, p. 123) quotes Clandinin's and Connelly's (1994) argument that the 'researcher is always speaking partially naked and is genuinely open to legitimate criticism from participants and from audience. Some researchers are silenced by the invitation to criticism contained in the expression of voice'.

We both, in our different ways, struggled with this fear, and for a while allowed ourselves to succumb to being silenced. Therefore, the opportunity to present at the Families, Identities and Gender Research Network Symposium on 'Emotion and the Researcher' (Morris & Davies, 2014) offered us a way to find a voice, and to satisfy our need to 'produce'. We were both delighted but full of trepidation and decided to frame the presentation as a further cycle of inquiry, inviting others present at the symposium to inquire with us into the theme. Whilst not without its challenges, this felt more consistent with the methodology, and also with our collaborative approach to teaching and therapy. We were also aware of our expectation that the context for this symposium might be reminiscent of the second wave feminist trend for women-dominant, or women-themed, events, with the hope that this might offer an appreciative context.

Gendered Voices

The lived experience of this inquiry predates our meetings together and includes our individual journeys in relation with 'gender'. There is almost 20 years difference between us, which we hypothesised would have a contextualising impact on our experiences of gender (in)equality and feminist theories.

During the project, Andrea gave birth to a son, her first child, whereas Mary's son and daughter were young adults. We had learnt to be mothers in different eras. However, we shared a curiosity about the meaning of gender, how our gender affected our lived experiences, how this had become stronger and at times weaker in our lives, our changing readings of feminisms, and an aware-ness that we had found ourselves at a point when the meaning we made of 'gender' was requiring increasingly more of our attention. We discussed our different feminist icons; our joys and concerns about the world our children were growing into; our noticing of shifting, and entrenched, attitudes in rela-tion to gender (in)equality; and our hopes and frustrations of and for societal changes. In this section, we try and capture something of the unfolding cycles in our emotional connecting and re-connecting to our declared interest in 'gender', including sections from letters that we wrote to each other during one cycle of inquiry.

Rationality and objectivity have traditionally been privileged across aca-demic disciplines and are culturally synonymous with male-ness. Subjectivity, irrationality and emotions are positioned as contaminants to gaining an empirical, pure view of the world as it 'really' is, culturally associated with subjugated classes, racial groups and women-ness (Jaggar, 2009). Feminist epistemologies have sought to raise the voices of the subjugated (Kemp & Squires, 2009b). Undertaking research *with* others brings the researcher into close proximity to the lived experience of the other and the emotional land-scape of their world. Qualitative, feminist and action research methodologies seek to locate the researcher within their research, as has been demonstrated with rigour, sensitivity and authenticity by the other contributors to this volume (see e.g., van den Scott, 2018 [this volume]).

Within the development of systemic psychotherapy theory and practice, 'gender' has been an important 'theme of difference' (Goldner 1991; Hare-Mustin 1987; Jones 1998). Yet, a prompt for us engaging in the project was our feeling that an implicit rule (unspoken) was developing in various con-texts, which prohibited conversations about social inequalities arising from gendered positions. We felt we were experiencing minimising, placatory atti-tudes and were angry at being silenced. Sharing these thoughts with each other was empowering, and we knew that we had to be cautious about being too complimentary to each other's position and to ensure that we allowed in critical voices. We had not, it seems to us now, given due consideration to the strength of emotions that would arise, and what it would mean for us that these emotions were evoked within our gendered selves. The aim of action research is not to generalise, but to offer a sense-making framework for expe-riences. Both our methodology and our social constructionist epistemology privileged feelings, subjectivity and lived experience. However, when we discussed with each other points of interest in both our therapeutic and consultative conversations with others, finding ourselves speaking 'as women' became challenging and it was hard to ignore the thought that we were 'having a bit of a whinge':

> I felt some sort of responsibility to uphold a 'woman's perspective', not only just in the therapeutic work we do, but also in the teaching and development of our own practices. I am not implying that my male colleagues are not attentive to gender-themes, far from it, but inevitably I identify with a position of struggle towards an egalitarian position that is embedded in a tradition of dis-empowerment (even though I recognise my white middle-class, educated background gives me more opportunities than many others including many men). (Mary to Andrea, March 2012)

A cycle of inquiry returned us to the literature, in particular the seminal ethnographic study exploring discourses of gender discrimination in the context of two technology companies (Kelan, 2009a, 2009b). Kelan noticed a tension for employees between lived experiences of discrimination and organisational/societal discourses of gender egalitarianism. Her concept of 'gender fatigue' refers to the apathy to oppose, name and address gender inequalities. Kelan suggests that in a sociopolitical climate of post-feminism and individualisation, either the 'victim' and/or the discriminator is held responsible for acts of discrimination. The notion of subjugating practices being perpetuated at the level of the group or at the level of society, are avoided, ignored or silenced. For Kelan (2009, p. 7), 'the systematic nature of discrimination is disguised. Even if women confront gender discrimination they often feel powerless to challenge it because they assume there are individual reasons for the situation rather than believing that gender might have a bearing'.

Within our enquiry, we risked minimising and dismissing the emotional responses from our gendered selves, and becoming active participants in our own silencing at a number of contextual levels: in accepting that female voices are not valid data; in agreeing that female knowledge is not 'proper' research; and in subjugating lived gendered experiences in favour of dominant discourses. We were actively co-constructing a world that perpetuates the superiority of research *about* rather than *with* people, and a world in which 'gender' has been *done*.

> I was shocked and appalled. I seemed caught in a paradox to say 'all is well, it isn't like it used to be', but knowing that things were far from great. If you keep saying the same thing, if you say that there is still discrimination, people do not listen. So we spend time thinking about how to say something differently, how to say something that can be heard by others. But how do we say something that is different enough to be heard, when what you need is to say the same thing as before? (Andrea to Mary, March 2012)

Jaggar's striking metaphor of 'outlawed emotions' fits well with our sense of being silenced: 'feminist and other outlawed emotions...may provide the first indication that something is wrong with the way alleged facts have been constructed, with accepted understandings of how things are...only when we reflect on our initially puzzling irritability, revulsion, anger or fear may we bring to consciousness our "gut-level" awareness that we are in a situation of coercion, cruelty, injustice or danger' (Jaggar, 2009, p. 191). Attenuating, listening and responding to the strong emotions we feel as researchers moves us closer to unmasking critical social constructs that harbour discriminatory ways of being with others. Asking questions of ourselves and others at the edges of such constructs provides opportunities for us to appreciate research as being so much more than knowing 'about' the world; research is an opportunity to promote social change (Riger, 2016). Furthermore, reflexivity offers researchers a frame for locating their own selves in the dynamic relationship between the researcher and the researched (Berger, 2015; Etherington, 2004).

ON BEING BOTH THE PRODUCT AND THE PROCESS OF INQUIRY

In this concluding section, we reflect on research as generating social change and the positioning of emotions. We suggest that one can chose to acknowledge and privilege the emotional responses of the researcher as both the process *and* the product of collaborative inquiry. We ask ourselves, looking back, what difference our research made to us and those we engage with, and offer some examples of how our inquiry continues to show itself in our lives as researchers, teachers, psychotherapists and women.

New Vocabularies

During the inquiry, we continually had to reassert to ourselves that what we were engaged in was of value, and not just for ourselves. A change then for both of us has been our relationship to approaching inquiry with an action research methodology. A process of first-person inquiry offered a compass for Andrea as she orientated herself to a new clinical context. Reflecting and inquiring on three years of practice that felt different to her previous experience, enabled her to share with others the nature of her work with people experiencing psychosis (Davies, 2016). Mary continues to supervise trainee Systemic Psychotherapists who are engaged in first-person inquiries into themselves as developing psychotherapists: she notices the impact on her supervisory practice of having a different *experiential knowing* in relation to collaborative inquiry processes. These processes demand high levels of self-reflexivity for both student and supervisor, including attending to the emotional responses in both the therapeutic and learning endeavours.

Andrea supervises trainee clinical psychologists and continues to be presented with the certainty of objective, reductionist research methodologies: she finds herself concerned that when we assert the methodology that a student is to engage with, we may also prescribe what worldview that individual should hold. Morally, should academics and researchers dictate epistemology? Framing methodological debates as a moral issue ties with the proposition to 'redescribe' research practices, and 'to speak differently in the face of an entrenched vocabulary' (Reason, 2003, p. 106).

Finding Voice

Arguably, we cannot step outside our ingrained cultural assumptions, but we can discover them. Engaging in this inquiry has highlighted for us how we are still influenced by 'entrenched vocabularies' within the discourses of research and gender. Our collaboration has also reawoken our awareness of discussions on feminism, leaving us both, in different ways, empowered to talk more freely about our thoughts on gendered positions. We realised that a post-feminist ethos had silenced us and we began again to find our voices, giving ourselves permission to critically engage with a range of ideas in relation to gender, identity and politics. Mary has written about and delivered a keynote lecture (Morris, 2016, 2017) tracing the links between the development of systemic psychotherapy and feminist theory, arriving at the contemporary challenges and tensions for therapists working in our cultural context, where gender identity is increasingly fluid. An impact of the lecture was to give permission for student groups to find their own voice in debating gender identity politics.

Talking in the Space Between

As systemic psychotherapists we are interested in the influence context has on people's understanding and ways of living. Earlier we have spoken about gender as context, and here we share our reflections of how and where our inquiry together shows itself in our conversations with clients. We notice that we are less constrained by concerns about imposing our own values as we have found new ways of articulating and questioning the usefulness of a binary gender description. It is our belief that human beings seek to categorise in order to make sense of and negotiate the world, yet the process of categorisation leads to much distress and often allows the misuse of power: 'these distinctions have become part of Western common sense, but we do not regard this as a sufficient argument for retaining them' (Rorty, 1999, p. xix). Our own realisation that we were in danger of co-constructing a world that perpetuates discrimination has heightened our curiosity as to how others may contribute to a context that confines and silences them. This is challenging to us; we must simultaneously and in equal measure value the right of individuals to define themselves, understand the impact of oppressive practices and honour the process of categorisation as sense making:

> We all know men who are nurturing and women who are not. Such an approach distracts us from the task at hand, which is to proceed from the fact of a gendered world, and then to use our special expertise as family therapists to document how this fact of life unfolds on intimate relationships – to describe it, capture its ironies, paradoxes, ambiguities, and dilemmas, and then to use our observations to assist those who come to us for help. (Goldner, 1985, p. 22)

We Cannot Not Be Female

We are situated within many discourses on what it means to be female, and how we should/could/ought to behave or even perform being a woman. We feel bolstered by reading about other women and men reclaiming the feminist label (Chimamanda Ngozi Adichie, Emma Watson, and Laura Bates of the Everyday Sexism Project to name a few), and challenged to take responsibility for our silenced voices and to speak out. This is not always easy; in fact, it is rarely easy. In beginning to re-describe for ourselves what it is to be the women we are, we have found new challenges in relation to how we think about gender. Butler (1990) claims it is 'no longer clear that feminist theory ought to try to settle the questions of primary identity in order to get on with the task of politics. Instead, we ought to ask, what political possibilities are the consequence of a radical critique of the categories of identity' (p. ix).

This is profoundly unsettling for feminists who grew up in the second wave era of feminism, yet this is the world we live in, the world our clients are struggling with and the world our children are constructing.

CONCLUSION

Researching our relationship to gender has, for us, inevitably involved an orientation that includes self-reflexive practices, acknowledging and connecting with emotions. We are aware that we have not offered a definition of 'gender' as such. This is not an oversight: our understanding of what *we* mean by gender has changed during the process of the inquiry and whilst we maintain a frame of gender as socially constructed, we have through our inquiry begun to critique the binary view of gender identity construction. In attempting to privilege qualitative action inquiry methodologies, we are aware that we could be criticised for falling into the binary, either/or trap of quantitative versus qualitative. We are also aware that the field of gender studies is fraught with tensions around dialectical distinctions, and that even the binary/non-binary distinctions can be seen as an either/or.

The more one critiques the dominant position and advocates for the nondominant view, the greater the risk that one will be viewed as 'disloyal' or dismissive of the dominant. It is possible to find value in both views, and it is at these moments that we find it more useful to occupy a 'both/and' position, so that we can value both strands of research methodologies, and multiple ways of doing (or being) gender(ed). Within our own practices, we have mentioned just a few of the changes we notice in our conversations with friends, relatives, colleagues, students and clients as a consequence of having engaged in this inquiry. Writing this chapter in itself has constituted a further cycle in our inquiry, and we anticipate more to come. Both of us are increasingly aware of the impact of shifting public conversations about gender identity that are seeping into our clinical work; more can be said and inquired into about this.

The frame of second-person collaborative inquiry brings the person of the researcher and the subject of the research together in such a way that emotions are integral to the research endeavour. Whilst we speak here predominantly from the collaborative position, we anticipate that the reader has gleaned sufficient reference to our differing first-person positions. Sharing our emotions with each other has 'disposed' us 'to action' (Maturana, 1988) and has also illuminated our lived experiences as the women, mothers, researchers, teachers and psychotherapists that we were, are and will become.

REFERENCES

Berger, R. (2015). Now I see it, now I don't: Researcher's position and reflexivity in qualitative research. *Qualitative Research*, *15*(2), 219–234.

Bradbury, H., & Reason, P. (2006). Conclusion: Broadening the bandwidth of validity: Issues and choice-points for improving the quality of action research. In P. Reason & H. Bradbury (Eds.), *Handbook of action research* (concise paperback edition) (pp. 343–51). London: SAGE.

Butler, J. (1990). *Gender trouble. Feminism and the subversion of identity.* London: Routledge.

Clandinin, D. J., & Connelly, F.M. (1994). Personal experience methods. In D. K. Denzin & Y.K. Lincoln (Eds.) Handbook of Qualitative Research. (1st ed., pp. 413–427). London: Sage.

Coleman, G. (2001). *An inquiry into gender and business education: In pursuit of mother-consciousness.* Ph.D. thesis, Centre for Action Research in Professional Practice, University of Bath. Retrieved from http://people.bath.ac.uk/mnspwr/doc_theses_links/ g_coleman.html. Accessed on March 16, 2017.

Davies, A. (2016). The art of looking like you are doing very little: Working on a psychiatric ward with people experiencing psychosis. *Context, 147,* 32–35.

Etherington, K. (2001). Writing qualitative research: A gathering of selves. *Counselling and Psychotherapy Research, 1*(2), 119–125.

Etherington, K. (2004). *Becoming a reflexive researcher.* London: Jessica Kingsley Publishers.

Goldner, V. (1985). Warning: Family therapy may be dangerous to your health. *The Family Therapy Networker, 9,* 19–23.

Goldner, V. (1991). Toward a critical relational theory of gender. *Psychoanalytic Dialogues, 1,* 249–272.

Grant, A. (2018). Shock and offence online: The role of emotion in participant absence research. In T. Loughran & D. Mannay (Eds.), *Emotion and the researcher: Sites, subjectivities and relationships* (Vol. 16). Studies in Qualitative Methodology (pp. 143–158). Bingley: Emerald.

Hare-Mustin, R. (1987). The problem of gender in family therapy. *Family Process, 26,* 15–17.

Higher Education Authority (2016) National review of gender equality in Irish higher education institutions report of the expert group. Retrieved from http://hea.ie/assets/uploads/2017/04/ hea_review_of_gender_equality_in_irish_higher_education.pdf. Accessed on March 16, 2017.

Heron, J., & Reason, P. (2008). Extending epistemology within a co-operative enquiry. In P. Reason & H. Bradbury (Eds.), *The Sage handbook of action research participative inquiry and practice* (2nd ed., pp. 366–380). London: Sage.

Jaggar, A. (2009). Love and knowledge: Emotion in feminist epistemology. In S. Kemp & J. Squires (Eds.), *Feminisms* (pp. 188–193). Oxford: Oxford University Press.

Jarrett, C. (2010). Feeling like a fraud. *The Psychologist, 23,* 380–383.

Jones, E. (1998). A feminist systemic therapy? In I. Bruna Seu & M. Colleen Heenan (Eds.), *Feminism and psychotherapy. Reflections on contemporary theories and practices* (pp. 189–202). London: Sage.

Kelan, E. K. (2009a). Gender fatigue: The ideological dilemma of gender neutrality and discrimination in organizations. *Canadian Journal of Administrative Sciences, 26*(3), 197–210.

Kelan, E. K. (2009b). *Performing gender at work.* London: Palgrave Macmillan.

Kemp, S., & Squires, J. (2009a). Introduction. In S. Kemp & J. Squires (Eds.), *Feminisms* (pp. 3–12). Oxford: Oxford University Press.

Kemp, S., & Squires, J. (2009b). Epistemologies. In S. Kemp & J. Squires (Eds.), *Feminisms* (pp. 142–145). Oxford: Oxford University Press.

Marshall, J. (1999). Living life as inquiry. *Systemic Practice and Action Research, 12*(2), 155–171.

Marshall, J. (2011). Images of changing practice through reflective action research. *Journal of Organizational Change Management, 24*(2), 244–256.

Marshall, J. (2016). *First person action research: Living life as inquiry.* London: Sage.

Maturana, H. R. (1988). Reality: The search for objectivity or the quest for a compelling argument. *Irish Journal of Psychology, 9*(1), 25–82.

McNamee, S. (1988). Accepting research as social intervention: Implications of a systemic epistemology. *Communication Quarterly, 36*(1), 50–68.

McRobbie, A. (2004). Notes on post feminism and popular culture: Bridget Jones and the new gender regime. In A. Harris & M. Fine (Eds.), *All about the girl: Culture, power and identity* (pp. 3–14). London: Routledge.

Morris, M. (2016). Gender and feminism: A personal journey with feminist ideas. *Gianfrancho Cecchin Memorial Lecture Family Institute Dysgu Conference,* University of South Wales.

Morris, M. (2017). The personal is political: The political is personal. *Context, 149,* 13–16.

Morris, M. & Davies, A. (2014). *Being both researchers and subjects: Attending to emotion within a collaborative enquiry.* Paper presented at Families, Identities and Gender Research Network, *Emotion and the Researcher Symposium,* Cardiff University, Cardiff.

Reason, P. (2003). Pragmatist philosophy and action research: Readings and conversations with Richard Rorty. *Action Research, 1*(1), 103–123.

Reason, P. & Bradbury, H. (Eds.) (2008). *The Sage handbook of action research participative inquiry and practice* (2nd ed.) London: Sage.

Riger, S. (2016). On becoming a feminist psychologist. *Psychology of Women Quarterly, 40*(4), 479–487.

Roberts, E. (2018). The 'transient insider': Identity and intimacy in home community research. In T. Loughran & D. Mannay (Eds.), *Emotion and the researcher: Sites, subjectivities and relationships* (Vol. 16). Studies in Qualitative Methodology (pp. 113–126). Bingley: Emerald.

Rorty, R. (1999). *Philosophy and social hope.* London: Penguin.

van den Scott, L. K. (2018). Role transitions in the field and reflexivity: From friend to researcher. In T. Loughran & D. Mannay (Eds.), *Emotion and the researcher: Sites, subjectivities and relationships* (Vol. 16). Studies in Qualitative Methodology (pp. 19–32). Bingley: Emerald.

Schön, D. A. (1991). *The reflective practitioner: How professionals think in action.* London: Ashgate.

CHAPTER 15

BLIND SPOTS AND MOMENTS OF ESTRANGEMENT: SUBJECTIVITY, CLASS AND EDUCATION IN BRITISH 'AUTOBIOGRAPHICAL HISTORIES'

Tracey Loughran

ABSTRACT

Purpose – *This chapter explores my responses to Carolyn Steedman's* Landscape for a Good Woman (1986) *as a historian and an educated working-class woman and considers the 'blind spots' in some commentary on the book. The aim of this study is to unpick understandings of subjectivity, class and education in certain kinds of academic text.*

Methodology/Approach – *The chapter draws on a qualitative analysis of works of history and cultural studies and reflections on the author's own emotions and experiences.*

Findings – *Education and class are equally important in the experiences of educated working-class people, but there are considerable difficulties in*

Emotion and the Researcher: Sites, Subjectivities, and Relationships
Studies in Qualitative Methodology, Volume 16, 245–259
Copyright © 2018 by Emerald Publishing Limited
All rights of reproduction in any form reserved
ISSN: 1042-3192/doi:10.1108/S1042-319220180000016016

communicating these different aspects of selfhood and in ensuring they are understood.

Originality/Value – *'Autobiographical histories' as a form, and the use of the first person in contexts where it is not usually accepted, provide new possibilities of identification and knowledge for marginalised peoples. 'Vulnerable writing' therefore has a political purpose.*

Keywords: Autobiography; history; cultural studies; subjectivity; class; education

INTRODUCTION

The summer of 1991, when I was 11, was a time of in-betweens, a high-definition moment bridging many 'befores' and 'afters'. My family was between homes, temporarily living with my paternal grandparents as we prepared to move from as-yet-ungentrified Tooting in south London to the not-quite-genteel, just-about-Surrey commuter town of Worcester Park. I was between schools, about to make the transition from primary to secondary education. Earlier in the year I had passed an entrance exam and gained a scholarship to a minor public school, and so I was also about to move from the state to the private sector; a movement that simultaneously propelled me forwards, to all that a good education could (and would, and did) bring, but has also kept me ever since in a perpetual awareness of origins (and therefore in some ways, in the same emotional space as the eleven-year-old). From simply existing in the world, I now had to earn my place in it.

In a few short weeks I left behind so many of the things that anchor us, that make us certain of ourselves – home, place, friends, the pattern of our days – and, ever since, liminality has defined my experience of the world. In a quite literal sense, education has led me to spend years in transitional spaces, shuttling between places of home, education and work: Surrey to London, London to Manchester, Manchester to Sheffield, Sheffield to Cardiff and Cardiff to Essex. But, of course, all this movement is no more than the outward and visible sign of an inward lack of grace, of the person caught between different ways of being, who does not fully or rightfully inhabit any of the available ready-made worlds of family or social milieu, and who has to somehow conjure her own belonging out of – perhaps not quite thin air, but imagination and chance, materials that make it difficult to feel anything but precarious.

Of course, no matter how singular all this feels, I am not alone. I am a historian, and so I know that my story is only a variation on the stories of countless scholarship girls and boys, of anyone whose education has led them to places that their own past selves would not have comprehended and that their families do not (will not) understand (LeMathieu, 2014; Steedman, 1997). I also know that for a historian to tell this story in this way is extremely rare. Using the first person to narrate a personal past as part of historical practice, the insertion of the historian's self into her History,[1] challenges some of the most cherished foundational myths of the discipline. In this chapter, I reflect upon my own relation to a seminal text which does speak in this way, Carolyn Steedman's *Landscape for a Good Woman* (1986). In thinking about how the subject position of the reader influences the meaning of the text, and arguing that this book encapsulates new ways of understanding what History might be, I move beyond the purely personal to reflect on the relationship between the personal and the political in historical writing.

I have chosen to orient this discussion around the relationship of historians to historical texts because we often unthinkingly replicate dominant disciplinary practices in our own writing; what we read shapes how we think, speak and write in complicated ways. The chapter is a stand against the projection of professional 'objectivity', and an impassioned plea for certain kinds of writing against others, on the basis that our claims about selfhood are always political, in all the spheres in which we operate. We are professional historians (or sociologists, or neuroscientists or literary scholars), but we are also citizens who live out our beliefs partly through our professional practice. We have a responsibility not to hide.

'OBJECTIVITY', EMOTION AND HISTORICAL PRACTICE

Ruth Behar is an autoethnographer who writes perceptively and powerfully about the simultaneous necessity and difficulty of putting 'the self who observes' into the text, a practice which for her is all about 'vulnerability' (Behar, 1996, p. 6). Writing vulnerably should not be mistaken for simple confession. To remain ethnographers, 'vulnerable observers' must always scrutinise 'the connection, intellectual and emotional, between the observer and the observed', and ensure that vulnerability is 'essential to the argument, not a decorative flourish, not exposure for its own sake' (Behar, 1996, p. 14). This kind of writing allows marginalised peoples to reclaim power and enables identifications that are smothered or simply denied being by more detached forms of expression. Behar therefore laments trends within contemporary anthropology that lead scholars away from personal connections to the field, including the proliferation of large research teams and the seductions of high theory. Still other scholars, she claims, have 'retreated to history, to the quiet of the archives and the study of the past, where presumably an observer can do less damage, not have to be quite so disturbingly present' (Behar, 1996, p. 25).

This is where the historian pauses. Certainly, research relationships with living people have different emotional resonances and hold higher stakes in the immediate moment of contact, than the connection between a historian and sources dealing with the dead: but History is not a retreat and the past is not quiet. As Michael Roper (2014, p. 172) points out, historical research 'operates under distinctive psychological conditions, wherein the desires, frustrations and pleasures of historical actors may communicate themselves to us, and in which we have certain emotional experiences, but in which the relationship is neither face-to-face nor reciprocal'. Over the past 30 years, intra- and extra-disciplinary debates have taught us over and again that historians cannot help but be 'disturbingly present' whenever they research and write (Jenkins, 1997). This quality of 'present-ness' is even more intense when historians consciously acknowledge and feel their deep moral responsibility to those who cannot answer back or (re)make their case, as several thought-provoking reflections on the affective dimensions of historical research testify (Burton, 2005; Robinson, 2010). For these reasons, 'empathy is not optional but an aspect of all historical work, no matter how seemingly impersonal' (Roper, 2014, p. 174).

Yet it is not difficult to understand why Behar, an outsider to the discipline, working in a tradition characterised by its own tortured relations of closeness/distance and 'Othering', would view History in this way. Since the nineteenth century, 'objectivity' has been the false idol of the historical profession (Iggers, 2011). On an intellectual level, most historians now accept the impossibility of 'objectivity' as conventionally understood; nevertheless, we continue to visit archives, insert footnotes into our texts and castigate hapless students who plagiarise or make things up. As the persistence of Holocaust denial vividly demonstrates, relativism is not a viable political or moral option. The appeal to evidence, and the disciplinary apparatus that ensures rigour in its use, helps to guard against these dangers (Fulbrook, 2002, pp. 164–184).

This ambiguous relation to the question of historical 'objectivity' is reflected in standard modes of historical writing. Historians, for the most part, expunge their presence from their texts. Helen Sword's survey of writing practices across the humanities, social sciences, and sciences found that only 40 per cent of historians employed either 'I' or 'we' in their writing, as opposed to 92 per cent of philosophers and 98 per cent of literary scholars. Instead, historians packed their prose full of subjectively weighted nouns, adjectives and verbs designed to sway readers to a particular point of view, leading Sword to conclude that of all academics, historians are 'the most clearly subjective – manipulative, even – in their use of language' (Sword, 2012, pp. 39–40).

This rejection of personal pronouns is both a matter of disciplinary habit and part of the individual historian's presentation of self. It is a management of the public expression of emotion and can be perceived as a perverse form of emotional labour (Hochschild, 2003). If 'all historical writing is autobiographical in the sense that authors seek to project a certain image of themselves' (Vinen, 2011, p. 533), then, paradoxically, the erasure of self in historical writing tells us much about the historian's values and the type of history she believes is important. An absent 'I' claims authority, and presents this authority as natural, through the elimination of self (Scott, 1991, p. 782). Historically, it is those who wield power who have been able to project their own worldview as 'objective', and in this way to naturalise it. Nowadays, the assumption of an 'objective' stance might be unthinking, but it is nevertheless a choice: a choice to identify with those capable of an erasure of self that is believed and perpetrated, rather than those forced, always and forever, to inhabit and to be judged by their unruly bodies. It is a stand with coloniser over colonised, oppressor over the oppressed, men over women, white over Black.

The use (or not) of personal pronouns also tells us something about how the historian conceives of his audience. A third-person omniscient narrator directs the reader; he assumes a quite explicit power over what the reader should think or feel; he does not engage in conversation or permit the possibility of alternative responses to those envisaged. In rejecting this tradition, autobiographical histories approach the reader in a different way; the 'I' presupposes a 'we'; it creates a relationship. But readers access, understand, and interpret texts in different ways, and they bring their own ideas about the authorial self to these encounters. Prevalent assumptions about literacy, education and social class can operate to hide the author's status as a highly educated person. As researchers, we often fail to recognise this position and to realise its importance, both because we share it, and because this is what we expect of the authors we read for academic purposes. Yet this subject position determines all kinds of things which affect our understanding: the way in which the author is able to speak, the personal history structuring her ability to speak in this way and decision to do so, and our own perception of ourselves as the audience to whom she speaks.

LANDSCAPE FOR A GOOD WOMAN

Carolyn Steedman's *Landscape for a Good Woman* is a truly original work of history. It is a book about class, gender and psychology; it is a work of autobiography, family history and social history. Writing in the 1980s, Steedman's starting point is that existing traditions of class analysis and cultural criticism cannot 'deal with everything there is to say' about the lives of working-class women such as her mother; women who were not forbearing saints, who desired the things of the earth and who voted Conservative not Labour (Steedman, 1986, pp. 6–7). The book is Steedman's attempt to provide interpretative devices which will make sense of her mother's life, the ways in which her own childhood was structured 'by the one my mother had lived out before me, and the stories she told about it', and how both these stories 'can be elaborated by the marginal and secret stories that other working-class girls and women from a recent historical past have to tell' (Steedman, 1986, p. 5).

To make sense of these stories, Steedman draws on several different interpretative traditions, most of which are not usually meshed, and certainly not in historical writing (Eley, 2005, pp. 172–181). The book contains elements of biography and autobiography: the 'I' of the author is a constant presence. But Steedman also places her own and her mother's stories in historical contexts (the north of England in the early twentieth-century; south London in the 1950s). The book is therefore also History. She exploits to the full the potential of (auto)biography to 'cut paths in and through the determined spaces of structures and cultures in which individuals are located', and to find a space that acknowledges lives as unique but still does not conceive them as 'wholly individual or free-floating' (Clarke, Hall, Jefferson, & Roberts, 1977, p. 57). Finally, Steedman draws on psychoanalysis to explore the importance of dreams, childhood and family relationships, and in her adoption of the form of the case-study.

I have never read anything quite like this book, and I doubt another work of history will ever have quite such an effect on me. I first read it when I was in my early thirties. At the time, I held a permanent lectureship in History at Cardiff University. I knew I was lucky; my path from PhD to permanent post in a Russell Group university had been remarkably smooth, with only two months of unemployment between viva and my first temporary position at the University of Manchester, and no unsalaried months since. But I did not feel safe. I could not seem to finish the book I was writing; it was not the kind of History I had set out to write, it was dry, it was dull, and it did no justice to its subjects. I felt dissatisfied with myself, with my ability as a researcher, and I agonised over whether this was really the profession for me. If I had known of any other viable options – if I had been able to imagine another kind of job that I could walk into, one that paid reasonably well, where people would treat you with a minimum of respect – then I might have quit. In time and space, I was a long way from that nervous eleven-year-old dreading the summer's end, but she was still there, fearing failure, the horizons of her world not so much smaller than mine.

So, with an identification that might seem facile, I read *Landscape for a Good Woman* as the words of one scholarship girl to another, from one formed in the crucible of the welfare state to one marked by its gradual dissolution. I read it with an almost painful stab of recognition, the kind that quickens and pulls you into life. Steedman was born in 1947 and raised in south London. She passed her eleven-plus, went to grammar school, gained a place at Sussex University, and went on to read for a PhD at Newnham College, Cambridge. I was born in 1979, raised and educated in south London. I gained a place at Sussex University (and left after a year, a first-generation university student unable to support myself financially and with parents who offered love, but no more immediately practical support), and went on to read for a PhD in History at Queen Mary, University of London. There are many convergences in this story. Above all, though, her text speaks to my experience of a working-class childhood which shaped who I am, and an education which has separated me from that childhood.

I recognise the class anger that is burnt into the soul, the acid flux knowledge of powerlessness that persists long after the barricades against it have been erected, long after the qualifications have been gained and there is money in the bank. Steedman (1986, p. 2) recalls a health visitor telling her mother that the house wasn't fit for a baby, and she says:

> I will do everything and anything until the end of my days to stop anyone ever talking to me like that woman talked to my mother. It is in this place, this bare, curtainless bedroom that lies my secret and shameful defiance. I read a woman's book, meet such a woman at a party (a woman now, like me) and think quite deliberately as we talk: we are divided: a hundred years ago I'd have been cleaning your shoes. I know this and you don't.

I think, less deliberately, as I read: *I know what this is like. I know what this means.* But this identification is not solely based in our shared past experience of working-class childhoods; it arises from our common training and modes of understanding, our shared professional orientation to the past. Steedman makes sense of stories by historicising them. This is a familiar language, a familiar position, and the power of this way of thinking is not separate from my emotional response to her text. It is a form of understanding which makes this emotional response possible. We are fellow-travellers through our education and profession, through History as well as our histories.

EDUCATED WORKING-CLASS WOMEN

I identify with *Landscape for a Good Woman* because Steedman and I are both educated working-class women. I borrow the phrase 'educated working-class woman' from Valerie Walkerdine, another child of the postwar boom who passed the eleven-plus and ended up as an academic (Walkerdine, 1990, p. 158). It is an inelegant phrase, and I like it for that reason. It is exact. It acknowledges not only a working-class childhood, but also the separation from origins that is an inevitable outcome of prolonged education and the choice of a different way of life to your parents. It acknowledges that education does not make you middle-class, but it does make you different from how you started out. It works *because* it doesn't quite sound right. It conveys the awkwardness which is an inescapable part of occupying this particular place in the world. It accords class and education equal importance, in a way that is often difficult for authors and for audiences.

To offer a perspective from the position of an educated working-class person, one that does not deny the past or the present of the observer, involves drawing on the evidence of subjective experience *and* education. The educated working-class person necessarily holds both perspectives within herself, but these dual elements of selfhood are less often recognised by those who do not share both elements of this subject position. This lack of recognition appears at times simply as a blind spot, no different from the many others that inevitably limit our vision, and at other times like a wilful assertion of power. It is related to the liminal status of educated working-class people, and particularly to the difficulties of negotiating contexts where other working-class people are less often found. Yet the claiming of a self that is educated *and* working-class is important, because in claiming this status, we make a broader social and political statement about what other working-class people can be and do, and how these achievements should be understood.

My subject position leads me to read *Landscape for a Good Woman* as a story/History about class, education and ending up somewhere far from where you started out. This is not the only way to read the book, and not the way it has most often been read. Many scholars have picked over the bones of Steedman's experiments in history and autobiography, and effused at length about her explorations of class, gender, childhood and subjectivity. But they are far less interested in the role of education in her story, and barely at all in Steedman's self-conscious stance *as a historian*. Nicola King states that although Steedman creates a vivid sense of her childhood, there is an absence at the heart of her text, as she does not convey an impression of her present life and experience – what she is 'now' is largely left out of the account (King, 2000, p. 34).

Well, is it? The author of a scholarly book which is simultaneously auto-biography and History, with a good smattering of psychoanalytic theory to frame it – that is who Steedman is now. The 'I' who produced this text is an academic writing for other academics, and that is integral to the narrative. We know where she ended up before we open the book. Readers easily miss this quite fundamental point because they are researchers used to reading texts by academics for other academics. Perhaps particularly for readers from a different class background to Steedman, who take educational attainment for granted, there is simply nothing to comment on here; all is normal, and there-fore not noticed. As the subjects of her work, Steedman's class and gender are more evident to readers than her education, which shapes the subject position from which she now speaks.

LOOKING FROM THE OUTSIDE IN

Yet the claim to educated working-class selfhood is fraught with difficulties. Liminality generates paradoxes and problems. If your audience recognises only your claim to be working-class, then this aspect of selfhood engulfs edu-cation and, with it, recognition of achievement and even full personhood. (This is, of course, another form of colonisation.) If your audience ignores or downplays your class status, then it feeds into an invidious assumption that it is not possible to be working-class and educated, that education some-how makes you not working-class; this assumption contributes to wider pat-terns of stigmatisation of working-class people and places. The author is also caught in another bind. It is as simple as this: to write as an educated work-ing-class person for an academic audience means that you do not belong to either world; you claim the insider's perspective at the exact moment, and in the exact manner, that makes your claim at best a half-truth (which is to say at least a half-lie); or, perhaps more kindly, a claim about memory rather than life as it is now lived. You become, willingly or not, 'an exiled native inform-ant, returning to interpret the culture of his childhood to the inhabitants of the world of his exile' (Lovell, 1990, p. 361).

These difficulties are illustrated by the historian Robert Colls' account of how Richard Hoggart's *The Uses of Literacy* (1957), a classic work of cultural studies, influenced his own worldview. In this work, the former scholarship boy Hoggart drew on his own working-class background to argue for the existence of a distinct working-class culture that embodied certain values, and was worthy of respect. Colls describes sitting in his bedroom as a 16-year-old grammar school boy in 1965, reading *The Uses of Literacy*, then looking out of the window and realising that what he saw below was a working-class community with its own culture. There was joy in this revelation – 'Hoggart had made me literate. All was new' – but also loss: 'In the beginning, I didn't know I belonged to a "culture", but at the moment when I realized I did, I felt estranged. This was a paradoxical condition, not willingly sought at the time and only half-grasped since' (Colls, 2004, pp. 283, 286).

Education, experience and estrangement are indivisible in this account. This 'flash of realization', Colls tells us, 'had everything to do with the book in front of me and nothing at all to do with what was happening down in the street – a street, I may say, that I had never thought about even though I had stepped into it a million times' (Colls, 2004, p. 284). His new understanding depended on his working-class identity and on his education; the kind of understanding gained was inseparable from the way that understanding was reached – in much the same way that my own understanding of Steedman is inseparable from both my working-class identity and my training as a historian.

At the end of his essay, Colls argues that the 'paradoxical condition' he initially presented to the reader was false, because 'Hoggart's book was part of the high culture of the community he described'. This book by another scholarship boy did not really alienate Colls from himself or the working-class culture it taught him to name; rather, it 'enriched and sharpened the world it addressed, and was part of' (Colls, 2004, p. 306). The logical conclusion of Colls' argument, and one I wish he had worked out in more detail, seems to be that we should not hive off the achievements of educated working-class people as somehow belonging 'out there', but instead claim them back for working-class culture and thus widen the definition of what that is. Part of me applauds this conclusion as a way of resisting the persistent stigmatisation of the working class. Another part fears that such claims actually lead to further academic colonisation of working-class experience, one that conflates observer/observed and in this way actually devours the experience of those who still have less money and less power; who could write books, who might write books, but from where they currently stand cannot even get anyone to listen.

LOOKING FROM THE INSIDE OUT

But what is the alternative? If class rather than education is emphasised when dealing with texts by educated working-class people, commentators fail to appreciate the position of privilege from which they read. They implicitly adopt the familiar position of voyeur of working-class life. It is an insidious way of denying the claims of working-class people to any cultural status or achievement beyond those described only in class terms. Alan Sillitoe persistently pointed out that his *Saturday Night and Sunday Morning* (1958) was simply a novel. It was not a 'working-class novel', a label that betrayed the 'narrow class standpoint' of reviewers, and it was certainly not an autobiography: 'the novel, while mirroring the sort of atmosphere I grew up in, is a work of the imagination in that all the actors in it are put together so that no identifiable characters came out at the end. I imagine novelists of the middle-class condition also perform in this way' (Marwick, 1984, p. 141; Sillitoe, 2008, pp. 5–6).

We can say something similar about the failure to recognise the importance of education and training, as well as class, in *Landscape for a Good Woman*. At different points in the text, Steedman tells readers that what they are reading is or is not History (Steedman, 1986, pp. 21, 127, 139, 142). But her later explanation for claiming it was not History is perverse; it is because her 'education and socialisation as a historian' tells her that she did no 'real empirical research for the book', and she 'wants real historians to know that I know this'. In other words, she wants other historians to recognise her as a historian, even if that involves denying that what she has written is History, and the recognition of what she has written as History would please her 'much more than anything else' (Steedman, 1992, p. 45). This is a claim about education rather than professional status; it is a plea for a book about who she *was* to be read with some recognition of who she has *become*, to acknowledge what she has done without making loss of part of herself the condition of recognition. It is a claim to be an educated working-class woman.

Anyone who tries to negotiate these complexities but lacks Steedman's own skill is even more liable to be misinterpreted. One of my most unpleasant experiences in the academic world occurred when I gave an early version of this paper at Cardiff University in 2014. An upper-class female academic took me to task for claiming a privileged identification with Steedman on class grounds (a claim of privilege that I had tried to avoid),[2] and for self-identifying primarily as working-class rather than as female (I don't: I am an educated working-class woman). I was able to see the irony in someone from a very different class background standing too close to me, raising her voice and talking over me to make it crystal clear that I was wrong about the ways in which educated working-class women can be misheard or silenced; and if I hadn't been so angry I would have laughed at the surreal part of her tirade about how I didn't know what working-class men were 'really' like (because, presumably, my grandfathers, father, brothers, husband, father-in-law, brother-in-law, and nephews are in some way less 'real' than the working-class men she had encountered in universities, or paid to do work in her house or garden); all the same, I thought twice about refining the paper and delivering it again, and I am thinking a third time now about publishing it.

CONCLUDING THOUGHTS

When I started attending my private school at 11, I moved into an environment where my accent marked me out. I stopped speaking unless spoken to. Other girls picked up on my glottal stops.[3] I have never wanted to change my accent, but I speak differently now, partly as a result of spending so much time with people from different class backgrounds, but partly because my habitual vocabulary when teaching and working is one I never heard in the accents of my childhood. I still mentally pause whenever I have to pronounce a word with a 't' in the middle. It feels wrong either to sound or not sound it. Even now, I meet people in professional settings who hear my voice and seem to mentally write me off; who express surprise that someone with a PhD and many publications to her name has read 'difficult' or 'long' books (their descriptions, not mine); who try to talk over me in meetings, and are offended when I will not stop. I will talk now, because I am tired of not being listened to, and because if people like me don't talk, people like them will never start to take our voices for granted.

We need to find ways of communication that enfold manifold understandings – of who we are and how it shapes what we do, of the limits of what we can know, of our power to speak and our powerlessness to control how we are heard. The working-class educated woman cannot be easy with the voice of the omniscient third-person narrator (who is, after all, always middle- or upper-class, and quite often male). She needs to claim the authority to say 'I': it can be articulated and heard partly because of those others who went before. I can say it because Steedman said it, and Steedman (and Colls) can say it because Hoggart said it. For those of us who often feel on the margins, simply to hear that 'I' speaking – an 'I' simultaneously like and unlike our own selves – is revelatory. It shows what is at stake when we research history, and even more so when we write it.

When we reject the personal voice, we are not only writing ourselves out. We are implicitly subscribing to an entire disciplinary tradition founded on the valorisation of 'objectivity', and the power and authority of white middle-class professionals. We are not just losing a voice; we are adopting one that is not our own. This is damaging, for ourselves and those we write with and for. In his study of the hidden injuries of class in early modern England, Andy Wood explores the psychic consequences for labouring people of buying into paternalist discourses, of suppressing their anger and biting their lips. He argues that deference to their social 'betters' did not simply reflect the existing social structure, but helped to constitute it; the adoption of deferential speech helped to maintain the hierarchical order (Wood, 2006).[4] In other words, in at least some contexts, we enable our oppressors to maintain their dominance partly by using their language, by taking it on as our own. As linguists know, 'habits of speech can create habits of mind' (Deutscher, 2011, p. 234), and as intellectual historians tell us, it is 'easy to become trapped and confined by the intellectual categories we inherit' (Dixon, 2008, p. 11). We need to act on this knowledge about language and how it shapes our possibilities.

To write an autobiographical history, or even to write in the first person, is a way of subverting convention and expectations: it is a way not only of repossessing the dispossessed, but of speaking ourselves; it is a matter of saying that the subaltern can speak,[5] but she must speak herself, and not through mimicry of the professional interlocutor. To write in this way is to change the traditional form of historical writing, and to claim the discipline and the profession as our own. To have 'the authority to define which parts of reality are picked out by a particular term, and what that term says about those realities, is to have a powerful influence on how others perceive and think about the world' (Dixon, 2008, p. 28). Writing from the self in this way is intensely vulnerable, but it is also an expression of power: for historically, the ability to choose how, when, in what form, and to whom to tell your story has been a rare gift. We need to wield this weapon, so that others like us can find different ways of speaking and of being heard. To 'speak in a way that matters', to 'drive a wedge into the thick mud of business as usual' (Behar, 1996, p. 166), is a political act, an act not only of resistance against a dominant culture but also a way of changing it.

NOTES

1. Throughout this chapter I use 'History' to refer to the discipline of History ('the work of historians; history-writing': Steedman, 2001, p. 146), and 'history' to refer to the individual and/or collective past.

2. What I actually said, and still stand by, is 'Steedman speaks to me because I share many of her experiences: as a south Londoner, as a working-class child, as an educated woman. Her critical analysis and her history can speak to other people in other ways, but the emotional response will be different or absent if they do not share elements of this personal history. This means that a middle-class reader will not understand her book in the same way as I do, but it also means that a working-class woman without formal education would not either, because the particular estrangement Steedman talks about, and which I recognise, is about class and education – not one or the other'.

3. The glottal stop is a voiceless stop sound made in the throat, often replacing a 't' in spoken English (e.g. for 'letter', 'le'er'). It is a usual feature of working-class London accents.

4. Wood is inspired by Richard Sennett and Jonathan Cobb's classic study of *The Hidden Injuries of Class* (1972).

5. 'Subaltern' refers to marginalised peoples, especially those relegated to lower status within hegemonic structures (see Spivak, 1988).

REFERENCES

Behar, R. (1996). *The vulnerable observer: Anthropology that breaks your heart.* Boston, MA: Beacon Press.

Burton, A. (Ed.) (2005). *Archive stories: Facts, fictions, and the writing of history.* Durham, NC: Duke University Press.

Clarke, J., Hall, S., Jefferson, T., & Roberts, B. (1977). Subcultures, cultures and class. In S. Hall & T. Jefferson (Eds.), *Resistance through rituals: Youth cultures in post-war Britain* (pp. 9–74). London: Hutchinson & Co.

Colls, R. (2004). When we lived in communities: Working-class culture and its critics. In R. Colls & R. Rodger (Eds.), *Cities of ideas: Civil society and urban governance in Britain, 1800–2000* (pp. 283–307). Aldershot: Ashgate.

Deutscher, G. (2011). *Through the language glass: Why the world looks different in other languages.* London: Arrow Books.

Dixon, T (2008). *The invention of altruism: Making moral meanings in modern Britain.* Oxford: Oxford University Press.

Eley, G. (2005). *A crooked line: From cultural history to the history of society.* Ann Arbor, MI: University of Michigan Press.

Fulbrook, M. (2002). *Historical theory.* London: Routledge.

Hochschild, A. (2003). *The managed heart: Commercialization of feeling.* Berkeley, CA: University of California Press.

Hoggart, R. (1958). *The uses of literacy: Aspects of working class life with special reference to publications and entertainments.* Harmondsworth: Penguin.

Iggers, G. I. (2011). The intellectual foundations of nineteenth-century 'scientific' history: The German model. In S. Macintyre, J. Maiguashca, & A. Pók (Eds.), *The Oxford history of historical writing: Volume 4, 1800–1945* (pp. 41–58). Oxford: Oxford University Press.

Jenkins, K. (1997). *The postmodern history reader.* Abingdon, Oxon: Routledge.

King, N. (2000). *Memory, narrative, identity: Remembering the self.* Edinburgh: Edinburgh University Press.

LeMathieu, D. L. (2014). 'Scholarship boys' in twilight: The memoirs of six humanists in post-industrial Britain. *Journal of British Studies, 53*, 1011–1031.

Lovell, T. (1990). Landscapes and stories in 1960s British realism. *Screen, 31*(4), 357–376.

Marwick, A. (1984). *Room at the top, Saturday night and Sunday morning*, and the 'cultural revolution' in Britain. *Journal of Contemporary History, 9*(1), 127–152.

Robinson, E. (2010). Touching the void: Affective history and the impossible. *Rethinking History, 14*(4), 503–520.

Roper, M. (2014). The unconscious work of history. *Cultural and Social History, 11*(2), 169–193.

Scott, J. W. (1991). The evidence of experience. *Critical Inquiry, 17*(4), 773–797.

Sillitoe, A. (2008). *Saturday night and Sunday morning*. London: Harper Perennial.

Spivak, G. (1988). Can the subaltern speak?. In C. Nelson & L. Grossberg (Eds.), *Marxism and the interpretation of culture* (pp. 271–313). Urbana, IL: University of Illinois Press.

Steedman, C. (1986). *Landscape for a good woman*. London: Virago.

Steedman, C. (1992). *Past tenses: Essays on writing, autobiography and history*. London: Rivers Oram Press.

Steedman, C. (1997). Writing the self: The end of the scholarship girl. In J. McGuigan (Ed.), *Cultural methodologies* (pp. 106–125). London: SAGE.

Steedman, C. (2001). *Dust*. Manchester: Manchester University Press.

Sword, H. (2012). *Stylish academic writing*. Cambridge, MA: Harvard University Press.

Vinen, R. (2011). The poisoned madeleine: The autobiographical turn in historical writing. *Journal of Contemporary History, 46*(3), 531–554.

Walkerdine, V. (1990). *Schoolgirl fictions*. London: Verso.

Wood, A. (2006). Fear, hatred and the hidden injuries of class in early modern England. *Journal of Social History, 39*(3), 803–826.

AFTERWORD

Tracey Loughran and Dawn Mannay

INTRODUCTION

More than four years ago, a group of open-minded and curious individuals came together to talk about how emotion had shaped their experiences as researchers. Over the course of two workshops, we heard about emotional experiences at academic conferences, in conducting ethnographic or oral history interviews, in reading sources and texts, in negotiating decisions about the care of patients and clients and in moving through different communities and places as researchers. These workshops replicated in miniature our wider experiences of emotion and research. We felt nervous anticipation at the prospect of sharing stories, previously untold, that were close to our hearts; joy, relief and recognition at hearing about the emotional journeys of others; and happy excitement at new discoveries, collaborations and friendships.

Alongside these positive emotions, there were also some rapid shifts in mood, perhaps to be expected when so many of us felt exposed and vulnerable. Some memories are especially vivid: one participant's bitter outpouring of resentment at the marginalisation of certain voices and experiences within the wider context of academia; jostling over perceived claims to greater emotional 'authenticity'; and flashes of anger at failures of understanding between speaker and audience. All these experiences are everyday parts of academic life, but with the spotlight on emotion, they felt particularly intense and meaningful over those two days.

Those workshops confirmed our growing sense that others were also desperate to find ways and places to reflect on the role of emotion within their research. More than this, however, the workshops simultaneously revealed

Emotion and the Researcher Sites, Subjectivities, and Relationships
Studies in Qualitative Methodology, Volume 16, 261–268
Copyright © 2018 by Emerald Publishing Limited
All rights of reproduction in any form reserved
ISSN: 1042-3192/doi:10.1108/S1042-319220180000016017

the limits of our own knowledge, and provided a practical demonstration of how emotion is conceptualised and deployed within research relationships and academic spaces. We felt there was much more to learn and much more to say. This volume has therefore endeavoured to explore multiple aspects of the operation of emotion in research. It has taken in different stages of the research process, from the formulation of research questions and methodologies to decisions about how and where to communicate findings. It has examined diverse sites, from fieldwork carried out face-to-face and online, on a different continent or in the researcher's home community, to clinical practice and academic conferences. Finally, it represents multiple disciplinary perspectives across the humanities, social sciences and healthcare sciences.

By directly addressing the nature and scope of social research and the impact of social relations on this research, the volume should be relevant to researchers in any discipline. We are proud of the contributions brought together here and feel that the volume is a valuable addition to an emergent field. At the same time, it is clear that there is still much for those interested in the relationship between emotion and research to learn and to do. At the close of this volume, then, we look forward to consider the directions that future explorations of emotion and research might take.

EMOTION MATTERS – BUT HOW, WHERE AND WHEN?

Our first conclusion is the most obvious. Emotion matters in research. We are not alone in reaching this conclusion. *Emotion and the Researcher* builds on an impressive body of research that has examined interactions between researcher and researched and sought to trouble this distinction (Delamont & Atkinson, 1995; Geer, 1964; Kulick & Willson, 1992). The contributors to this volume owe a great deal to scholarship that has examined how research (especially fieldwork) shapes and constructs subjectivities, emotional selves and intimate relations (Barbalet, 2010; Coffey, 1999; Roper, 2014; Smart, 2007; Ward, 2016). Explorations in autoethnography, autobiography and reflexivity have shown us how we might find new ways of thinking and writing about emotions in research (Behar, 1996; Kuhn, 1995; Steedman, 1986; Walkerdine, Lucey, & Melody, 2001). Part of the work of this volume has been to consolidate and extend the insights from this earlier scholarship, and in doing so, to showcase its importance.

Despite this existing body of work, the volume has nevertheless surprised us as editors with its revelations of how emotion is ever-present in research, permeating the entire process and even going beyond it. Our contributors discuss emotions in fieldwork (whether other people are present or not), in analysis, in writing-up, in relationships with colleagues, in conferences, in collaborations, and how emotions inflect relationships with a range of people that are neither researcher or researched but connected in some way. The openness our contributors demonstrate about their own concerns and shortcomings will act as a guide for current and future researchers. Often, we do not hear about how others feel unprepared for the emotional demands of research or wonder how they will cope. Knowing that others have been in the same situation and have come out the other side is immensely consoling. We hope that readers will find practical inspiration in these confessional chapters.

Our second conclusion is, perhaps, equally obvious, but more disconcerting. Emotion undoubtedly infuses and influence every research encounter – but some kinds of researcher are more willing, or more able, than others to acknowledge and reflect upon what this means. We can discern several divisions here, each of which illustrates the unequal distribution of power within and outside academia. The most evident divide is between disciplines. Contributors to this volume are drawn from a wide range of disciplines, but none from the 'hard' sciences or from clinical medicine. This is not because emotion is absent from these fields. It has been several decades now since philosophers and historians first demonstrated the social construction of scientific knowledge (Jordanova, 1995; Latour & Woolgar, 1986), while a more recent vogue for medical memoirs provides ample evidence of the intense emotions of clinicians at work (Byron, 2014; Gawande, 2014; Kalanthi, 2016; Marsh, 2014).

However, we were unable to recruit any contributors from these fields. Our initial call for the workshops extended across Cardiff University and was therefore circulated to colleagues in the biosciences, dentistry, medicine, optometry, pharmaceutical science, chemistry, computer science, earth sciences, engineering, mathematics, physics and astronomy – but scholars in these fields did not respond. In putting this volume together, we made an effort to recruit a researcher in clinical medicine to increase the range of the work, but proved unable to find someone comfortable with the aims of the book and able to commit the time required. This perhaps suggests either that scholars working in the 'hard' sciences and clinical medicine do not perceive emotion as having the same kinds of influence on their research, that they are less interested in interrogating this influence if they do recognise it, or that their disciplines lack an academic language or vocabulary that would enable such reflection.

It is no coincidence that the fields unrepresented here are also overwhelmingly male. With one (honourable) exception, all contributors to this

volume are female; likewise, only two of the attendees at the Emotion and the
Researcher workshops in 2014 were male. We can become too easily accustomed to this gendered cleavage of disciplines and of specific topics within
and across disciplines, but it is worth stopping for a moment and considering what it means for our practice as scholars. The essayist and novelist, Siri
Hustvedt (2016, pp. 90–91), who has also published on neurobiology and philosophy, describes herself as

> embody[ing] the masculine/feminine, serious/non-so-serious, hard/soft divide in my own
> work. When I publish a paper in a science journal or lecture at a conference in the sci-
> ences, I find myself on male terrain, but when I publish a novel, I stay squarely in female
> land. The audiences at public events vary accordingly, from about 80 percent male in the
> sciences and philosophy to exactly the reverse at a literary reading or event.

As Hustvedt (2016, p. 91) notes, this 'gendered geography' becomes the
context for how we work, and for how our work is seen.

This division of scholars who are willing to publicly discuss how emotion
influences the research process along gendered lines is one of the strongest
pieces of evidence that, as Craig Calhoun argues, the dualism that has characterised Western approaches to reason/emotion is not a historical artefact.
Rather, this dualism 'itself affects the ways in which people deploy notions
of both reason and emotion' (Calhoun, 2001, p. 52). We might then view the
preponderance of female contributors to this edited volume on emotion in
research as evidence of the same operation of power that colonised rationality as a masculine domain, but is now widely perceived as profoundly damaging to men unable to fully inhabit their emotional selves (de Boise, 2015,
pp. 45–69).

Conversely, however, we might also point to the absence of Black and
minority ethnic (BAME) perspectives within this volume as evidence of
the continued lack of presence and power among these groups in academia
(Bhopal, 2018). In 2015–2016, the last year for which statistics are available
at the time of going to press, no Black academics had worked in senior management at any British university for the previous three years. Universities
employed more Black staff as cleaners, receptionists or porters than as lectur-
ers or professors (Adams, 2017; HESA, 2017). BAME scholars are simply not
'here' in British academia, and that is the main reason for their lack of representation in this volume (and one which, if we had our time again as editors,
we would do more to remedy). Moreover, if emotion has been stigmatised
and associated with marginalised groups, then reclaiming emotion is an act
of power – but it is more difficult for those who lack representation, who 'do
not quite inhabit the norms of an institution' (Ahmed, 2017, p. 115), to align
themselves with a potential source of stigma. The gains are too recent, and

there is still too much to lose. The comparison with social class is instructive here. While academics from working-class backgrounds may continue to feel marginalised in many ways, researchers explicitly or implicitly claim working-class status in this volume, and have been able to do so partly because other scholars did so before them (Reay, 2017; Steedman, 1986; Walkerdine et al., 2001). With greater representation, the risks of owning emotion lessen.

EMOTION AND SUBJECTIVITY, SCIENCE AND RIGOUR

Nevertheless, it can still seem risky to talk about emotion in research because, as we discussed in the introduction to this volume, disciplinary conventions actively work against the admission of emotion. Perversely, as academics we perform an inordinate amount of emotional labour to establish the guise of objectivity (Goodwin, Jasper, & Polletta, 2001, p. 15). Even within the human and social sciences, the workings of emotion in research are still most often acknowledged where they are least escapable. Ethnography, a discipline dependent on subtle interactions with others, took a reflexive turn before most other fields (Dube, 2007, pp. 26–27). Reflexivity is still found most often in fields that have borrowed techniques from ethnography to guide interactions with living participants, such as qualitative social science or oral history (Bornat, 2010), and it is notable that the majority of contributors to this volume draw on these traditions.

This point leads on to our third conclusion, and one that is more complex and unexpected. In our view, it is essential that writing on emotion, subjectivity and research remain open, fluid and questing – in short, that it remains risky. Reflexivity must be more than a reflex (Collins & Gallinat, 2010, p. 4). In the introduction to this volume, we implied that the ideal of objectivity retains its power across different disciplines partly because it is so ingrained in our everyday practices. Authors 'perform' the self within the text, and this 'textual performance' is at least partly an effect of their narratives on the imaginations of readers (Summerfield, 2013, p. 349). The more a 'performance' complies with what we expect, the more it aligns itself with power, and the less power it has to provoke thought. As Robert Darnton (1986, p. 227) argued in a different context:

> By situating his narrative in a standard way, drawing on conventional images, and blending stock associations, a writer puts across a meaning without making it explicit. He builds significance into his story by the way he recounts it. And the more ordinary his manner, the less idiosyncratic his message.

If writing on emotion and research is to remain imaginative, inspiring and innovative, it must not slip into an easy convention where the technical vocabulary of 'reflexivity' serves the same purpose as an appeal to 'objectivity' once did.

This appeal to fluidity is a plea to always remember what we can and cannot know. In writing about emotion in research, we enter marginalised terrain. To report back from that terrain, we have to adopt 'a discourse of knowledge form that can be understood and accepted within the dominant Western frameworks of knowledge and culture' (Edwards & Ribbens, 1998, p. 3) – a way of thinking originally hard-earned that eventually comes all-too-easily to us as researchers. If we fall into the trap of adopting a standardised language to communicate about emotion in research, then we risk becoming trapped in this same discourse. Other risks are attendant upon this, not least that we fail to investigate the particularity or universality of our own emotional responses. If we assume that everyone else feels and responds as we do, we simply 'project ourselves into the other and in so doing, obscure the reality of the other's experience' (Lanzoni, 2012, p. 288). As Rebecca Solnit (2014, p. 88) argues, 'pretenses at authoritative knowledge are failures of language: the language of bold assertion is simpler, less taxing, than the language of nuance and ambiguity and speculation'.

It is easy to see why, even in the domain of research on emotion, the creation of standardised vocabularies and approaches appeals. We are still in thrall to the scientific model and seduced by its promise of prestige. Equally, as researchers, we want to advance knowledge. We fear the loss of rigour that threatens whenever we depart an established path; we want certainty, and so we turn to the models established by science. But we need to learn to live with uncertainty:

> Science is about control, control of vocabulary and method, so the same results can be replicated again and again. Its models are often frozen, even when researchers attempt to describe dynamic processes. But absolute control is impossible. There are always leaks. Subjectivity cannot be eliminated from the story of doing science, which does not discredit the scientific method and all the discoveries that have been made in its wake. (Hustvedt, 2016, p. 117)

The main contribution of this volume, then, might be to show that there is more than one way to understand emotion in research and more than one way to write about it, without losing rigour. Our contributors reveal their joys and heartaches, but they also adopt and generate diverse approaches that ensure they retain a critical perspective. They demonstrate the possibility of a 'controlled application of their subjectivity' (Hans-Ulrich Wehler, cited in Roper, 2014, p. 92).

In editing this collection, we have gained a wealth of knowledge, developed more nuanced understandings of emotion, and gained a deeper appreciation of its place within and beyond interdisciplinary applications. We hope that readers have enjoyed a comparable experience in journeying through the valuable and moving accounts offered across *Emotion and the Researcher: Sites, Subjectivities and Relationships*. More than this, we hope that some readers are inspired to do what we did more than four years ago – bring some interesting and open-minded researchers together in a room, and invite them to be honest about what matters to them in research. We guarantee it will be worth the effort – and we look forward to reading the results.

REFERENCES

Adams, R. (2017). British universities employ no black academics in top roles, figures show. *Guardian*, January 19. Retrieved from https://www.theguardian.com/education/2017/jan/19/british-universities-employ-no-black-academics-in-top-roles-figures-show. Accessed on January 8, 2018.

Ahmed, S. (2017). *Living a feminist life*. Durham, NC: Duke University Press.

Barbalet, J. M. (2002). *Emotions and sociology*. Oxford: Blackwell.

Behar, R. (1996). *The vulnerable observer: Anthropology that breaks your heart*. Boston, MA: Beacon Press.

Bhopal, K. (2018). *White privilege: The myth of a post-racial society*. Bristol: Policy Press.

Bornat, J. (2010). Remembering and reworking emotions: The reanalysis of emotion in an interview. *Oral History*, 38(2), 43–52.

Byron, T. (2014). *The skeleton cupboard: Stories of sanity, madness and hope*. London: Pan Macmillan.

Calhoun, C. (2011). Putting emotions in their place. In J. Goodwin, J. M. Jasper, & F. Polletta (Eds.), *Passionate politics: Emotions and social movements* (pp. 45–57). Chicago, IL: University of Chicago Press.

Coffey, A. (1999). *The ethnographic self: Fieldwork and the representation of identity*. London: SAGE.

Collins, P., & Gallinat, A. (2010). The ethnographic self as resource: Introduction. In P. Collins & A. Gallinat (Eds.), *The ethnographic self as resource: Writing memory and experience into ethnography* (pp. 1–24). New York, NY: Berghahn Books.

Darnton, R. (1986). The symbolic element in history. *Journal of Modern History*, 58(1), 218–234.

de Boise, S. (2015). *Men, masculinity, music and emotions*. Bsingstoke: Palgrave Macmillan.

Delamont, S., & Atkinson, P. (1995). *Fighting familiarity: Essays on education and ethnography*. Cresskill, NJ: Hampton Press.

Dube, S. (2007). Introduction: Anthropology, history, history anthropology. In S. Dube (Ed.), *Historical anthropology* (pp. 1–73). New Delhi: Oxford University Press.

Edwards, R., & Ribbens, J. (1998). Living on the edges: Public knowledge, private lives, personal experience. In J. Ribbens & R. Edwards (Eds.), *Feminist dilemmas in qualitative research: Public knowledge and private lives* (pp. 1–23). London: SAGE.

Gawande, A. (2014). *Being mortal: Illness, medicine, and what matters in the end.* London: Profile Books.

Geer, B. (1964). First days in the field. In P. E. Hammond (Ed.), *Sociologists at work* (pp. 372–398). New York, NY: Basic Books.

Goodwin, J., Jasper, J. M., & Polletta, F. (2001). Introduction: Why emotions matter. In J. Goodwin, J. M. Jasper, & F. Polletta (Eds.), *Passionate politics: Emotions and social movements* (pp. 1–24). Chicago, IL: University of Chicago Press.

HESA (2017). *Staff at higher education providers in the United Kingdom 2015/16.* Retrieved from https://www.hesa.ac.uk/news/19-01-2017/sfr243-staff. Accessed on January 8, 2018.

Hustvedt, S. (2016). *A woman looking at men looking at women: Essays on art, sex, and the mind.* New York, NY: Simon & Schuster.

Jordanova, L. (1995). The social construction of medical knowledge. *Social History of Medicine, 8*(3), 361–381.

Kalanthi, P. (2016). *When breath becomes air.* London: Vintage.

Kuhn, A. (1995). *Family secrets: Acts of memory and imagination.* London: Verso.

Kulick, D., & Willson, M. (1992). Echoing images: The construction of savagery among Papua New Guinean villagers. *Visual Anthropology, 5,* 143–152.

Lanzoni, S. (2012). Introduction: Emotion and the sciences: Varieties of empathy in science, art, and history. *Science in Context, 25*(3), 287–300.

Latour, B., & Woolgar, S. (1986). *Laboratory life: The construction of scientific facts.* Princeton, NJ: Princeton University Press.

Marsh, H. (2014). *Do no harm: Stories of life, death and brain surgery.* London: Weidenfeld & Nicolson.

Roper, M. (2014). The unconscious work of history. *Cultural and Social History, 11*(2), 169–193.

Smart, C. (2007). *Personal life: New directions in sociological thinking.* Cambridge: Polity.

Solnit, R. (2014). *Men explain things to me and other essays.* London: Granta.

Reay, D. (2017). *Miseducation: Inequality, education and the working classes.* Bristol: Policy Press.

Steedman, V. (1986). *Landscape for a good woman.* London: Virago.

Summerfield, P. (2013). Concluding thoughts: Performance, the self, and women's history. *Women's History Review, 22*(2), 345–352.

Walkerdine, V., Lucey, H., & Melody, J. (2001). *Growing up girl: Psycho-social explorations of gender and class.* Basingstoke: Palgrave Macmillan.

Ward, M. (Ed.). (2016). *Gender identity and research relationships* (Vol. 14). Studies in Qualitative Methodology. Bingley: Emerald.

INDEX